# LABOUR AS AN INTERNATIONAL PROBLEM

MACMILLAN AND CO., Limited
LONDON · BOMBAY · CALCUTTA · MADRAS
MELBOURNE

THE MACMILLAN COMPANY
NEW YORK · BOSTON · CHICAGO
DALLAS · SAN FRANCISCO

THE MACMILLAN CO. OF CANADA, Ltd.
TORONTO

# LABOUR AS AN INTERNATIONAL PROBLEM

*A Series of Essays comprising a Short History of the International Labour Organisation and a Review of General Industrial Problems*

BY

G. N. BARNES
ARTHUR FONTAINE
DR. SHOTWELL
EMILE VANDERVELDE
MINORU OKA

ALBERT THOMAS
W. A. APPLETON
H. B. BUTLER
SOPHY SANGER
E. JOHN SOLANO

EDITED BY

## E. JOHN SOLANO

MACMILLAN AND CO., LIMITED
ST. MARTIN'S STREET, LONDON

1920

*COPYRIGHT*

# TABLE OF CONTENTS

PAGE

INTRODUCTION. By E. John Solano - - - - xiii

## CHAPTER I

### THE SCOPE AND PURPOSE OF INTERNATIONAL LABOUR LEGISLATION

By G. N. Barnes

I. General Principles of Policy - - - - - 3
II. International Labour Organisation - - - - 13
III. The International Labour Office - - - - 28
IV. The Triumph of Combination - - - - - 30

## CHAPTER II

### HISTORICAL SIGNIFICANCE OF THE INTERNATIONAL LABOUR CONFERENCE

By Dr. J. T. Shotwell

I. The Shadow of Revolution - - - - - 41
II. The Conference and International Trade Unionism 44
III. International Labour Legislation as a Domestic Problem - - - - - - - - - 47
IV. The Problem of National Independence - - - 54
V. The Conference and the League of Nations - - 64

## CHAPTER III

### INTERNATIONAL TRADE UNIONISM

By W. A. Appleton

I. Industrial and Political Activities - - - - 69
II. Aims of the "Trade Union International" - - 74

## CHAPTER IV

### LABOUR LEGISLATION IN JAPAN

#### By Minoru Oka

PAGE

I. Industrial Conditions in Japan - - - - 85
II. The Japanese Factory Act - - - - - 88
III. Provisions of Factory Legislation - - - - 91
IV. Enforcement of the Factory Act - - - - 93
V. Future Labour Legislation in Japan - - - 94
VI. International Labour Conventions:
    Japan's Relation to Labour Conventions - - - 96
    Effect of Labour Conventions in Japan - - - 96
    Special Treatment of Countries in Special Circumstances - - - - - - - - - - 98
VII. General Considerations - - - - - - 100

## CHAPTER V

### LABOUR REFORMS IN BELGIUM.

#### By Emile Vandervelde

I. Special Circumstances in Belgium - - - - 105
II. The Problem of Unemployment - - - - 108
III. The Cost of Living and Rate of Wages - - - 114
IV. The Economic Effects of an Eight-hour Day - - 117
V. The Need of Economic Freedom - - - - 128

## CHAPTER VI

### PRACTICAL PROBLEMS OF INTERNATIONAL LABOUR LEGISLATION

#### By Sophy Sanger

I. Initial Difficulties - - - - - - - 135
II. Preventive Measures in Unhealthy Processes - 137
III. Preventive Measures against Accidents - - - 142
IV. Reduction of Hours and Night Work - - - 144
V. Child Labour - - - - - - - - 146
VI. The Protection of Mothers - - - - - 149
VII. The Berne "Labour Charter" - - - - - 152
VIII. Conclusion - - - - - - - - 157

# TABLE OF CONTENTS

## CHAPTER VII

### A REVIEW OF INTERNATIONAL LABOUR LEGISLATION

#### BY ARTHUR FONTAINE

PAGE
I. DEFINITION OF INTERNATIONAL LABOUR LEGISLATION - 161
II. CAUSES THAT LED TO INTERNATIONAL LABOUR LEGISLATION - - - - - - - - - 164
III. THE BIRTH OF INTERNATIONAL LABOUR LEGISLATION - 167
IV. FIRST EXPERIMENTS IN INTERNATIONAL LABOUR LEGISLATION - - - - - - - - 171
V. THE BERNE CONVENTIONS - - - - - - 175
VI. A PROGRAMME OF INTERNATIONAL LABOUR LEGISLATION 190
VII. GENERAL CONCLUSIONS - - - - - - - 191

## CHAPTER VIII

### THE WASHINGTON CONFERENCE, 1919

#### BY H. B. BUTLER

I. COMPOSITION OF THE CONFERENCE - - - - - 198
II. ORGANISATION - - - - - - - - 203
III. THE WORK OF THE CONFERENCE - - - - - 211
IV. FUTURE PROBLEMS - - - - - - - - 238

## CHAPTER IX

### THE TASK OF THE INTERNATIONAL LABOUR OFFICE

#### BY ALBERT THOMAS

I. ORGANISATION OF THE OFFICE - - - - - 250
II. THE OFFICE AND THE EVOLUTION OF SOCIAL REFORM - 262
III. THE FUTURE OF THE OFFICE - - - - - - 268

## APPENDIX I

### THE LABOUR SECTIONS OF THE PEACE TREATY

GENERAL PRINCIPLES - - - - - - - - 273
PERMANENT ORGANISATION - - - - - - - 275
Chap. I. Organisation - - - - - - - 276
Chap. II. Procedure - - - - - - - - 281
Chap. III. General - - - - - - - - 289
RESOLUTIONS - - - - - - - - - - 290

## APPENDIX II

PAGE

RESOLUTION PASSED AT THE BERNE CONFERENCE, 1906 - - 291

## APPENDIX III

DRAFT CONVENTIONS AND RECOMMENDATIONS ADOPTED
BY THE INTERNATIONAL LABOUR CONFERENCE AT
WASHINGTON

PAGE

Draft Convention limiting the hours of work in industrial undertakings to eight in the day and forty-eight in the week - 294

Draft Convention concerning unemployment - - - - 305

Recommendation concerning unemployment - - - - 308

Recommendation concerning reciprocity of treatment of foreign
workers - - - - - - - - - - 310

Draft Convention concerning the employment of women before
and after childbirth - - - - - - - - 310

Draft Convention concerning the employment of women during
the night - - - - - - - - - - 315

Recommendation concerning the prevention of Anthrax - - 319

Recommendation concerning the protection of women and
children against lead poisoning - - - - - - 320

Recommendation concerning the establishment of Government
Health Services - - - - - - - - - 322

Draft Convention fixing the minimum age for admission of
children to industrial employment - - - - - 323

Draft Convention concerning the night work of young persons
employed in industry - - - - - - - - 327

Recommendation concerning the application of the Berne
Convention of 1906 on the prohibition of the use of white
phosphorus in the manufacture of matches - - - - 332

## APPENDIX IV

DRAFT CONVENTIONS AND RECOMMENDATIONS ADOPTED
BY THE INTERNATIONAL LABOUR CONFERENCE—
GENOA, 1920

PAGE

Recommendation concerning the limitation of hours of work in
the fishing industry - - - - - - - - 334

# TABLE OF CONTENTS

ix

Recommendation concerning the limitation of hours of work in inland navigation - - - - - - - -   PAGE 334

Recommendation concerning the establishment of national seamen's codes - - - - - - - - -   336

Draft Convention fixing the minimum age for admission of children to employment at sea - - - - -   336

Recommendation concerning unemployment insurance for seamen - - - - - - - - - - -   339

Draft Convention concerning unemployment indemnity in case of loss or foundering of the ship - - - - -   339

Draft Convention for establishing facilities for finding employment for seamen - - - - - - - -   340

## APPENDIX V

MEMBER STATES AND GOVERNING BODY OF THE INTERNATIONAL LABOUR ORGANISATION - - - - - -   344

# LABOUR AS AN INTERNATIONAL PROBLEM

## INTRODUCTION

BY

## E. JOHN SOLANO

Formerly of the Ministry of Labour, and a Deputy-Director of Labour Supply,
Ministry of National Service

# INTRODUCTION

## I

WHEN the statesmen of the belligerent nations met in Paris in 1919 to terminate the most murderous war in history, it was natural that they should try to devise some practical means to secure for mankind the state of universal peace. With this object, they established the League of Nations. Many people, their minds still obsessed by the stress of warfare which so long occupied and oppressed them, think of the prevention of wars as the only means of attaining universal peace and commonly imagine this to be the sole object of the League of Nations. Because more than one great and populous nation still stands outside the League and because some nations after joining it have engaged in wars, people are inclined to be sceptical as to its usefulness and to regard its objects as an unattainable dream. The value of the League of Nations, however, cannot be judged solely with relation to the prevention of wars because that is not the only important international function for which it has been established. It was expressly declared by the Treaty of Paris that the desired state of universal peace could be realised "*only if it is based upon social justice.*"[1] By this declaration, the governments of the allied peoples —including those of Japan and India—definitely announced their sympathy with the aspirations of the wage-earners throughout the world for progress in industrial reforms, for improvement in their conditions of life and for adequate remuneration. They called upon other peoples to join the League of Nations and to co-operate with them in establishing the League, with its ideals of humanity, upon a strong foundation of universal social advancement based on the principle that the worker shall no longer be regarded as a commodity or article of commerce. To enable this task to be carried out they created, by the Peace Treaty, an autonomous body known as the International Labour Organisation[2] with definite functions and powers to be exercised under the League of Nations, and they laid down certain general principles to govern the policy of this organisation which in effect constitutes an international charter for the physical, moral and intellectual well-being of the industrial workers of the world.[3] They further arranged that questions affecting the well-being of workers should be considered annually, or more often if necessary, at international labour con-

[1] Appendix I. p. 275 (Preamble—first paragraph).

[2] A list of the member states of the International Labour Organisation, together with names of the Governing Body and Directors, will be found in Appendix V. The regulations governing its organisation and procedure are contained in Appendix I. pp. 276-290.

[3] See Appendix I. pp. 273-275.

ferences, and they drew up for discussion at the first of these conferences which was held at Washington in 1919, the most important list of industrial reforms ever advocated by the leaders of a group of states for approval and adoption by the legislatures of all peoples.[1]

Thus its occasional intervention to avert wars does not constitute the only, nor even the primary work of the League of Nations. If it is to justify its existence, its energies must be concentrated ceaselessly in helping to solve the vital, social and economic problems of our day which involve dangers to the domestic peace of every nation—dangers in some respects as disastrous and wasteful as the ravages of war. If the worth and promise of the League of Nations to-day is judged by the actual achievements of the International Labour Office in this field of troubled potentialities during the short time since its inception, no thoughtful man will remain doubtful as to the usefulness of the League or take a hopeless view about its future.

This book has been written with the object of explaining the constitution, functions, procedure and policy of the International Labour Office, and to provide a short record of its work ending with the conventions and recommendations passed at the International Seamen's Conference, held in Genoa in July 1920.[2] It also includes a short review of the history

[1] See footnote, p. 205, for the Agenda of the Washington Conference.
[2] See Appendix IV.

of international labour legislation. The book was
conceived in the form of a series of essays by authorities in different countries because the questions with
which it deals must be considered throughout from
international points of view, and also because the
solution of industrial problems which are complicated by special circumstances—such as those prevailing in Asiatic and tropical lands or in countries
where the revival of commerce has been checked
through the widespread devastation of industrial
regions due to war—gives rise to questions which
should properly be discussed by the representatives
of the countries concerned. The Editor has been
fortunate in securing for this work the co-operation
of a group of distinguished international authorities,
all of whom, with the exception of Mr. Appleton,
the President of the International Federation of
Trade Unions, are directly associated with the International Labour Organisation—some were entrusted
with the task of bringing it into being, some have
taken part in its conferences and others are now carrying on its work in various administrative capacities.

The writers of Chapters I.-VI. all laboured under
two difficulties, namely: the risk that the time which
would elapse before their work could be published
might make their chapters seem to some extent out
of date, and the necessity of committing themselves
to conjectures as to future developments which might
prove wrong. These difficulties were unavoidable
having regard to the scheme of a book which dealt

step by step first with the work of creating the International Labour Organisation, then with a careful consideration of how far its procedure, functions and policy would successfully meet the great and obvious difficulties connected with the solution of intricate international industrial and social problems, and lastly with the actual results of the first tests of the new organisation at the labour conferences at Washington and Genoa. While the thanks of the Editor are due to the contributors who consented to write under difficult conditions, it is the fact that the passing of time and subsequent developments have generally vindicated their judgments and the opinions they expressed—as will be seen for instance by a comparison of the chapters written by Mr. Barnes, Mr. Oka and Miss Sanger, with Mr. Butler's most interesting and detailed description of the proceedings of the Washington Conference in Chapter VIII. Nevertheless, in fairness to contributors it must be borne in mind that they deal with separate phases of the development of the International Labour Organisation, or with concrete problems necessitating conjectures made in certain phases of its development, during a period under review of about two years.

A short reference to the main subject of each chapter—on which further comment will be made later—will be useful at this point, to explain the scope and arrangement of the book. In the first two chapters, Mr. G. N. Barnes and Dr. Shotwell, who

were both delegates of their respective countries to
the Labour Commission on International Labour
Legislation at the Paris Conference which brought
the International Labour Organisation into being,
deal principally with the constitution, functions and
procedure and policy of that body.  The historical
interest and value of these contributions is heightened
by the candour with which the writers discuss a subject full of inherent difficulties due to class jealousies,
national susceptibilities and the considerations of
diplomatic usage which govern official international
deliberations.   Mr. Barnes' remarks regarding the
bitter opposition to the Trade Union movement in
its earlier phase, the changed attitude of governments
and employers with respect to the legitimate aspirations of organised labour and the developments of
modern commerce which make the settlement of industrial disputes a national rather than a class
interest, are extremely interesting as showing that
the trend of social forces, together with the solidity
of the workers' interests throughout the world, has
gone far towards creating a need for fresh efforts to
attain progress by a wider combination than that of
Labour alone; that is to say, through the co-operation
of all the elements of human industry—workers,
employers and governments.[1]

Dr. Shotwell's description of the constitutional difficulties which confronted the delegates of the United
States on the Labour Commission at the Paris

[1] See pp. 30-37.

Peace Conference is instructive as showing how the procedure of the International Labour Organisation was modified by American amendments. The American chapter of the book is a notable contribution to contemporary thought. It indicates the historical significance of the International Labour Organisation as a great and far-reaching development of democratic institutions, because its procedure brings the ordinary citizen of different countries, representing industrial activities in labour and capital, together with the representatives of governments, to make international labour laws which depend, not upon treaties settled by diplomatists, but upon public opinion in every country as expressed through national legislatures, to make them binding.[1]

Mr. Appleton, whose contribution follows, was set a difficult but all-important task in defining the policy of International Federation of Trade Unions towards the new official International Labour Organisation. He deals, as Mr. Barnes also does in his chapter, with the conflicting forces which animate the labour movement to-day and discusses their causes.[2] With Mr. Barnes he advocates an ordered and constructive policy of industrial reforms as the surest means of attaining social progress. Mr. Appleton wrote his chapter before Mr. Jouhaux and Mr. Oudegueest, who are respectively the Vice-President and General Secretary of the International Federation of Trade Unions, were both

[1] See p. 50.        [2] See pp. 71-72.

elected at the Washington Conference to be members
of the governing body of the International Labour
Office,[1] thus facilitating the realisation of Mr. Appleton's most important general conclusion as to the
desirability of co-operation between his world-
organisation of workers and the new Labour Office,
provided that the complete independence and efficacy
of the former are in no way impaired.[2]

Mr. Oka and Mr. Vandervelde, whose chapters
follow next, were also respective national delegates
of Japan and Belgium on the Labour Commission at
the Paris Peace Conference. These contributors deal
with conditions in their countries which involve an important principle of international legislation under the
Labour Organisation of the League of Nations. The
labour sections of the Paris Peace Treaty made allowance for the fact that differences in climate, habits,
customs, economic opportunity and industrial traditions might make the immediate attainment of uniform
conditions of labour in all countries impossible.[3]
They affirmed the principle, however, that all industrial communities should endeavour to regulate labour
conditions as far as their special circumstances permitted, so as to attain what, for practical purposes,
would amount to relative uniformity with the conditions already prevailing in, or adopted by other

---

[1] Personal particulars regarding each of the members of the Governing Body will be found in footnotes to pp. 241-242.

[2] See p. 80.

[3] Appendix I. p. 273, Article 427, second paragraph.

member states. Japan is an important example of a country in which special circumstances must affect international legislation. The initiative and energy of her people have enabled her within a short space of time to break from the immemorial habits and traditions of her native industries, and to become one of the leading nations of modern commerce and manufacture. It is therefore interesting, from an international point of view, to study her recent economic progress and the peculiar labour problems to which it has given rise, more especially as the attitude of the Japanese Government and employers with regard to industrial reforms must sooner or later exercise a direct influence in other Asiatic countries. Mr. Oka's hope that his country would co-operate in a liberal spirit with western nations in carrying out universal industrial reforms under conditions, having regard to special circumstances, of relative uniformity in different countries, was amply justified by the progressive policy of Japan at the Washington Conference which opened an era of immense importance and fateful change in the history of Asiatic peoples.

Mr. Vandervelde, in dealing with the special circumstances which affected Belgium, had a difficult task. He was writing of what were transient conditions due to the ravages of war, which he knew would materially alter so far as they affected Belgium for better or for worse long before his chapter could be published, and which were at the same time highly com-

[1] See pp. 216-220.

plicated. These conditions, of course, still prevail in varying degrees of acuteness in other European countries, and may continue to do so for some time. Therefore, even though the marvellous recovery made by the Belgian people from the consequences of war has mitigated the difficulties described by Mr. Vandervelde as complicating both the revival of industry and labour reforms in his country, much of what he says regarding those difficulties applies in a relative sense to other states which are confronted with them. In these countries, Mr. Vandervelde's remarks regarding the measures taken in Belgium to solve the problems of reconstruction through relief measures and organisation, together with his suggestions as to mass production, standardisation, the installation of modern plant and other plans for reviving industry and facilitating labour reforms will be read with interest.[1]

The contributions of Miss Sophy Sanger and Mr. Arthur Fontaine commence what is practically a new section of the book. In the preceding chapters the writers have dealt mainly with the constitution, functions, procedure and policy of the International Labour Organisation ; in the remaining chapters the writers give a short review of the movement towards making international laws to regulate industrial conditions for the benefit of workers, from its commencement down to the work done at the conferences held at Washington and Genoa in 1919 and 1920. These writers all speak with authority on their subjects.

[1] See pp. 122-126.

Miss Sanger, who was formerly Legal Secretary to the British Womens' Trade Union League, and Secretary to the British Section of the International Association for Labour Legislation which for many years did much valuable work in laying the foundation of labour reforms based on international law, is now officially connected with the International Labour Office at its headquarters in Geneva. Mr. Arthur Fontaine, Director of Labour in the French Ministry of Labour who was elected chairman of the Governing Body of the International Labour Office at the Washington Conference, has had a long experience of the subject on which he writes, and is in a sense the pioneer of international labour legislation as he negotiated the first labour treaty which can properly be classified under this head.[1] In her chapter, Miss Sanger deals with a number of important industrial reforms which stood in the agenda of the Washington Conference, and are now the subject of its conventions and recommendations. Her contribution is valuable in view of the fact that as an active member of the International Association for Labour Legislation she studied the problems connected with these and other reforms, and prepared the ground for their universal application to industry as laws long before they attracted the present general attention.

Mr. Fontaine, in his most useful historical review, summarises the whole of the developments which

[1] See p. 169 (last line), and p. 170.

have culminated in the establishment of the International Labour Office, and the great impetus given to international co-operation for carrying out industrial reforms by its policy of holding annual conferences to consider proposals for this purpose. Mr. Fontaine traces the various activities which carried the movement for equalising labour conditions in different countries, from the initial stage of sporadic agitations to the first results in reciprocal treaties between two nations, and subsequently to the later developments which led to the labour conferences held at Berne. Mr. Fontaine ends his review with the Paris Peace Conference, where as already stated international labour legislation was established as one of the functions of the League of Nations. In reading the chapters written by Mr. Fontaine and Miss Sanger, it becomes clear how much the present generation owes to those who struggled for so long in the face of discouragement and seemingly insuperable difficulties to give effect to the idea and the basic principles of founding industrial reforms on international law. Their labours have enormously facilitated the creation of the International Labour Organisation and prepared the ground by much thought, effort and experience for the programme of reforms which are embodied in the conventions and recommendations of the Washington Conference. It is not too much to say that the origin and initial success of the Labour Organisation of the League of Nations lies to some extent in the activities which resulted in the international conferences held at Berne before the war.

The first results of the work of this new organisation at the Washington Conference are dealt with by Mr. H. B. Butler who is now Deputy Director of the International Labour Office, and who, as Assistant Secretary to the British Ministry of Labour, first conceived in its main outlines the scheme proposed by the British Government at Paris in order to make international co-operation in the economic field an essential part of any plan elaborated by the allied nations to secure universal peace. Mr. Albert Thomas, the distinguished statesman who is now Director of the International Labour Office, concludes the series of essays. Mr. Thomas is a historical scholar who has been identified with political and social progress in France both as a writer and as an active worker in public affairs. His responsible post as the French Minister of Munitions during the war added to his already wide knowledge of industrial conditions and labour problems. He therefore brings a trained and thoroughly experienced intellect to bear on the great constructive task entrusted to his guidance. In his chapter, Mr. Thomas besides discussing general questions of procedure and policy describes in detail the departmental organisation he has established with approval of the Governing Body to enable the International Labour Office to carry out its work.[1] The scope, variety and importance of this work is indi-

[1] See pp. 250-260.

cated by the nature of this organisation which will probably be amplified in the future. The events described by Mr. Butler in his chapter constitute an achievement of extraordinary significance in human affairs, as one example alone will show. Any attempts to bring industrial conditions in Asiatic countries into line with those in Europe and America and to establish legislative reforms in Asia through the most advanced democratic methods, by agreement between Asiatic governments, employers and workers, would have been flouted as utterly impossible a few years ago. Yet such attempts were initiated with success at Washington where international co-operation to settle controversial and even dangerous questions was daily proved to be a practical possibility. Courage was certainly the key-note of the Washington Conference. Boldness, vision and imagination are certainly the three characteristics of the organisation which Mr. Thomas has created and describes in his chapter as the instrument through which the Office of the International Labour Organisation is to achieve its purpose.

With the Appendices, the book comprises a concise volume of comprehensive and recent information in connection with one of the greatest experiments ever attempted by man for the benefit of man. It is hoped that it will be useful to persons occupied in public affairs because it concentrates thought upon the solution of the most urgent and difficult social problems of our time. It is also hoped that the information contained in the book will help to attract a certain amount of general attention and sympathy in regard to the work of the International Labour Office, because the success and value of its efforts will ultimately depend upon the judgment of public opinion and it is essential, if the new organisation is to have a fair chance of success, that public opinion in all democratic countries should as far as possible be well-informed regarding its nature and objects.

## II

To make the information in these pages as complete as possible, it is necessary to refer shortly to recent developments regarding two questions — namely, the constitution of the Governing Body of the International Labour Office, and the Labour Conference held at Genoa on matters concerning maritime workers.

Under Article 393 of the Paris Peace Treaty, the Governing Body of the International Labour Office is composed of twenty-four persons : twelve representing governments, six elected representatives of employers' delegates, and six of the workers' delegates.[1] Of the twelve states represented, eight are those of chief industrial importance, the other four being elected by the government delegates of the remaining states. An organising committee appointed at Paris to make arrangements for the Washington Conference, drew up a list of eight states

[1] Appendix I. p. 278.

of chief industrial importance, and as no rule had been laid down to determine the relative industrial importance of different countries, they invited objections to the list. Sweden, Canada, Poland and India claimed inclusion in the list, India addressing her claim direct to the Council of the League of Nations, as under the Treaty the Council has to decide any question as to which are the eight states of chief industrial importance. It was expected that the Council would give its ruling on the four objections lodged, before the Washington Conference was held, so as to enable the Governing Body to be set up regularly. Owing, however, to difficulties connected with America's inclusion in the League, this was impossible. A difficult situation then arose. It must be remembered that there was no question regarding the elected representatives of the employers or workers. But until the eight chief states of industrial importance had been authoritatively determined, and the twelve representatives of their governments chosen with complete unanimity, the Governing Body could not be constituted regularly. Yet it was necessary to set up a Governing Body at the Washington Conference, to arrange for the next conference. In these circumstances, the Selection Committee [1] at the Conference decided to accept the provisional list of eight states drawn up at Paris and to proceed with the

---

[1] This body was elected by the Conference to direct its proceedings, and consisted of six members, twelve government, six employers', and six workers' representatives.

election of the Governing Body despite the technical ir-
regularity of its constitution owing to the objections
which had been raised. India, China, Persia and Siam
took no part in the elections and India protested,
while Denmark was only selected until such time as
America should join the League of Nations. When
the election was completed, out of twenty-four
members elected by three groups of delegates
—governments, employers and workers—the governments of non-European states throughout the
world had only four representatives on the Governing
Body.[1] The delegates of twenty Latin-American
countries expressed their dissatisfaction with this
state of affairs, and a resolution expressing disapproval of the constitution of the Governing Body,
moved by a South African delegate and supported
by the delegates of other countries, was carried at
the Conference by a majority of five votes. The
appeal pressed by India was heard at the Council of
the League of Nations at San Sebastian in June 1920,
when it was rejected.[2] The Secretary General of the

---

[1] See pp. 241 and 243.

[2] The decision of the Council was as follows :
" Considering the special circumstances in which the members of
the Governing Body of the International Labour Office were elected,
and in view of the fact that the substitution of India for a country
already represented on the Governing Body would entail a complete
revision of the list of members, the Council considers that if the claim
of India in this respect be upheld, this alteration should not in any
case come into operation before the expiry of the mandate granted
to the selected countries, that is to say, before 1922." In justice to
India it should be mentioned that her claim seems amply justified
upon official statistics of both production and the number of workers
engaged in industrial occupations such as shipping, transport, mining,

League was instructed " to consider in conjunction with the International Labour Office methods of drawing up a list of states according to their importance." In effect, therefore, the Council of the League of Nations—on whom this responsibility rests—has decided to postpone any change in the constitution of the Governing Body of the International Labour Organisation until 1922, when it will be re-elected under definite rules for determining the relative industrial importance of different countries, and possibly under rules for deciding the proportional representation of European and non-European states. Meanwhile the Governing Body has already appointed a committee to study the whole matter, which will report its conclusions to the International Labour Conference of 1921.

The question of an eight-hour day for maritime workers gave rise at one time to a doubt concerning the object and powers of the Genoa Conference. The seamen claimed that the Washington Conference had already decided the adoption of an eight-hour day and a forty-eight-hour week for maritime

and textile, steel and iron manufactures. The mileage of Indian railways exceeds that of France or Britain. Her agriculture occupies 71,000,000 of workers ; her maritime workers number more than those of any other country except Great Britain ; her mines, transport services and industries employ 20,219,000 workers as against 4,946,000 for Italy, 2,006,000 for Japan, 1,708,000 for Belgium and 925,000 for Switzerland. India's annual export of manufactured goods, worth £58,000,000, exceeds in value the annual export of manufactured goods of the last mentioned countries. These figures are taken from a statement published by the India Office, dated April 4, 1920.

workers,[1] and that the business of the Genoa Conference was to be limited to applying this principle.
Mr. Barnes, however, who was a representative of
labour and a British Delegate at the Washington
Conference, does not hold this view, and it seems
that most of the delegates who voted for the convention dealing with hours of work at Washington
understood that its application to seafarers was left
open for decision at a later international conference.
This, at any rate, is the view that prevailed. At the
Genoa Conference a majority of votes, including
the united votes of all the seafarers' delegates from
every country, were cast in favour of an international
convention establishing an eight-hour day and a
forty-eight-hour week for maritime workers, but this
majority was short, by a very narrow margin, of the
two-thirds necessary to pass the convention, and the
conference accordingly decided against applying the
principle of an eight hour day to seafarers. Altogether, 48 votes were cast in favour of the proposed
convention, as compared with 25 votes against it.
Sixteen governments and three shipowners voted in
favour of it, as compared with 7 governments and 12
shipowners against it. The 16 governments in favour
of the convention, including France, Germany, Italy,
Greece, the Netherlands, Canada and Australia,
cast 26 votes, and represented about 10,980,000 tons
of shipping. The 7 governments against the convention, including Great Britain, Spain, Japan, Denmark

[1] Appendix III. Article I. (d), p. 295.

and Norway, cast 13 votes, and represented about 25,570,000 tons of shipping.[1] Among the shipowners' delegates who voted against the convention, and against their governments' delegates at the same time, were those of Canada, Germany, Sweden, Italy and Greece ; while the British, Japanese and Danish shipowners voted with their governments. India, with Finland and Switzerland, abstained from voting. Countries like Poland, Roumania, Czecho-Slovakia, Uruguay and Venezuela, with inconsiderable shipping, voted in favour of the convention.

This short analysis of the votes leads to interesting conclusions. In the first place, the votes of the component states of the British Empire, on a question concerning an industry of peculiar and vital importance to the Empire, were not cast in the solid block which, it was feared in some quarters, might give Great Britain a predominant influence in the League of Nations. In the second place, the facts that a large majority of the government delegates voted with the workers' delegates as against the employers and other governments, and that the workers' vote was solidly united, bears out in a striking manner the accuracy of the prediction made by Mr. Barnes in his chapter written long before the Washington Conference, to the effect that the fear of workers that their delegates would be opposed and out-voted by the government and employers' delegates at the conferences of the International Labour Organisation

[1] Figures taken from Lloyds' Register of Shipping.

was unfounded because, in his opinion, the Labour delegates would tend to cast block votes on matters vitally concerning the workers' interests, while the government delegates would tend, for the reasons he gave, to support the Labour vote instead of combining with the employers' delegates as against the workers.[1] Though in this instance the result desired by the workers was not attained, it must be remembered that at the Washington Conference where Mr. Barnes' prediction was equally justified, a long programme of important industrial reforms, long desired by the workers, was voted for their benefit with the help of both government and employers' delegates and embodied in the conventions and recommendations of the conference.

Despite their disappointment on the question of the eight-hour day, the Genoa Conference was in no sense a failure from the workers' point of view, as the conventions and recommendations passed at the conference will serve to show.[2] Limitation of space prevents discussion in these pages either of the important matters contained in these conventions and recommendations or of the arguments advanced for and against an eight-hour day for seafarers. It is clear nevertheless that the application of this principle to their industry is not easy, especially while ships are at sea as distinct from periods when they lie in port. The difficulties involved vary in degree

[1] See pp. 24-25 and 26-27.
[2] Appendix IV.

as they affect different classes of men, such as sailors, stokers and stewards on passenger ships. Asiatic and African seafarers again present separate problems, and the Indian group of this class, as already stated, is the most numerous in the world after the British seamen, of whom they are fellow citizens. The proposed convention at Genoa, moreover, included all mercantile marine officers within the scope of its provisions except those who kept no watch, namely, captains, chief engineers, doctors and pursers. A rigid eight-hour rule for seafarers—however desirable it may be on moral and general grounds—might therefore necessitate triplicating the ships' officers and crews at present found adequate for efficiency and safety, at least during sea voyages, and might also necessitate reducing them to some extent during periods in port. When it is realised that at present there is an element of uncertainty as to how far international conventions can be applied simultaneously, uniformly and strictly, in the different member states of the League of Nations owing to the various systems of giving effect to laws which exist in them; and that at least two numerous and important groups of maritime workers would stand outside the eight-hour day rule—had it been passed at Genoa—in the Indians already referred to and the seamen of the powerful American mercantile fleet, whose country has not yet joined the League of Nations—it will be easy to understand the caution of the government delegates of the great sea-carrier nations in refusing to commit themselves without further consideration to a convention, which apart from the inherent difficulties of applying it to the shipping industry at once, might have placed their countries at a very serious disadvantage in competition with the mercantile fleets of rival nations who were not bound by its provisions.

Although no government delegate at the Genoa Conference advanced any such reason for an adverse vote, these relevant considerations are nevertheless obvious. Whether or not they influenced any decision at Genoa, they serve to illustrate clearly another important point made by Mr. Barnes in his chapter as to the difficulty in the way of industrial reforms caused by the fear that the expense they involve might put progressive nations and employers alike at a disadvantage in competing successfully with their less progressive rivals in commerce.[1] This difficulty can only be overcome through an international agency which periodically brings governments, employers and workers together to consider industrial reforms, to discuss their several points of view regarding them, and to act together with the object of making the introduction of industrial reforms actually or relatively uniform and simultaneous in every country, and which, moreover, possesses international sanctions enabling it to supervise the application of reforms to industries in each contracting state and to deal effectively with cases

[1] See pp. 4-5.

of default. The only agency in the world to-day which can carry out all these essential functions is the International Labour Organisation of the League of Nations.

It is satisfactory, for this reason, to note that the controversial matters dealt with in the preceding paragraphs, which the national susceptibilities and conflicting class interests involved rendered potentially dangerous, and which in each case resulted in disappointing powerful groups of nations and workers, have in no sense weakened the constitution of the International Labour Organisation or lessened the goodwill towards it and faith in its efficiency of any governments, or of employers and workers as a class in any country. The member states concerned in the objections made to the constitution of the Governing Body at Washington, took part in the subsequent conference at Genoa. The maritime workers, after the Genoa Conference, met at Brussels in August, 1920, under the auspices of the International Seafarers' Federation, to consider a variety of questions concerning their welfare, and also to decide what action they should take as the result of the failure at Genoa to apply the forty-eight hour week at sea to their industry. With respect to the limit of working hours, a resolution was first proposed calling upon maritime workers to commence an agitation in every country with the object of forcing governments to legislate granting seafarers an eight-hour day, and a forty-eight-hour week at sea with a forty-four-hour week in port,[1] and an international rate of wages, and failing such legislation, to commence an international campaign for a general strike of seafarers in every country to enforce their demands. The proposal for calling an international strike of seamen was eventually, for a time, abandoned in favour of an extremely significant and interesting alternative. The Conference of the International Seafarers' Federation adopted a suggestion that Mr. Thomas, the Director of the International Labour Office, should be asked to receive a delegation of maritime workers with a view to obtaining the assistance of his Office in arranging a joint meeting between the shipowners and seafarers for the purpose of trying to reach a friendly settlement, before taking the drastic action of a general strike—to which, however, the Congress decided to resort for an unlimited period, should the International Labour Office fail to effect a satisfactory settlement on the question of the limit of working hours.

Thus the International Seafarers' Federation, representing the organised maritime workers of every nation, passed at the Brussels Conference what practically amounts to a vote of confidence in the International Labour Organisation. This was done after the Genoa Conference, which some have prematurely considered as finally abortive regarding the settlement by this

---

[1] A Bill legislating for an eight-hour day for seamen is to be introduced in the British Parliament by Mr. Sexton, M.P.—a member of the Labour Party.

organisation of the question of an eight-hour day for seamen. That various difficulties and disappointments should have arisen in commencing the work of a body so novel as the International Labour Organisation both in connection with its constitution, which represents the bulk of civilisation, and in connection with functions which concern legislation for the upraising of the mass of mankind, is not surprising. The astounding fact is that these difficulties should have been so few, and so amenable, with patience, to satisfactory settlement. The confidence in the International Labour Organisaion shown by the governments, employers and workers of almost every country in the world, despite difficulties and disappointments, may justly be attributed to general recognition of the facts that the functions of this organisation, both at the periodical conferences and through the International Labour Office, are honestly, impartially and efficiently performed, and to a conviction that the measures of reform periodically referred to it for adjustment will be carried through sooner or later to practical results, so as to ensure improvement in the conditions of workers combined with justice to employers, and above all with due regard in every case to be paramount interests of the whole nation of which both workers and employers are sectional groups.[1]

[1] See pp. 265-6 and 269-270.

## III.

It is impossible to prophesy regarding the future of the International Labour Organisation. There is in any case no space in these pages for more than the briefest reference to a few of the many vast and intricate questions embraced by the world-wide policy of this organisation which seem, at the present time, to give hope for its ultimate success. In the spirit which animates its policy the International Labour Organisation possesses one of the strongest elements of success. It sprang into being from a great longing for peace in the hearts of men utterly weary of strife. It perpetuates in a settled determination, the impulse which united peoples of every race at the end of the war in efforts to safeguard the world against passion and violence as the means by which man should attempt to attain his desires. But above all, in each country attached to it, this organisation draws and keeps together the leaders of Capital, Labour and the Nation as a whole, in the spirit which impelled men throughout the years of war to compose their differences and to make common efforts and sacrifices for the common good. By keeping alive this spirit the International Labour Organisation opens the way to improve social conditions throughout the world by the irresistible moral forces of conciliation, reason and law.

The success of the Washington Conference was undoubtedly due in a large measure to the influence of this spirit of good will between the component groups of each nation and between the various peoples who assembled, not merely to deliberate, but to act. Miss Sanger and Mr. Fontaine show in their chapters that some of the identical reforms in the long list approved at Washington, within the short space of a month, were unsuccessfully pressed upon the public opinion of a group of nations now about to adopt them for some time before the more or less abortive Berne Conferences at which they were last discussed. The reforms in question were then neither less just nor less necessary than they are to-day. The nations who failed to give effect to them were not then less humane or less civilised than they are to-day. Their failure to adopt these reforms generally in the past may, as Miss Sanger points out, have been due partly to the facts that at the time of the Berne Conferences no regular machinery existed for bringing international labour conventions into being and for making them generally and uniformly applicable in pursuance of a consecutive policy, and also that non-government elements, such as organisations of employers and workers, were excluded from these conferences and were unable to influence the government delegates to whom they were limited. Yet the main obstacle to industrial reforms before the war was a selfish and narrow social spirit, which caused men to consider vital questions of public welfare almost entirely from the standpoint of their private or class interests. To-day, through the necessities of war, men of all the great industrial countries in the world have learnt to some extent to subordinate these interests to the broader claims of national expediency. The war for a time broke down many barriers between nations and between different classes in the chief industrial states. It taught both men and nations to understand and sympathise with one another. It accustomed both men and nations to depend on one another. Men and nations developed the habit of overcoming difficulties to enable them to act together for their common benefit. As a result, the discipline of war in unity, co-operation and sacrifice has for a time given society in the great belligerent industrial countries greater powers of elasticity and cohesion for moral purposes. Throughout the world the war has awakened a new spirit in public and international affairs. It was this spirit—not the framework of the International Labour Organisation itself—which enabled the delegates of governments, employers and workers from over forty nations to agree in one month at Washington upon a varied and useful programme of industrial reforms to be submitted to their respective legislatures for adoption as state laws within a year or eighteen months.[1]

If this spirit of goodwill survives and continues to manifest itself in co-operation between employers and workers for the systematic solution of industrial problems in the national as well as in the international sphere, it must tend to hasten the development of another factor of hope for peaceful social progress

[1] Appendix I. Article 405, p. 283.

—namely, the education of workers as to the relation of the concrete industrial reforms they desire to the whole field of general social and economic problems. To a great extent, the more intelligent workers already recognise clearly that in the complicated and nicely interrelated conditions of modern commerce and social intercourse their claims, except perhaps in the narrowest of local disputes, can no longer be limited wholly to simple issues of wages and hours or confined entirely to the respective interests of the workers and employers directly concerned. In time, the mass of workers everywhere, through the educative influence of the consultative methods of solving industrial problems on the principle embodied in the International Labour Organisation, will come to realise how intricate are the more important questions which have to be solved in working out a new and better industrial order. The work of the different sections of its Office in every member state, in carefully studying and collecting reliable information regarding industrial questions in close touch with the Trade Unions and associations of employers, should help in educating both the workers and the general community as to the nature and true proportions of various problems of social progress. As their knowledge and experience of these problems increase, the workers will realise that their interests as producers cannot be considered without having regard to their interests as general consumers, because these dual interests are more or less inseparable. They will realise that industrial questions which affect the interests of any important group of workers also affect directly the interests of other groups, both as producers and consumers, together with the interests of the whole nation of which the workers are part. They will realise that factors which tend to affect adversely the producing and purchasing power of the general community must react in suffering, soonest and most severely, upon the workers both as producers and consumers. They will realise in regard to the international aspects of this problem that, in some important respects for reasons stated by labour leaders and others in this book, the social progress they desire must in some measure be uniform in all countries.

In these reflections, the attention tends to become fixed on the white peoples of Europe, America and the Britannic groups of nations. Yet these peoples constitute but a part and the more certain elements of the whole international problem of social and industrial progress. Looming colossal against the future is the most uncertain calculation in the whole fascinating adventure of the International Labour Organisation—the crowded humanity of Asia, silent, inscrutable to western eyes, remote by ages of time from western customs, usage and thought, but infinite in its unstirred potentialities of intellect, energy and material wealth. It seems impossible to bring to the western mind any conception of the mentality and social systems of the peoples of

Asia. Perhaps they comprise a majority of human beings. Tremendous distances, natural barriers and remoteness from the sea cut the mass of them off from contact with western peoples and their ideas, mechanical devices and restless progress. Habit and poor communications cut most of them off from contact with the rest. Most of them live in little communities, each imprisoned in a small locality which is wholly self-sufficing for their crude needs. They are not linked together as a whole by interdependence for the necessities of life as in western communities. The position of the women is peculiar to Asia. To a great extent they are virtually slaves to the men. Many millions of them are kept secluded in their houses the whole of their lives. The mental isolation of the mass of oriental peoples from all movements of thought is absolute. They cannot read or write. Ignorance makes them resentful and suspicious towards innovations in a scheme of life which custom and tradition, ancient beyond computation and hallowed by religious authority, has fixed immovably in every detail of social intercourse. It is as though human existence, steeped too long in an immensity of sunshine, had become baked in a brittle mould which change can only break to pieces.

It is clear that Asia, as a whole, is far from beginning to approach a stage of industrial development which relates even remotely to western conditions. It is, in fact, a vast agricultural community with native local industries to which the western machinery for solving labour problems is inapplicable because such problems do not arise. In places, however, notably in Japan, India and parts of China, modern industries are being developed and workers are being organised on western principles. The International Labour Organisation therefore will chiefly be concerned at present with these industrial developments rather than with the whole continent of Asia, although all the important Asiatic communities except Russia are among its member states.

With regard to modern industry in Asia, Mr. Oka calls attention to one fundamental question on which the International Labour Organisation may exercise a profound influence for peace on the whole industrial future of that continent. He states that at present Japan is not troubled with the class wars and antagonism between Capital and Labour which afflict western communities, and anticipates that the friendly co-operation of employers and workers for the settlement of industrial questions under the procedure of the International Labour Organisation, may be applied also to the settlement of purely national and domestic issues between them with the result that his country may be spared the internal dissensions which have marred the rise of modern industry in Europe and America.[1] It is true that the absence of antagonism between Capital and Labour in Japan is due to some extent to the fact that modern industry has not yet created in that country a numerous class

[1] See pp. 97-8.

of industrial workers in the strict sense of the word. But in the probable event of industrial developments in Asia following the tendencies of those in western countries, differences due to conflicting class interests must sooner or later arise between employers and workers. If these differences are allowed to augment the disturbing effects of other western influences which are slowly permeating Asiatic peoples, so as to destroy the grip of religion, custom and respect for personal authority which now holds them together and guides their lives, without these effects being counteracted through strong constructive forces built into their communal existence as the basis of changing conditions, then Asia is in danger of being plunged into worse confusion of mind and social chaos than that which to-day depopulates and devastates Russia, whose miseries may spread in a flood of madness across that continent, eastward and southward to the seas.

The policy of the International Labour Organisation is thus an essential principle of constructive statesmanship in Asia, quite apart from its safeguards to peace in connection with the inevitable if gradual adoption by eastern peoples of western industrial methods. From the point of view of western workers, it is an essential principle of progress for other reasons. By ensuring that wages, hours of work and other conditions of the employment of Asiatic workers shall, as far as possible, be made relatively uniform with that of labour standards in the west, the policy of the International Labour Organisation will protect the largely unorganised Asiatic workers from injustice, hardship and exploitation, and will raise their general conditions of employment at a bound to a level which approximates comparatively to that of western countries. This policy will also protect western workers against competition from ill-paid Asiatic labour and against dangers of unemployment and obstacles to the social and industrial reforms which they desire, arising from handicaps to western commerce based on social progress, as compared with oriental commerce based on cheap production without regard to the welfare and rights of workers. The policy of making labour conditions in modern Asiatic industries as far as possible relatively uniform with those of western countries will in no sense retard the industrial development, true prosperity and progress of oriental countries. On the contrary, this policy should materially expedite their advancement, as Mr. Oka points out, by facilitating progress based upon domestic peace and co-operation to the avoidance at the best of wasteful hindrances through class wars and industrial conflicts, and at the worst of catastrophic evils which may arrest their progress for a generation. On the other hand, the developments of properly regulated modern industries in Asiatic countries need not necessarily constitute a threat to the prosperity of western workers. For a long time to come and perhaps permanently, their interests will be bound up with peaceful progress in Asia, the industrial development of which in a modern sense must be an infinitely slow and gradual process, during which oriental peoples must depend very largely on western workers for the supply of innumerable products. Asia, as already stated, may contain a majority of mankind who have not yet commenced their exodus from the prison of the past to the modern world with its freedom of opportunities. It must be remembered that millions of these people are living in cramped poverty within reach of unknown quantities of undeveloped wealth. They are paralysed by ignorance in a world which is continually being transformed by scientific activities. To-day, they are satisfied with the simplest possessions which serve the fewest possible human needs. But when these peoples, perhaps at some not distant future, commence their great migration into modernity, however slowly their progress and growing prosperity may increase their purchasing power and enlarge their wants, it is possible that for an indefinite period the markets of Asia may find the entire productive resources of the world too limited to supply their demands.

The fear of unfair competition, both on the part of employers and workers, unless labour conditions are made comparatively equal and unless social reforms are made relatively uniform in all countries is undoubtedly a serious obstacle to progress, which is not of course confined to the case of oriental countries, but applies generally to all industrial states. For this reason, the attainment of uniform progress is an essential condition for the success of the policy of the International Labour Organisation. To some extent its power to fulfil this essential condition will depend upon the care and good judgment with which the international labour conference introduces modifications in its general conventions and recommendations with respect to particular industries in any country, to make allowance for the special circumstances which affect them. It will also depend upon the efficacy of the legislative and administrative machinery in different countries for passing labour laws, and for enforcing their strict application to regulate industrial conditions. Fortunately, so far as oriental countries are concerned, the development of modern industries on an important scale is at present largely confined to Japan and the British Dependencies where ample machinery exists for legislating on labour laws and for enforcing them, and where public opinion, which is to be the driving force of social reforms through international labour legislation, can make its influence felt. Generally speaking, the oriental countries which lack effective legislative and administrative machinery for modern purposes are not yet the homes of large-scale modern industrial developments, and in these cases there will be ample time to consider the solution of difficulties regarding the regulation of industrial conditions before they arise. For immediate purposes, certain strong factors of influence will help to render effective the policy of the International Labour Organisation for making labour conditions and social reforms relatively uniform in all countries. Firstly, its branch establishments or the representatives in member states of its sections dealing with Intelligence, Health, Hours of Work, Industrial Methods and Wages, will provide reliable information gathered from independent sources including associations of employers and workers, regarding any special circumstances by reason of which the International Labour Conference is asked to postpone or modify the application of labour legislation to particular industries in any country.[1] Secondly, the tendency of the workers' delegates from the countries concerned will be to oppose strongly any proposal at an international labour conference which modifies or postpones in their case benefits granted to the workers of other countries in which they will naturally desire to share fully and equally. This tendency was illustrated at the Washington Conference in a striking manner by the attitude of the Japanese workers' delegates, when the proposal to modify the application of the eight-hour day to Japanese industries was being considered.[2] As a rule, also, the tendency of the workers' delegates to cast block votes at the Conference on matters concerning labour interests will operate against the modification or postponement of industrial reforms in special cases, unless they are clearly proved to be essential in the national interests, as was the case at Washington with regard to the question of Japanese working hours.

[1] See pp. 253-259.          [2] See pp. 218-220.

It was, of course, recognised at the Paris Peace Conference that relatively uniform social progress in different countries depended on two essential conditions, namely, that once industrial reforms were embodied in the conventions of the International Labour Conference, they should be the subject of punctual legislation and strict application in all countries. Accordingly, special provisions were inserted in the labour clauses of the Peace Treaty to secure these results.[1] These provisions confirmed by the Treaty obligations of nearly all civilised nations constitute a wonderful development of democracy. They add a new and effective safeguard for uniform social progress to those provided by the functions of the International Labour Office, and by the power of organised labour in every country to voice its grievances and to bring pressure to bear upon its government to remedy them including any lapse regarding its treaty obligations to effect industrial reforms. It is now possible for any recognised body of organised workers or employers in any member state, either directly or through their government, to charge the government of another nation with breach of faith towards its workers, and if necessary to cause it to be arraigned before the Tribunal of the League of Nations for judgment which may involve corrective measures of an economic nature being taken against it conjointly by all the member states of the League.

[1] Appendix I., Articles 408-420, pp. 284-289. See also pp. 17-20.

There are indications that the solution of labour problems on an international basis, especially those relating to unemployment, may be complicated by factors which, however closely they may relate to labour conditions, constitute in fact a distinct group of questions.   For instance, Mr. Vandervelde argues that for smaller industrial states, like Belgium, which possess a restricted home market and an industry capable in full operation of a volume of production greatly in excess of home requirements, the possibility of introducing industrial reforms in relative uniformity with those in force in great industrial countries and perhaps at all, may depend upon the grant of compensative advantages to the small industrial countries, in the shape of facilities for obtaining raw materials and access to the foreign markets of the world for the sale of their surplus products.[1]   The hope expressed by Mr. Oka in his chapter that the International Labour Conference would enlarge its policy so as to aim at international co-operation for the distribution of raw materials, was followed at the Washington Conference by a debate on the motion of Mr. Baldesi, the Italian Worker's delegate, regarding the international control and distribution of raw materials, which obtained a strong measure of support.[2]   More recently, an international conference of miners assembled at Geneva in 1920, passed a resolution calling on the International Labour Office to take steps to create an organisation for the inter-

[1] See pp. 129-130.        [2] See pp. 101 and 225-227.

national control and distribution of coal. These manifestations of an impulse towards international co-operation for the solution of economic questions are both interesting and significant. But if they lie in the sphere of practical politics to-day, they fall within the functions of the Economic Section of the League of Nations rather than within those of the International Labour Organisation. To introduce general economic questions at this stage into the field of legitimate labour reforms may result in complicating and retarding the solution of the urgent and difficult problems they present.

Even if extraneous questions are excluded from the consideration of industrial reforms, and if all its present member states and their component groups co-operate loyally to make the policy of the International Labour Organisation a success, the question arises whether this policy can possibly prove a permanent and complete success until all industrial nations and perhaps all civilised states are members of the Organisation. Germany and Austria were both admitted to it as member states without having to await their formal inclusion in the League of Nations, but the vast populations of Russia and the United States of America—that land of big ideas—still stand outside both the League and its Labour Organisation. Thus the two most populous communities in Europe and America are not yet identified with the international machinery for initiating social reforms which was created in Paris. It is the force of circumstances—not the force of conscience or of conflicting ideals—which prevents the great industrial democracy of the United States, for the moment, from co-operating with other nations in a task which aims at improving the condition of industrial workers throughout the world. The reversal of her traditional foreign policy, the new conception of her relations with a world filled with unrest and the readjustments of legislative and constitutional practice involved by this question, together with the sharply conflicting domestic issues which have confused and complicated it, are among the peculiar difficulties which make America hesitate to assume the political obligations of membership in the League of Nations as a sudden commitment. But whatever may be the cause of her hesitation, it is certainly not disagreement with the social ideals and moral purposes of the International Labour Organisation, which, of course, is linked to the League.[1] It is possible, therefore, that following the precedent of Germany and Austria, America may join the International Labour Organisation independently of her inclusion in the League of Nations. It is surely inconceivable that the American people, with their generous sympathies and love of progress, can keep aloof indefinitely from taking their part in the international scheme for the social elevation of mankind which they, together with other democratic peoples, have helped to establish. It is more probable that the common ideals which unite

---

[1] See Dr. Shotwell's remarks, pp. 65-66.

America to other great democracies, and which recently impelled her at her own time to combine with them in fighting for the cause of liberty, will also impel her at her own time to combine with them to promote the cause of social peace and progress as a member state of the International Labour Organisation, whether or not she ultimately enters the League of Nations.

The problem presented by Russia with regard to the international scheme for social reforms initiated at Paris is undoubtedly difficult. But the lapse of time since the Soviets were established has made it possible to estimate the proportions of this problem and even to notice certain general tendencies that may lead to its solution by ultimately bringing Russia into accord with the majority of civilised states in regard to common action for social progress. The principles of Bolshevism, and the social and economic consequences of their practical application in Russia are too generally known to need recapitulation. After the revolution, Russia might have come into kindly, prosperous relations with the western democracies to whom she was allied in the war. Had she done so, the movement for universal peace and social progress would have received a vital reinforcement. Unfortunately, her present autocratic rulers declared war on Democracy, with the result that Russia became cut off from intercourse with western civilisation, and remains a universal danger to both peace and social progress. The foreign policy of the new Russian autocracy, consists in organising active conspiracies in all countries and especially in the great industrial democracies, to incite the workers to wage heavy civil war against their fellow-citizens with the object of imposing a tyrannical class despotism upon the general community.[1] It is of course impossible to foretell what misfortunes may not befall any country in future through social unrest. At the present time, however, the senseless crime of waging civil war for social or political objects which they have the power to realise by peaceful means is, as might be expected, repugnant to the mass of educated workers in the industrial democracies. Bolshevism, nevertheless, has become an active and dangerous factor of social unrest throughout the world.

Men are apt to attribute the cause of the present acute and universal unrest to the economic and other consequences of the war. The war may have given strength and direction to industrial unrest; but the cause of it existed long before the war in the outworn and ill-conceived industrial conditions of our time. The inequalities and social evils of these

[1] The Pamphlet containing the reply of the Moscow Communist or Third International to the (British) Independent Labour Party, published by H. C. Glass, 15 Belleisle St., Glasgow, July 1920 (price 4d.), explains the Bolshevist plan for social progress through universal civil war. With happy stupidity Moscow has from time to time invited deputations of workers from different countries to come and see in Russia the advantages they may hope to enjoy—by adopting the humane and liberal Soviet ideals of universal brotherhood and social advancement through the massacre of their fellow citizens by the workers—in the spectacle of a people perishing slowly from merciless oppression, famine, pestilence, want and the wastage of civil and foreign wars.

conditions in western countries generally, increased and became accentuated throughout the period which saw the development of modern industry with its enormous accumulations of wealth. At the same time, the spread of education stimulated the workers to formulate and demand remedies which their right of combination and political franchise was giving them a growing power to enforce. To-day, the workers, armed with knowledge and political power and possessed to some extent of the control of industry, demand fundamental readjustments of the economic and industrial order of society. Those who hastily condemn the impatience which tempts sections of workers to try and improve their conditions by violent or revolutionary measures, do not realise the intolerable sense of grievance caused by these conditions especially among the younger generation. It is doubtful in our ignorance of later social history, if even well-informed men realise how great and wrong has been the neglect of industrial workers in European countries, till yesterday. The tardy declaration of Civilisation at Paris in the year 1919 that workers must no longer be regarded merely as " articles of commerce," and the subsequent declaration of Civilisation at the Washington Conference concerning the extent to which the mothers and children of workers, regarded as industrial assets, might at last be protected against serious evils, are in fact accusations against cultured man for his lack of humanity and his complacent disregard of his social obligations in the past. Thoughtful men of all classes in civilised countries are now awake to the need of prompt and generous social reforms. Have they awakened to this need in time ? Can they meet it by ordered and peaceful methods ? Are they prepared to make the sacrifices which these methods involve ?

These questions may be answered in the near future. The task of improving the intricate industrial and economic system of society must be a very long and difficult process. In every country it will necessitate the solution of a host of local and national problems, many of which will also have to be considered from an international point of view. All over the world this work will demand infinite patience, ingenuity and creative effort. It will also require sympathy and understanding between the different classes whose conflicting interests must somehow be harmonised before new and better social conditions can be stabilised anywhere. Workers on one hand will have to exercise wisdom and restraint. The general community on the other hand must acknowledge its enormous unpaid moral debt to the workers and must determine to discharge it without delay, ungrudgingly and in full. Even then, if the work of social reform is to be systematically and thoroughly done, it must be done gradually and comparatively slowly. If it is to be accomplished peacefully and is to create a lasting social order, it must be established firmly upon principles of justice. Finally, so far as peaceful social progress demands uniformity or relative uniformity in all countries, it must be based on some effective system of international co-operation.

These, in bare outline, seem to be the essential conditions of ordered social progress in future. They demand much of human nature. But neither in sacrifices nor in efforts for co-operation between classes or nations do they demand so much as the recent war, by which the victorious peoples claimed to have saved civilisation from injustice and wrong, only to find themselves, together with their late enemies, faced by the common task of saving it from these very defects in its social constitution. Delay in commencing this task will only aggravate these defects and make peaceful remedies either difficult or impossible. For immediate practical purposes it is probable that society will have to choose one of two alternative methods for dealing with them. The former is the peaceful and constitutional method, based upon co-operation and mutual understanding between different classes and nations. The latter involves bitter class conflicts which, to-day, may result in extending the Russian political experiment to other countries with consequences, in social upheavals and industrial ruin, of which no man can forsee the end.

It is here that the extraordinary value of the International Labour Organisation in the present crisis of human affairs becomes apparent. Despite the active class antagonisms, individual selfishness and tendencies towards extreme courses which characterise our time, society is undoubtedly vitalised by a strong sanity, a spirit of conciliation and a sincere desire to rid its system of evils and injustice. These moral forces should, in time, enable men in every civilised country to achieve social progress by peaceful ordered methods. In themselves, however, these moral forces would avail little without some instrument of policy to give prompt, practical effect to social reforms throughout the world. Happily, such an instrument exists. Through the International Labour Organisation, a majority of nations are actually engaged upon the task of advancing the welfare of industrial workers upon a basis of co-operation between all nations, as well as between the workers, the employers and the general community in every country. The essential condition of success for this organisation, in its mission of universal justice and humanity, is the patient and loyal support not only of the governments of its member states, but also of their employers and workers. If this essential condition can be fulfilled, the policy of the International Labour Organisation may prove of the utmost benefit to mankind as a paramount influence for social peace and progress in every land. It does, at any rate, provide a practical method by which the whole human race may work together to release the world from the grip of inherited wrongs and past mistakes and to build, however slowly, new conceptions of justice, peace, morality and freedom into the structure of society.

E. JOHN SOLANO.

# THE SCOPE AND PURPOSE

OF

# INTERNATIONAL LABOUR LEGISLATION

BY THE RIGHT HON.

## G. N. BARNES, M.P.

Ex-Cabinet Minister
Delegate to the Labour Commission on International Labour Legislation
Paris Peace Conference

I. GENERAL PRINCIPLES OF POLICY

II. INTERNATIONAL LABOUR ORGANISATION

III. THE INTERNATIONAL LABOUR OFFICE

IV. THE TRIUMPH OF COMBINATION

A

# CHAPTER I

## THE SCOPE AND PURPOSE OF INTERNATIONAL LABOUR LEGISLATION

### I. GENERAL PRINCIPLES OF POLICY

"This that they call the organising of labour is, if well understood, the problem of the whole future for all who in future pretend to govern men."   *Carlyle.*

IN an industrial sense the modern world will be recast with the march of science and the pressure of events. As improved facilities for transport and communications link nations closer together, no nation will or can be a law to itself.   The much vaunted self-determination of political theorists will become subordinated to world needs.

Moreover, "Labour" has to be reckoned with. The workman is rising in the scale of knowledge and under the impulse of new needs is demanding a better place in the scheme of things.   That can best be secured to him if the common sense and humane instincts of men throughout the world impel them to surmount all difficulties in the way of raising the general standard of life among the working classes, especially in countries where this standard is low.

The difficulties in the way of improvement, considered from an international point of view, are the same on a larger scale as those with which we are familiar in the national sphere. Nations are deterred from carrying out reforms because they fear that the added cost of production consequent on these reforms will handicap them, as regards competition in international trade, just as individual employers in a country fear reform— even when they sympathise with the demands of their workers for better conditions—because they think that the cost of these reforms may handicap them in competition with their trade rivals at home and abroad.

The difficulties in the way of improving the general condition of workers throughout the world, on a comprehensive and systematic plan, have hitherto been far greater than those incidental to improvements in any country, owing to the absence of any organised international effort for bringing pressure to bear with the object of securing simultaneous and uniform progress in all countries—such as the efforts of the Trade Unions, for instance, have secured for workers as a whole in Britain. In one country or another— it may be after years of agitation—definite progress is attained, and laws are passed regarding conditions of employment which benefit the workers of that country as a whole. There has seldom, if ever, been any progressive movement which has similarly benefited workers as a class throughout the world. This condition of affairs tends to retard progress so far as simultaneous international progress is concerned. For those countries which move in the van of progress in labour reforms are subject, owing to the relatively high standard of welfare among their workers, to definite disadvantages in competition with peoples whose wage rates, standard of living and conditions of labour compare unfavourably with those established among progressive peoples. The latter may derive certain advantages, if better organisation and improved methods of production accompany high wages and increased comfort among the workers. But governments and employers alike, in existing circumstances, are naturally averse to risk handicapping themselves by improving labour conditions, and this undoubtedly reacts prejudicially upon the cause of general progress. Hence the need for some international organisation which could promote a simultaneous, if relative, advance towards better conditions and a higher standard of life for workers throughout the world.

What are the difficulties in the way of realising this ideal, and how can they best be overcome in existing circumstances ? Some people who consider international labour legislation to be the true solution of this problem, urge the creation of a super-parliament of nations with power to enforce its decrees on all peoples, and they would proceed at once to invest parliament with the power of imposing penalties upon defaulting nations, in order to secure compliance with its decrees. Such a plan would be doomed to fail in its purpose. Some nations would certainly refuse to consent to it, and those which did so might incur serious disadvantages in consequence. This, at any rate, has been the result of some experiments already attempted in the field of international legislation. The Berne Conferences of 1906 and 1913 were attended by representatives of most European countries, but some of these have not yet ratified the conventions drawn up by their representatives. Those nations which have ratified and observed the Berne conventions have risked doing so to their economic detriment.

In establishing an organisation for international labour legislation, it is therefore essential to secure the co-operation of as many nations as possible. To do this successfully it is important to eliminate from the scheme, as far as possible, coercive measures to enforce the observance of the conventions agreed upon by the representatives of the contracting states. National honour, public opinion, the moral obligations of good faith and diplomacy should be relied upon, and should almost invariably suffice to secure the observance of conventions, provided that they are practicable and based upon justice and good reason. Conventions, of course, must be drawn up with great care and with full consideration of any special factors which may render their observance difficult or impossible in the case of any particular state.

In the light of these remarks, let me proceed to set out the main provisions of the scheme of international labour organisation which was recently endorsed by the Peace Conference at Paris and which will hold its first meeting at Washington in October 1919. First let me point out that the membership of this international labour organisation is confined to states which are members of the League of Nations. Thus countries which are not members of the League—including ex-enemy countries—are for the moment excluded from the international labour organisation. No international labour organisation, however, can be complete or wholly effective which does not ultimately include Germany and Russia. For my part I should be disposed to favour their early admission as members of the organisation.[1] Meantime it is true that most of the industrial nations of the world are at the moment included in its scope.

If the scheme of the organisation is considered, it will be seen that care has been taken in defining the conditions of membership not to impinge upon national susceptibilities. It would have been bad policy to impose conditions upon nations which might have hampered the League of Nations at the beginning of its career. Apart from this consideration, it would equally have been bad policy to have made it difficult for nations to join the international labour organisation of the League. It is, therefore, a fundamental principle of this organisation that its provisions are elastic and adaptable to the widely varying conditions of government, life, customs, climate and industrial development which distinguish its member

[1] Germany and Austria are now member states.—Editor.

states.[1]  As will be explained later, this essential
condition unfortunately involves inequalities regarding
the nature of the obligation resting upon the member
states to observe the conventions of the International
Labour Conference.  This, however, is unavoidable at
the present juncture.

Thus the outstanding features of the scheme are
firstly, that the International Labour Organisation
becomes part of the League of Nations and, secondly,
that its machinery is made adaptable to the varying
conditions governing the life and industry of its various member states.  While the International Labour
Organisation includes all the member states of the
League of Nations, it does not attempt to impose
rigid and uniform conditions of membership upon all
those states.  The former of these features is, I think,
wholly good.  It identifies labour problems with the
preservation of the peace of the world.  It makes the
due observance of international obligations, in regard
to labour problems, not only a matter for attention
but of necessity for action on the part of the League of
Nations, and thereby brings the League into sympathy
and intimate contact with the everyday life of the
mass of workers.

The second of the two features just referred to I
regard as a regrettable necessity.  We were up against
facts and as Burns says :—

> "Facts are chiels that winna ding
> And daurna be disputit."

[1] Appendix I. Article 427, p. 273.

Take, for instance, the case of a federal government which is a member state of the International Labour Organisation. The constituent states under the central federal government are not and cannot be separately represented on the Organisation; yet, under some federal constitutions, the constituent states have reserved to themselves, as against the central federal government, the right to adopt legislation in regard to labour. In such cases it is obvious that no international organisation, either through or over the head of the central federal government, could lay down the law to its constituent states upon matters as to which they are independent of their own central government. In other words, the international organisation could not impose conditions upon constituent states which could not be imposed upon them by their own federal government. We had, of course, to recognise this fact and act accordingly. We provided that the findings of International Labour Conferences might be cast in the form of recommendations which could be passed on by federal governments to their constituent states, leaving those states to apply them—if they apply them at all—in their own way. We further provided that even if findings were cast in the form of conventions for countries in which the central government was supreme with regard to labour legislation, that these findings could be treated as recommendations and dealt with accordingly by a federal government,[1]

[1] Appendix I. Article 405, p. 283.

unless, of course, the convention dealt with a subject on which the federal legislature had power to legislate in the constituent states, when these states would be bound by the action of their federal government.

If, as I believe, public opinion is always in the last resort the impelling force in effecting changes in human relations, then it may be that despite the lack of obligation on the part of constituent states under a federal form of government, the moral force of public opinion will compel eventual agreement by them with the policy of the League of Nations. Recommendations will at least go to constituent states from their respective federal governments and will be accepted or otherwise as public opinion may decree.

Let us consider, for example, how this question may be dealt with in the United States of America as compared with another country. The Washington Conference may decide to cast its findings in the form of a convention in regard to the non-employment in factories of children under a given age. It may fix the age at fourteen for Great Britain and America. The non-federal government of Great Britain would be under obligation to submit the convention to its national legislature for ratification and enforcement, but no such obligation would or could rest upon the United States Federal Government, because the federal legislature may not at present be competent to make laws restricting the employment of children in the constituent states of the Union.

The findings embodied in the convention would,

however, go to the states of the American Union
as recommendations, through their federal government. They might be accepted by some states,
if public opinion in them was ripe for such a
change, while they might be rejected in others.
For these anomalies the only remedy is public
opinion and Trade Union action. Pressure for the
adoption of the convention limit of fourteen years,
exerted by the friends of children in each state, would
be the only means of carrying out this reform and I
think it would succeed. At the worst, the complete
adoption of the convention throughout the United
States would only be a question of delay. A delegate
representing labour organisations in America would
be present at the Conference and would be under a
moral obligation to see that effect was given to its
decisions. Moreover, American educational and social
welfare organisations which have the interests of
children at heart would work for the adoption of
reforms, as against possible apathy or opposition.

The difference in degrees of industrial development
and the widely varying climatic conditions which
prevail in various countries will also prove factors of
difficulty in the way of international labour legislation. In India, for instance, a girl of fourteen is of
marriageable age and her physical development, as a
rule, is far in advance of that of a child of fourteen in
Northern Europe and America. In India also there
is a patriarchal system of native industry established
by ages of immemorial custom. Under this system

the working day is long, but hour for hour, as compared with the working day in countries with highly developed industries, it is relatively far less productive. In Japan the same thing is true in a minor degree. In both countries also wages are adjusted to a much lower standard of living. While the delegates to the labour section of the Peace Conference were fully alive to the need of improvement in the conditions of labour in these two countries, they realised the absolute necessity for making allowance in respect of factors peculiar to them by which they differed so widely from other countries represented at the Conference. Accordingly they felt that their efforts for improvement should be directed to attaining a simultaneous and relative progress in all countries, rather than a rigid uniformity in progress which would have confronted certain countries with a sudden and profound revolution of change, set them an impossible task at the outset of their efforts for improvement and perhaps resulted in their withdrawal from the League of Nations.

We therefore provided that, in framing conventions and making recommendations, the International Labour Conference should have due regard to climatic conditions, the absence of a highly developed industrial organisation, the want of an abundant supply of machinery, or any other special circumstances peculiar to them through which certain member states differ in a marked degree from the others. We also provided that the Conference should be free to suggest the modifications in their general recommendations

and conventions which might be applied to the special
conditions in any country, so as to secure a relative
progress regarding it as compared with the general
progress in other countries.    If an eight hour day,
for instance, should be decided upon for countries in
which the working day is one of nine hours and in
which industrial development is advanced, then a ten
hour day might be recommended for countries in the
East where the working day is one of twelve hours,
in which climatic conditions are different from Europe
and America and where industrial development comparatively speaking is in its infancy.    There are, of
course, evils to which these considerations do not
apply.    Poison is poison all the world over.    Every
country is concerned in the suppression of poisonous
conditions and the recommendations and conventions
of the Conference would, in regard to these, apply to
all countries alike without modification.    But the
object of the work of the Conference will in all cases
be the same, namely, to educate public opinion and
enlist sympathy in all countries for the task of establishing industry throughout the world upon a foundation of fair remuneration and healthy, decent, conditions of life for the workers.

## II. INTERNATIONAL LABOUR ORGANISATION

Before explaining shortly the organisation through
which the business of the Conference on international
labour legislation will be conducted, it is necessary
to make clear the relation of the Conference to the

general scheme of the League of Nations.  The Conference is, of course, a part and development of the League of Nations, and its recommendations or draft conventions must be deposited with the Secretary General of the League of Nations and communicated by him to each of the states which are members alike of the League and of the Conference.  The Conference, however, as regards its constitution and organisation is a self-contained body, the powers and functions of which are in fact entirely distinct from the general functions of the League of Nations.[1]  The International Labour Office, or headquarters of the organisation, will be at the seat of the League of Nations.[2]  It will act in the closest possible co-operation with the Secretary General of the League who will be under obligation to assist the Labour Office in any emergency.  At the seat of the League of Nations, the International Labour Office will be under the control of its own Director who will be provided with separate accommodation and a permanent staff.

The supreme authority of the Permanent Organisation for the International Regulation of Labour Conditions—known as the International Labour Organisation—is of course the International Labour Conference, which it is arranged shall meet annually. At the International Labour Office, the controlling authority under the Conference is the Governing Body, under whom is the Director and his staff.  The com-

[1] Appendix I. Articles 387-391, pp. 276-7.
[2] Appendix I. Articles 392-399, pp. 278-280.

plete nature of the International Labour Organisation, and its relative independence regarding the exercise of its functions, will be seen by comparing it with the permanent organisation of the League of Nations. The supreme authority of the League is, of course, the Assembly of the Nations, which corresponds to the International Labour Conference. Under this supreme authority is the Council of the League—corresponding to the Governing Body of the Conference, and under the Council is the Secretary General who corresponds to the Director of the International Labour Office.

With regard to procedure,[1] the Governing Body will act as the executive for the Conference. The Governing Body will meet periodically at short intervals, and can be called together specially if necessary. It will be the business of the Governing Body to prepare the agenda for annual Conferences from information sent to it from the different affiliated countries, either from governments or from responsible non-government sources such as industrial organisations of employers and workmen. The agenda must be circulated by the International Labour Office four months before the meeting of a Conference, so as to enable the governments concerned to instruct their delegates on the policy to be followed and also to enable governments to object, if they think proper, to any item placed on the agenda. Items to which objections are raised may, however, be discussed subsequently and dealt with, if it is decided

[1] Appendix I. Articles 400-407, pp. 281-284.

to do so, by two-thirds of the delegates attending a Conference.

In the event of it being decided that a question is to be discussed at a Conference it will be the business of the Labour Office, under the supervision of the Director, to collect all the information obtainable in regard to the question, and to prepare draft conventions based upon such information. There will thus be definite proposals prepared for submission to the annual Conference, which can, however, be modified or expanded as the result of its deliberations. Proposals in their final form must obtain two-thirds of the votes before being adopted by the Conference.

From this point the procedure becomes somewhat complicated, because of the inequality already referred to regarding the nature of the obligation incurred by different member states respecting the conventions drawn up by the Conference. It has been decided that the Conference shall cast conventions or recommendations for the consideration of member states, leaving them free to adopt or reject them, subject to two conditions—firstly, that conventions or recommendations adopted by the Conference shall be submitted to the competent legislative authorities of each country, and secondly, that in the event of acceptance of a convention by the legislative authority of a non-federal government, such government shall come under the further obligation to give effect to the convention by legislation or otherwise.

Let us trace the proceedings throughout from the

Conference stage. On a convention or recommendation being adopted by two-thirds of the votes cast, it has to be sent for registration to the Secretary General of the League of Nations, who in turn sends it through the proper channels to each of the member states. These states are then required to submit it to their competent legislative authority or authorities within twelve months from the end of a Conference, unless unforeseen circumstances arise, when the time may be extended to eighteen months. In the case of a recommendation, the countries concerned are required to submit it to the competent authority and to inform the Secretary General of the action taken, but are under no further obligation. In the case of a convention which is duly ratified by the competent legislative authority of any state, the state concerned is required to communicate the fact of ratification to the Secretary General of the League of Nations, and to take the necessary steps to give effect to the provisions of such convention.

In the event of failure on the part of any member state to submit a convention or recommendation to its legislative authority or authorities as required, any other member state is entitled to refer the matter to the Permanent Court of International Justice of the League of Nations. If, after acceptance by its legislative authority, a non-federal government fails to ratify and to give effect to a convention, then it is open to the Governing Body, either on its own initiative or on complaint being made to it by any member state,

to make representations to the defaulting government
and to publish such representations and the reply, if
any, which it may elicit from such government.
But the Governing Body may go further. It may
apply to the Secretary General of the League of
Nations to set up a commission of enquiry to deal with
the matter. Provision is made for the constitution
of such a commission within six months of the League
coming into existence. Each member state of the
League of Nations is under obligation to nominate
three persons of industrial experience who shall be
members of a panel, and it is further stipulated that
one of each three shall be a person of independent
standing and that the other two should represent the
workmen and the employers respectively.

The Secretary General, on application being made to
him by the Governing Body to constitute a Commission
of Enquiry, will select three members from this panel—
one from each representative class on the panel—
to serve on the Commission of Enquiry and also
appoint the chairman. The members of the panel
nominated by the complainant and defaulting states
are not eligible to serve on the Commission. The
Commissioners are required to make enquiry and
submit a report to the Secretary General. If their
finding is against the defaulting state, they are also
required to indicate what steps are, in their judgment,
necessary to remedy the grievance of which complaint
has been made. They may also recommend what
economic measures, if any, may be taken by the League

of Nations against the defaulting state, as a penalty
for default, if such state fails to make an appeal in
time or appeals unsuccessfully, and, in either case,
continues in default.

It will be noted that provision is made for a defaulting state to remedy any grievance alleged against it
before any question of penalties for default can
arise. Even in the event of its failure to do so the
imposition of any punitive economic measures which
may be recommended to the League in the report of
the Commissioners remains in suspense. After the
lapse of time for the appeal, or after an unsuccessful
appeal, however, the punitive measures sanctioned by
the League may be taken against the defaulting
state by the government of any other member
state.

The report of the Commission of Enquiry will be
sent by the Secretary General of the League of Nations
to the defaulting state as well as to the complainant
state, and they will be asked to say within a month
if they accept the recommendations made therein.
If not, an appeal may then be made by either state
to the Court of International Justice of the League of
Nations, which may affirm, reverse, or vary the decisions of the Commissioners. The decision of the Court
of International Justice on the matter is final. It will
thus be seen, that before any action can be taken on
any question affecting the interests of any member
state, the state concerned is given every opportunity
of falling into line with the general policy of the

League by remedying voluntarily any grievance alleged against it by another member state.

A most interesting and important feature of the scheme is the provision by which any properly constituted industrial association of employers or workers in a member state can make direct representations to the International Labour Office regarding the failure of any state to carry out its obligations respecting the conventions or recommendations of the Labour Conference. The Governing Body may at its discretion communicate these representations to the state complained against, for its observations.[1] This provision will undoubtedly quicken public interest in the proceedings of the Conference by bringing industrial associations of employers and workers into direct touch with the International Labour Office at all times and independently of their delegates. It will also bring the pressure of public opinion in all member states to bear upon the subject of international labour reforms, and will prove a powerful factor of influence in ensuring observance of the conventions dealing with the reforms which are adopted from time to time by the International Labour Conference. This provision will also tend to stimulate co-operation between workers throughout the world for the promotion of their interests and will add both weight and responsibility to the measures they adopt to attain this end.

It is necessary at this stage to note the constitution of the authorities in whom, under the League of

[1] Appendix I. Article 411, p. 285.

Nations, powers are vested to deal with the international issues under discussion; namely the Conference and the Governing Body of the International Labour Organisation. The functions of both authorities have been referred to shortly in this chapter and are fully set out in the text of the Peace Treaty in the appendix to this book. The constitution of both authorities is such as to create, and justify, confidence in them. Each member state is represented on the Conference by delegates who ensure that the interests of the state as a whole are duly safeguarded and are not subordinated to sectional interests, while sectional interests of capital and labour, on the other hand, are also assured that due consideration will be given to their claims. The International Labour Conference and its organisation are so constituted that governments, employers and workers alike might all regard the Annual Conferences of the Labour organisation as an opportunity for initiating highly practical labour reforms, and not merely as a convenient medium for expressing vague idealistic aspirations.

If the Conference were intended to be no more than a convenient opportunity for the interchange of opinions or the collection of information upon international labour questions, then there would have been no need for the careful balance which has been effected in framing its constitution as regards the relative proportions of the government and non-government delegates who will represent each state.[1] It must be

_____
[1] Appendix I. Article 389, p. 276.

remembered that each member state undertakes specific obligations in regard to the conventions and recommendations of the Conference. It is therefore right that the governments of these states should not be over-ruled at the Conference by the votes of their non-government delegates who represent sectional interests, not the interests of the nation as a whole. In accordance with this principle it has been decided that the Conference should be attended by four delegates from each member state who are to be appointed by their respective governments. Two of these four are to be the government representatives, one is to represent the interests of the employer and the other to represent the interests of the workers in each state. To ensure in turn that the employers' and the workers' delegates shall in each case be truly representative of their sectional interests as a whole, each government is under obligation to appoint these non-government delegates to the Conference in agreement with the industrial associations of employers and workers, where such organisations exist, in their respective countries.

The Conference on International Labour Legislation will therefore consist of delegates, half of whom will represent the governments and the other half the employers and workers of each member state. So that the conventions and recommendations of the Conference shall be based on a thorough and scientific consideration of the subjects with which they deal, provision has been made to place necessary technical and special advice at the disposal of the Conference. For this purpose each delegation has the right to take to the Conference two technical advisers on each topic, and any one of these advisers may change places with the delegate at any time, at his discretion. When questions especially concerning women are to be considered, one at least of these advisers is to be a woman.

Principles analogous to the above have also been applied to the constitution of the Governing Body. That is to say, as the respective governments of the member states have, altogether, half the representation on the Conference which gives direction to their policy, it has been decided that the Governing Body under the Conference shall be constituted in like manner. The Governing Body, accordingly, is to comprise twelve representatives of governments and twelve non-government representatives; six representing employers' and six representing workers' organisations. The apportionment of the government representatives is to be on the basis of eight for the eight chief industrial states and four for the other states—the latter to be selected by the delegates at a Conference representing the smaller states. The twelve delegates of the workers and employers respectively are also to be selected by the employers' and workers' delegates at a Conference. This system of representation is, I think, reasonable. It gives governments the power to safeguard the interests of states as a whole, and it also gives the representatives of the two great

sectional interests in each industrial country power to
make their influence felt. Their representation on the
Conference is undoubtedly another factor which will
add to the responsibility and influence of associations
of employers and workers generally, and it should help
materially in getting the recommendations and conventions of the Conference adopted and put into
practice in their respective countries.

The main objection to this system of representation
is, that the workers—for whose benefit the organisation
has been established—may be out-voted at the Conference by the representatives of governments and
employers should they combine their votes, because
the workers' representation stands in a proportion of
one to three as compared with that of governments
and employers combined. This objection, however,
is based on the assumption that the workers' delegates
at the Conference will be opposed by the delegates
of both governments and employers. Such an
assumption, I venture to say, is wrong. Past experiments in international labour legislation have
shown that governments have on the whole adopted
a favourable attitude regarding the aspirations of
the workers.

It requires no gift of prophecy to say that
governments will tend to do more, not less, for
workers in future. The contrary view fails to give
weight to the increased power of the worker in
all democratic governments, due to the fact that
the mass of workers everywhere are organising

themselves for political action and becoming a more powerful influence in the life of nations. As this process continues, the government representatives at the International Labour Conference will inevitably tend to co-operate more closely with the representatives of the workers. The policy of all democratic governments reflects an earnest and growing desire to improve the lot of the worker. If the government delegates at a Conference are chosen from among men who fairly reflect public opinion in their respective countries— and I have no doubt but that this will be the case—then the sympathy of these with the workers' delegates is assured. The government delegates, moreover, with their administrative training and experience, will give the workers' delegates valuable help in the difficult and often delicate work of giving practical form to the aims of labour through international legislation.

May not at least as much be said for the delegates who will represent employers at the Conference ? As a class British employers, at all events, have undoubtedly been influenced profoundly by recent events. There is, I believe, a sincere desire on the part of the vast majority of them to do what they can to improve the lot of the worker in every possible way. The Conference will prove of material assistance in helping them to realise this desire by providing the means by which one of the principal obstacles in the way of its realisation may be removed, namely, the fear, already referred to, that if higher wages and better conditions for the worker are conceded by employers in one country, they will be handicapped in competing against their rivals in countries where wages are kept low and industrial conditions remain bad. Simultaneous and relative progress in the conditions of industry in all countries through international labour legislation, as the result of careful deliberations at the Conference, will, I believe, abolish this evil in time and enable employers throughout the world to co-operate with the workers and the representatives of their governments in maintaining steady and universal progress in the improvement of labour conditions without the fear that uneven progress will involve the penalties of loss or ruin to those who are most progressive.

There is another aspect of the question of labour representation at the Conference to which attention should be drawn, namely, the method of voting by the delegates. Instead of the delegates voting together as a block for each country, they will have the right to vote separately and independently as individuals.[1] There are two reasons for this rule. In the first place, the Conference will deal with matters of domestic concern, which may be the subject of disagreement among the different delegates of any country. In the second place, the system of voting by individuals independently will encourage a broad outlook on international labour problems and will tend to foster a spirit of international unity—two important factors which are not only in harmony with the whole project of the

[1] Appendix I. Article 390, p. 277.

League of Nations, but which are essential elements
for the success of the International Labour Conference.

The employers and workers of any member state
will therefore be free to associate themselves with the
employers and workers of other countries, in matters
concerning their mutual interests.   The government
delegates will, of course, have the same right of splitting
their votes or voting with other nationalities, although
it is probable that in most matters these delegates
will vote according to the wishes of their respective
governments.   This mode of voting will be an interesting as I believe it to be a novel experiment.   It
remains to be seen how it will work out, but on the
whole I am inclined to think that it will work well.   It
must be remembered that the questions selected for
inclusion on the agenda of each annual Conference
will previously be decided upon by the members
of the Governing Body of the International Labour
Organisation in consultation.   It is, therefore, right
to assume that the government delegates will be
sympathetic in their attitude with regard to the
matters placed on the agenda with their concurrence at the suggestion of the other representatives.
Even if the workers' delegates were not assured of
the sympathy of their government colleagues on the
Governing Body, their position will be strong as they
are certain to command a labour block vote at the
Conference on every question which vitally concerns
the interests of workers.   Thus, for example, at a

Conference of say one hundred delegates, representing twenty-five countries, the united workers' delegates might cast twenty-five votes in favour of resolutions put forward by a workers' delegate from any country. On the other hand, it is extremely improbable that the whole government and employers' delegates at the Conference would cast a solid block vote against the workers' resolution. If, therefore, these resolutions are practicable and founded upon justice and good reason, they are likely to be carried at the Conference despite the fact that the workers' delegates are in the minority.

### III. THE INTERNATIONAL LABOUR OFFICE

Before concluding these remarks on the International Labour Organisation it is necessary to refer to one of the most important functions of the Labour Office. As already explained, it will be the duty of the Director to collect and furnish to the Conference the fullest information from international sources regarding subjects which are placed on the agenda for discussion. Besides this special information the Director will publish a journal in such languages as the Governing Body decide, which will deal generally with matters of interest connected with labour problems considered from an international point of view. In order to collect this information the Director will enter into definite relations with those departments of different governments which deal with questions relating to labour or with such representatives as governments may appoint for this purpose.

Thus the Director will be called upon to exercise delicate as well as important duties. Under his direction the Labour Office should become a reservoir into which will flow a constant stream of information from all parts of the world for the use of the Conference and for the education of public opinion in all countries regarding industrial problems. Information will be gathered in each country relating to such matters, for instance, as the age at which juvenile labour is first employed in industry wherever the law forbids the employment of juvenile labour before any age ; to what extent education is provided for juveniles before and after the age at which industrial employment is commenced ; the length of the normal working day in each country, the extent to which it is regulated by the law, and to what extent a government invites the advice and co-operation of industrial organisations of employers and workers in dealing with industrial problems. Further instances of information which may usefully be collected by the Labour Office are the extent to which legislation in different countries insists on preventive measures to safeguard workers against accidents ; forbids the use of poisonous ingredients in manufacture ; and how far it regulates the conditions under which women and juveniles work.

The Labour Office, in fact, will be the eyes and ears of the organisation behind the Conference. The system of intelligence which it perfects will form an additional link between the International Labour Conference and industrial associations of employers and workers in each member state—which are already linked with its constitution through their delegates— because the International Labour Office will certainly rely upon industrial associations throughout the world to assist it in the collection of accurate and complete information upon all questions connected with labour conditions in different countries. The constant demand of the International Labour Office for information, together with the annual Conferences on International Labour Legislation, will tend to stimulate industrial associations in all member states to perfect arrangements for supplying accurate information concerning their own sections of industry. Thus the International Labour Office, through its intelligence work for the Conference, will become the mainspring of activities which will make for closer sympathy and better understanding between different nations and will assist workers throughout the world to co-operate for their common good.

## IV. THE TRIUMPH OF COMBINATION

The right of combination, for which workers in the past fought so hard and so long, finds no place in the scheme of the Conference except by implication—but its full recognition is there all the same. As already explained, the governments of the member states

represented at the Conference, while being recognised
as the national units and the connecting links with the
International Labour Office, are expressly bound to
recognise the industrial associations of employers and
workers in their respective countries and to appoint
their non-government delegates to the Conference in
agreement with these industrial associations. This
marks a tremendous advance in public recognition
regarding the right of workers to combine to promote
their interests. To measure its importance, the past
struggles of workers for the right to combine must be
recalled, together with the vehemence of the opposition they encountered.

It is not too much to say that the factory workers
in the early days of the last century were regarded
pretty much in the same light as the slaves of the
South American cotton plantations—merely as
potential wealth producers for their betters—and
outside the pale of equal citizenship. The workers'
agitation for better conditions of life and employment, by organised combination, was at first
ruthlessly suppressed, either by the use of force on
the part of the government or by the insidious but no
less effective employers' boycott. To be a member
of a Trade Union was to risk liberty. To be a spokes-
man for Trade Unionism was to get "the sack"
whenever a convenient opportunity occurred. Even
the legalisation of the Unions proved, at first, a delusion and a snare.

In Great Britain, Trade Unions were legalised by the

law of 1824 ; yet, within ten years subsequently,
English agricultural labourers were actually sentenced
to long terms of imprisonment in exile for the offence
of forming an Agricultural Labourers' Union.  For
years afterwards the legitimate use of Trade Union
funds was not granted the necessary protection of the
law ;  peaceful persuasion was banned by the application of the law of conspiracy ;  and generally speaking,
the workers' hard-won recognition of the right to
combine was effectively negatived.   Economists added
their theories to the forces of opposition.  They argued,
for example, that to attempt to improve the lot of the
workers except by reducing their numbers by limiting
their families, was tantamount to flying in the face of
providence.  All this opposition to the attempts of
the workers to secure better conditions of life and
labour by collective effort was in force throughout a
time when the power of the individual workman to
bargain for his labour was being reduced to a nullity.
The old-time friendly and intimate relation between
employer and employed was rapidly passing.  Small
employers were being absorbed by companies and
syndicates which had neither bodies to be kicked nor
souls to be damned.  I am not going back on these
things to open up old sores or to revive bitter con-
troversies of the past, but rather to explain, in part at
least, the psychology of many workers in Britain at
the present time.

The old opposition to the legitimate efforts of workers
for progress to better things, resulted naturally in a

certain attitude of mind on the part of the workers in regard to the national forces they saw arrayed against them. Parliament, judges, economists, employers—all in the van of opposition to the workers—animated them more or less with lively distrust and antipathy. The workers demanded to be left to work out their destiny in their own way. Some among them regarded this opposition against them as a war made by certain powerful classes in the community against the workers as a class. They argued that the obvious remedy lay in retaliation, that is to say in class war waged by the workers against other classes. Advocates of this theory are active among our workers to-day. They regard themselves, in a sense, as outlaws in the existing social scheme and they spend their time in fomenting trouble of some kind, not so much to get any immediate material benefit for the worker as to paralyse and destroy the existing order in the vague hope of creating a new world from the chaos of its ruins. True, they are a minority, but they must be reckoned with. In doing this there is need for never-failing sympathy, patience and due regard to the fact that these men are the product of days when every man's hand was against the worker, and he had to rely upon his own right arm alone for his emancipation from injustice and wrong.

Happily there is a better spirit now abroad. The old conceptions of the worker's lot in life and the opposition to his right to improve it have gone the way of all errors. There is in all democratic countries a general recognition of the rights of the worker, as well as the need for improvement in regard to the conditions of his life and work, as the only possible foundation of a healthy, prosperous, peaceful community. For some years the Trade Unions have been regarded as the trustees of the workers' interests and their leaders as the advocates through whom workers can bargain on terms of equality with employers and the government regarding their interests. There could be no more striking illustration of the change of public opinion regarding industrial combinations of workers than the recognition of their right to representation in the International Labour Conference. Trade Unionists no longer find themselves opposed as disturbers of the peace or tolerated as necessary evils. They are recognised as co-workers with other organised forces for the common good.

The worker has won the right of combination. He has now to perfect a more efficient, comprehensive and powerful system of combination which will not only be national but international in scope. The better organisation of workers will tend to stimulate organisation among employers, and will in this way facilitate, by rational collective action, the avoidance as well as the settlement of industrial disputes which are ruinous alike to employers, workers, and the nation and which are aggravated by the confusion or anarchy to which independent action on the part of individuals or small sections of workers and employers gives rise. Apart from its other moral advantages the growth of organised co-operation among workers and employers will help materially in the scientific development of production upon a large scale which is an essential condition and the very foundation of our industrial prosperity and social welfare in the future.

One inevitable result of the development of large scale production will be that, in future, governments will become larger employers of labour than they are to-day, because some industrial enterprises, as for instance the supply of electric power, will become too vast to be safely left in private hands even if the financial burden involved could be borne by private funds and credit. It is inevitable, apart from future industrial developments of this nature, that governments must concern themselves more closely than hitherto with the settlement of industrial disputes, because such disputes will become more and more matters of vital national concern. This need, again, will demand a more efficient and wider combination of workers to facilitate the settlement of complicated questions concerning the interests of vast numbers of workers, through the agency of a few representatives appointed by them to safeguard their interests.

The obstacles to the organised combination of workers no longer arise through the opposition of governments, employers, or economists. These old opponents have been converted to the value of combination, both among employers and workers, as an essential condition for establishing industry

upon sound economic principles and, above all, upon
the well-being of healthy, efficient and prosperous
workers.  The difficulties in the way of the progress
of combination, curiously enough, arise now from the
workers themselves.  It is caused mainly by over-
lapping and conflict among various combinations of
workers with regard to the functions they exercise.
There are too many Trade Unions and too little
Trade Unionism.  Happily, efforts are being made
by the most influential and representative labour
leaders in all countries to rectify existing anomalies
on the lines of federation and amalgamation.  The
combination of the Trade Unions themselves is
being slowly—and I am afraid painfully—reorgan-
ised to suit modern requirements, so as to unite
their forces and their functions in accordance with
a common will and purpose.

In this task, workers in all countries will undoubtedly
be assisted by the creation of the annual Conference
of the International Labour Organisation established
under the League of Nations.  The representation of
workers from every country at this Conference is
indeed the triumph of the workers' struggle for the
right of combination in the past, and in it lies the
brightest hope for progress in the future.  The Conference holds in it the seeds of a vast and far-reaching
international combination, not only of workers but of
governments and employers—indeed of all the human
forces of industry.  The express object of their co-
operative efforts is to establish the production of

wealth throughout the world on a foundation of justice and welfare for the workers. It is for the workers throughout the world to combine in one great brotherhood for the realisation of this ideal and, in doing so, to forge a potent bond for the preservation of unity and peace among all peoples.

G. N. BARNES.

# HISTORICAL SIGNIFICANCE

OF

# THE INTERNATIONAL LABOUR CONFERENCE

BY

## JAMES T. SHOTWELL

Professor of Columbia University, and American Delegate to the Commission
on International Labour Legislation, Paris Peace Conference

I. THE SHADOW OF REVOLUTION

II. THE CONFERENCE AND INTERNATIONAL LABOUR
ORGANISATIONS

III. INTERNATIONAL LABOUR LEGISLATION AS A DOMESTIC
PROBLEM

IV. THE PROBLEM OF NATIONAL INDEPENDENCE

V. THE CONFERENCE AND THE LEAGUE OF NATIONS

# CHAPTER II

## THE HISTORICAL SIGNIFICANCE OF THE INTERNATIONAL LABOUR CONFERENCE

### I. THE SHADOW OF REVOLUTION

THE only way to understand the significance of an institution is to see it in its historical setting, not alone with reference to the narrow sequence of causes which produced it, but also with reference to that broader current of events which determines our point of view.

The International Conference for Labour Legislation has history behind it ; but it is a somewhat confused and little appreciated history, which has never been set forth clearly for the understanding of the general public.[1] This may in part account for a strange failure on the part of that public to appreciate the significance of what was done at Paris. But the little interest which it stirred in those whose lives had been passed in the consideration of the problems with which it deals is harder to explain. Not until the first Conference was actually summoned for Washington was there any serious consideration given by Labour to its

[1] A short review of this history is contained in Chapter VII. of this book.

41

possibilities. Then when it was too late to enlarge those possibilities without seriously altering the whole structure, the importance of the first world parliament of industrial democracy began to dawn upon the leaders of both labour and capital—though not seldom the dawn was a cloudy one.

The immediate setting for the creation of the Conference was the announcement by Clemenceau at the first general session (Séance Plenière) of the Peace Conference that the first steps towards the organisation of the Peace Conference itself would be the creation of three Commissions, the first to examine the responsibilities for the war, the second to deal with the crimes committed in the war, and the third with international labour legislation. Whatever the assembled diplomatists may have felt upon hearing this announcement of the questions to be considered first, it produced a degree of surprise that almost amounted to bewilderment in that part of the audience which never hesitated to express its feelings. The journalists present came away from that first general session seeking light from any and every quarter where they might find it, in order to explain to the readers " back home " how the Conference was proposing to set about the actual business of securing the peace of the world. Their surprise at the prominence of international labour legislation was not due to any lack of interest in labour problems, but to the fact that up to the very moment of this announcement no word had reached the public that the Conference, which had ostensibly

met mainly to draw boundaries and set nations in
their places on the map, had any intention to move
industrial problems to the fore. The programme laid
down in this solemn session was therefore far removed
from what either journalists or the general public
seemed to have expected.

There were two conjectures as to why the Conference
had taken this step. The first was that the real
masters of policy, the great Powers, had not reached
agreement as to how they were to proceed in the settlement of the larger issues before the Conference, and
that as there was need to give some outer indications
of activity in the meantime, the public and the
smaller Powers were being put off with something of
general interest to keep them occupied. The other
was that the governments of Europe were nervous in
the face of a rising industrial unrest, with unknown
Bolshevistic possibilities, and had, therefore, to offer
to Labour a definite and formal recognition at the very
opening of the Conference, both to justify themselves
with reference to the war in the past, and to hold
forth the hope of a larger measure of international
labour agreements in the future.

Whether the governments of Europe were nervous
or not in the winter of 1918-19, there was plenty of
reason for uneasiness. We have now become so used
to the Bolshevist régime that we cannot any longer
realise how deeply it first stirred the passions of all
classes in Europe—the bourgeois with fear, the radicals
and revolutionaries with uneasy hope. Then the wild

fires of revolution in Germany seemed to presage
universal anarchy, and at least one or two of the
governments represented at Paris were thought to
stand in daily danger of being overthrown.  The long
shadow of Russia could not be obliterated from Europe.

In such circumstances the holding of international
labour Conferences at Berne by the Socialists and
the Syndicalists or Trade Unionists, who proposed
once more to take up the broken threads of their
pre-war organisations, had more than ordinary significance.  This meeting was meant and taken as being
more or less of a challenge to Paris,—the revolutionary
and industrial international organisations as against
the governmental.  It was this aspect of the meeting
in Switzerland, as much as what was regarded as
the rather premature attendance at it of German
delegates, which kept the more conservatively
nationalistic Labour leaders—especially from America
—from participating.

## II. THE CONFERENCE AND INTERNATIONAL LABOUR ORGANISATIONS

The work of the Commission for International
Labour Legislation of the Peace Conference has, therefore, first of all, to be measured against that of these
international organisations of European industrial
democracy.

Fortunately comparison is not difficult, for both
Internationals, the Socialist and the Trade Union,
drew up definite propositions embodying the principles

upon which they wished to see world peace.
When one examines these pronouncements, however,
from the standpoint of labour, with reference to its
own claims as such in the settlement, one is struck
with the fact that a large part of the programme they
laid down had nothing to do with economic matters
at all, but concerned things so remote from the
factory and workshop as the Balkan boundaries or
colonial adjustments. This in itself is a significant,
and withal an inspiring fact, which seems to have
attracted little attention,—that the first attempt of
industrial democracy to frame a programme for
foreign affairs should have so little to do with labour
itself.

The " War Aims " which Labour had put forth
at various times in the latter stages of the war, and
which were largely evident in the pronouncements of
Berne, had covered the whole wide range of social
justice and laid down general principles for international dealings without regard to the limitations of the
particular demands of the workers. The leaders
of industrial democracy were engaged upon the
larger task of laying the basis for the new world-
order, which they hoped to erect, so that democracy
might be safe in the future to go ahead with its
plans and its dreams of economic progress. So
deeply were they impressed by the interdependence
of reforms at home with international peace that
their main preoccupation in the suggested settlement
was to secure first an enduring peace as a condition

for the reforms which could then follow. Consequently the programmes of Berne were predominantly political instead of economic.

A statement of the demands of Labour *for itself*, due in the first instance to the Trade Unionists, was ultimately adopted unanimously by the Conference as a whole in the form of a "Labour Charter." This document is the one product of the Berne congresses which is to be measured up against the labour section of the Treaty. Interest in it is not lessened by its obvious German ancestry, embodying as it does the points laid forth in a proposal of the International Labour Office in the earliest days of the Armistice. This "Labour Charter" was, therefore, more than a revolutionary document. It was a constructive programme as well, and may yet play a large rôle in the future history of international labour ideals. But it exhibited those elements of irresponsibility for results which are to be found so generally in the programmes of an opposition. In this case the opposition was two-fold—German, and anti-governmental or revolutionary. The propositions it advanced were, therefore, thorough-going and without those modifications which are imposed by responsibility.

At the same time it must be admitted that they embodied the point of view of a large and powerful element in the labour world of the allied countries, and furnished in fact the one definite expression of the demands of labour which might serve for a clue to the Peace Conference. Yet the Commission for

International Labour Legislation of the Peace Conference was hindered as well as helped in its work by this pronouncement of the Berne Congress, for it was at once clear that no international body limited by the responsibilities of power could proceed as freely to draw up for execution projects which it might regard as desirable, but which were often impossible to apply at a given moment and in given circumstances. The result was bound to be that whatever was done by the Conference in Paris, would seem ineffective and partial by comparison with the programme laid down by the International Conferences at Berne.

### III. INTERNATIONAL LABOUR LEGISLATION AS A DOMESTIC PROBLEM

There is a second limitation to the work of the Commission for Labour Legislation which became only too evident as that work progressed, and which has marked the history of past international attempts at labour legislation. The method of securing legislation by way of treaty is at best a poor device. Few states are inclined to bind themselves in definite contracts with their neighbours concerning the treatment of their own industrial problems, and the history of past international labour legislation is slight and obscure. As a matter of fact it was this very obscurity which puzzled the newspaper correspondents at Paris as to the meaning of the Commission itself, for in the past only two general agreements had been reached by way of international convention, and these concerned only night work for women and the prohibition of the manufacture of sulphurous matches. When one compares these two slight clauses with the enormous mass of labour codes in the different countries—enormous and rapidly increasing—one realises how relatively ineffective has been the method of procedure by way of the Treaty.

How then could the Paris Conference make good, limited as it apparently was to this method of procedure and faced with all the variety of problems that concerned the World Congress meeting in the midst of such social unrest and turmoil as the world was then passing through ?

The situation was certainly not promising, and yet the very difficulties of the case made the solution which was urged all the more remarkable. The British Labour Delegation to the Peace Conference made a proposal that instead of centering attention solely upon any specific claims of labour which might be inserted in the Treaty, there should be erected an annually recurring International Labour Parliament and an International Labour Office, which could keep pace with the progressive changing demands of the labour world, and so secure, not one single Labour Charter, but a never-ending series.

The idea was a large and fruitful one. So far as Labour was concerned, the Peace Conference of Paris would be but the first step in a continuous process ; and the Treaty, instead of being a final document, was, in so far as it was concerned with industrial problems, but the first clauses of a document which was to be continued by future congresses through future treaties. It would thus be the beginning of a continuous co-operation on the part of Labour, Society, and Governments.

The contribution of the British Delegation, however, was much more than a statement of a policy—it proceeded to offer the details of a definite plan by which the policy could be realised, a plan which when first presented to the Commission on International Labour Legislation, was already elaborated in the articles and clauses of a proposed section of the Treaty of Peace, and contained most of the essential elements of the plan as later adopted. Indeed, from the standpoint of diplomacy, it is possible that the plan as first presented was too detailed; for it had not been whittled to fit all of the constitutional objections which participating governments were forced to raise against it, and therefore the first phase of the discussion tended to be rather critical and negative, because the larger principles underlying it were more or less taken for granted. But, on the other hand, this detailed plan of a constitution for Labour was a pleasing contrast to the unformed generalities which were all that a number of the other sections of the Peace Conference had to begin with ; and, all things considered, it is possible that future historians may find in this well developed proposition the most original and suggestive experiment of all those which

D

were advanced at a Conference at which the whole scheme of world politics was in discussion, if not on trial.

The distinctive contributions which marked the International Labour Constitution as original and of particular significance, are in the first place the recognition of non-official representation in an official international body, and in the second place the provision by which the action of that international body was to be related with that of the various governments.

For the first time in the history of international law it was proposed to permit unofficial delegates—mere citizens of different countries representing home interests in labour or capital, to vote with similar representative citizens of other countries, independently of the action of the representatives of their governments, and so to help actually to bind those governments towards certain international policies and treaties.

It was clear that some device would have to be found for the limitation of the powers of these non-official representatives, and yet it was necessary that that limitation should not be carried to the point of endangering in any way the reality of their work. As the Commission was warned more than once in the course of its proceedings, Labour was tired of words and empty and delusive promises and would not be interested in the erection of any institution which was devoid of power. If, however, power were to be given to men irresponsible to their governments, it was taking that power from the governments themselves. This brought one into a very dangerous dilemma, for if the power to make labour treaties were to be taken over by a body containing so large an element of unofficial representatives, what about the power to enforce the treaties ? Should the governments be held responsible for carrying out propositions arrived at and agreed upon in the formulation of which they had been partly shut out ? The result would be to make a government little more than a police force for the administration of regulations arrived at by these Industrial Parliaments ; in short, there would have arisen something like a World State under the aegis of Industrial Democracy and the International Parliament of Labour would be the most august legislating institution in the world, over-riding government not only within itself but in the subsequent carrying out of its decisions.

This dilemma gave rise to a long discussion. The more revolutionary section of the Commission, represented especially by the brilliant Secretary of the French Confédération Générale du Travail, was strongly for proceeding at once with the bolder policy which would endow the International Labour Parliament with the powers of a genuine legislature and bind the constituent countries to the carrying out of its decrees. This point of view was apparently shared in greater or less extent by those qualified to speak for labour in all the continental countries—a fact of much significance in estimating how far towards industrial

confederation the continental countries might proceed.
Great Britain and the United States, however, and still
more Japan, were reluctant even to consider such a
revolutionary point of view, and stood out strongly
against the notion that the time had come for the
recognition of a world state, even where the impulse
to common action was so strong. For the United
States, which at best had come against its will into
the arena of world politics, any such suggestion as that
its government should abrogate its control of such
domestic affairs as industrial legislation, seemed
almost automatically to exclude it from participation
in the scheme. Japan was equally reluctant from
another reason, for its industrial problems were as yet
so unlike those of Western Europe, that it could hardly
be expected to place itself at the mercy of an international body in which it would have so slight a voice.
Since there was no power to compel the representatives
of any state in Paris to accept a parliament endowed
with such prerogatives it was clearly necessary to find
some device by which the Parliament of Labour should
have sufficient authority to justify its existence in the
eyes of Labour as a real force for securing legislation,
and yet not set itself up as a super-government in
opposition to existing governments.

It was this dilemma which brought forth the second
and most ingenious contribution to the British scheme,
namely that the power of the International Parliament
be limited to secure the submission of its legislation
to the legislatures or other competent authorities of

the participating states. In the field of International Labour Legislation, the Foreign Offices and other bureaucratic intermediaries shall not interfere ; no recommendations of the proposed parliament can be smothered in the files of a reactionary diplomatic official ; they must be brought within a given time to the attention of Parliament or Congress or whatever law-making body the country may possess.

Beyond that, international compulsion cannot go towards securing the adherence of the participating Powers ; so that all the World Parliament can do is to lay its conclusions before the highest tribunal of public opinion in each country, and leave it to that body to decide whether it shall adhere or not.

In the long history of political theory it would be hard to find an experiment more interesting and suggestive than this proposed delicate machinery for transmitting to Powers jealous of their reputation and their standards of social morality, the forceful suggestion of international co-operation in matters which have hitherto lain exclusively within their jurisdiction. On the face of it there is no derogation of sovereignty whatever ; the International Parliament has no power to make legislation, but simply to suggest it. In reality, however, that suggestion, if passed by a two-thirds vote, comes to the various countries with an authority which somewhat resembles the device by which the British officials once governed the titular rulers of Egypt. It will be hard to believe that any state should be willing to write itself down as so backward in its ideals of social justice as to refuse to accept laws which are to be of otherwise universal adoption. The forces of progressive opinion will be given a leverage, by way of comparison and direct appeal, which should impel each state to go as far as possible towards meeting the demands of the yearly Conference.

In a word, the essence of the plan is to throw back upon public opinion in the various countries the responsibility for carrying on social legislation. By seizing upon this sound principle in the assignment of responsibility for passing legislation, it would be possible to exact from the participating states a degree of responsibility for such laws as they did accept, which otherwise could not have been exacted.

### IV. THE PROBLEM OF NATIONAL INDEPENDENCE

This brings us to the third main point in the British proposal, the question of the enforcement of International Labour Legislation, once it had been agreed upon. A long and very intricate section of the plan deals with this—too long and too intricate for the casual reader—and possibly it may be found to have gone too much into detail in a matter so intricate that it is impossible for us now to foresee just how it will work out. However that may be, the plan has the merit of frankly facing the difficulties of the situation and offering a number of alternative lines of action. The problem here is the most delicate of all. Can international action go so far as to interfere in the internal affairs of a sovereign state to pronounce upon the success or failure of its administration ? That would be the recognition of a World State in the most sensitive part of government machinery—the power to enforce law ; and yet it was the sense of every person concerned with it in the Labour Commission at Paris, that unless some provision were made to ensure the carrying out of the proposed legislation the whole enterprise would be rendered nugatory through the failure of those states to apply it for which it was more especially designed. International Labour Legislation would in the nature of the case be always minimum legislation. Its purpose would be to bring up the backward states to as near the standards of progressive countries as possible, in order that progressive states themselves should not be kept behind by the existence elsewhere of conditions permitting exploitation of labour and so causing unfair conditions of competition. Since experience has shown that these same backward countries might attempt to meet the situation by placing legislation on the statute books which was never intended to be carried out, the provision for overseeing the enforcement of labour legislation was of fundamental importance. Yet nothing can run more counter to the principles of national sovereignty as understood and applied throughout the world than this interference with the enforcement of law.

Here then was a further step towards the recognition

of that limitation on sovereignty which is implicit in the concept of the League of Nations. It would have been a serious innovation to have permitted the government of one state to raise objections to the way in which the government of another state was carrying out its own laws in a field which had always previously been regarded as distinctly a home affair. But the British scheme went even further than that; it proposed to allow bodies of private individuals in one state to pass judgment on the way in which the laws of another state were being carried out, and to interfere in order to secure better enforcement, thus going a long way towards the breakdown of that conception of sovereignty as absolute which was the ruinous doctrine upon which the old régime, before the war, was based. It was a bold and novel proposition, and if it were to be frequently invoked might conceivably accomplish as much mischief as good. But as drawn up, it is rather a negative than a positive provision. It stands in the background of the plan for international legislation with the threat of interference in the home life of the participants in case they do not behave. It is a recognition of the interests of all in the conduct of each of the governments of the world, and will be heeded without formal enforcement to the extent that the laws proposed have the general support of world opinion, and also to the extent of the vitality of the League of Nations, of whose constitution this is one of the most vital, if little recognised elements.

In the course of the debates in the Commission, it became more and more evident that while the plan was the product of the British delegates, the need for an international organisation was much stronger on the Continent than elsewhere. Labour laws, like labour movements, tend to break through boundary lines on the map, when those lines are drawn across a Continent so small and intricate as the Continent of Europe. Therefore the Continental representatives for the most part were in favour of making the scheme as rigid and binding as possible, and of frankly erecting a sort of International Industrial Super-State which should enforce both legislation and administration upon the various governments. The British proposal avoided the crucial point in the scheme for the creation of a Super-State by leaving untouched the power of the different national parliaments to pass their own laws ; but it supplied all the mechanism for enforcement that the Continental representatives could desire.

The American representatives, however, were unable to agree even to this compromise, in the form in which it was originally presented. For even such a partial scheme as this was carrying them beyond the limitations of their constitution as well as against the traditions of their industrial history. In the President of the Commission, Mr. Gompers, the United States had supplied a delegate who represented the major force in American industrial history, the American Federation of Labour. The policy of this organisation had always been to "keep out of politics." While gladly availing itself of labour legislation, it had steadily maintained a policy of remaining aloof from purely political questions and of bringing the direct pressure of its organisation to bear upon either of the great political parties of the country as occasion demanded. It, therefore, had always regarded its proper sphere as distinctly economic. To participate in the international constitution might involve a break with its non-political traditions, for it implied concentrating upon legislative action in home affairs rather than upon direct action as in the past. However, the American Federation of Labour had already taken steps in this direction during the war, particularly since its Buffalo meeting in 1917, and indeed the genius of Mr. Gompers had already discerned the inevitable widening of the sphere of action of his Federation, so that while conscious of the momentous character of his decision as a possible turning point for labour policy in the United States, he accepted the situation to which the war had finally brought American labour, along with that of Europe, and lent his co-operation as far as it was possible.

But it was not possible to co-operate freely. The Constitution of the United States prevented that. Practically all the labour legislation of the United States is state legislation, and the States can have no relations with foreign governments. How then could the United States participate in the proposed international labour legislation if the country as a whole possessed no organ either for securing a uniform and universal adoption of the proposed international labour laws, or for the enforcement of these laws if they should be enacted, except in the very limited fields over which the Federal Government had unquestioned juris-diction ? These difficulties were laid before the Commission with great cogency by both Mr. Gompers and his colleague, Mr. Robinson, in the earlier sessions of the Conference, and for a time it seemed as though an impasse had been reached which made it impossible for the United States to participate in the plan. The country would find itself in an intolerable situation if it were to share in the passage of propositions through the international body, which it would have no way of either enacting into law through Congress or of enforcing through the Federal authority.[1]

To be sure, there were certain indications in American

[1] This is not the place for a detailed discussion of the legal questions involved in American participation. It is possible that it may yet be found that the constitutional limitations indicated above do not necessarily apply after all. A treaty becomes the supreme law of the land, and therefore it has been held that action by treaty involves any necessary extension of the field of federal control to execute its provisions. A precedent already exists for thus overcoming divergent state laws by treaty action, in the case of a treaty protecting migratory birds which was made with Canada and is binding on the whole country, in a matter outside the reach of federal legislative action. But it would have been hazarding much for the representatives of the United States at Paris to have based upon this precedent their assent to an international obligation to apply it in the manner proposed. Moreover, even if the legal argument should turn out to admit of acceptance of the scheme, there was much to be said against using it, if it should result in any enlargement of the control of the Senate, instead of that of Congress as a whole, over labour matters. Fortunately the alternative to a treaty, recommendation for legislative action, would not be open to this objection.

industrial history that the time was approaching
when labour legislation would become more and more
a national, and less a state affair.  A way had been
found for the national enforcement of a law to
prohibit the use of phosphorus in matches ; and
another law had attempted to prohibit child labour
under certain conditions by stretching the powers of
inter-state commerce control to prohibit the commerce
of articles in the making of which there had been child
labour.  But this child labour law had been declared
unconstitutional by the Supreme Court as late as the
summer of 1918, so that the supreme judiciary of the
United States had declared itself, almost at the very
moment at which the Peace Conference was held, as
against any stretching of the constitution so that
labour legislation could be undertaken by Congress
through the inter-state control of commerce.  On
the other hand, the action of the Supreme Court in
limiting the power of Congress to its traditional
sphere, seems hardly likely to be final.  No sooner
had the Court pronounced its decision than the next
Congress at once passed a new Child Labour Law
which both Houses accepted simultaneously ; and
this time it proposed to go even further than it
had before, and boldly enforce the law by its power
of taxation.

The public opinion of the United States was obviously working towards the recognition of national
labour legislation by way of Congress, in place of the
old method of state action, and if the Supreme Court

should again declare the new law unconstitutional, it is even possible that a constitutional amendment could be secured which would definitely place labour legislation within the power of Congress. But the representatives of the United States at Paris could not anticipate history, and although signs at home were more and more evident that the temper of the country would not stand any longer the obstruction which it had been meeting from a few backward states, such as North Carolina and Mississippi, in securing rudimentary principles of labour legislation, Mr. Gompers and his associates could not risk guaranteeing any such interpretation of American political tendencies in an international agreement. They had to take the situation as it actually was, with all the historic limitations of the Federal Government. They were, therefore, in a very difficult position, for were they to interpret the position of the United States Government in this International Congress as simply being one of traditional impotence they would be lending a leverage to the perpetuation of that impotence by allowing it to remain the basis of an international policy at a time when other governments were assuming the new obligations. Moreover, much depended upon the participation of the United States in the proposed world organisation. In the face of a Europe on the verge of revolution, the effect of American abstention would be to strengthen that conservative reaction which was a highly unsafe policy to pursue, and at the same time to lessen the effect of the participation of the United States in securing social justice in other lines.

The solution of the difficulty was found in a compromise. And the compromise, as so often happens, enlarged instead of lessened the scope of the proposed International Labour Conference. That body might present its conclusions to the participating governments in the form of recommendations for labour legislation, instead of simply as treaties to be adopted by them. At first glance this seems like enfeebling its action by permitting an evaporation into rhetoric, and so the American suggestion was interpreted by the continental representatives on the Commission who were anxious to endow the international organisation with the sanctions of a real government. They claimed that to allow the Conferences in the future freedom to vote mere recommendations instead of drawing up treaties, would tend toward weakened influence, and they feared that the recommendations would not carry sufficient authority to secure adoption in the different countries. On the other hand, it was pointed out by the American representative that the possibility of falling back upon recommendations when treaties could not be arrived at would give much larger scope for the work of the Conference, by enabling it to take action not only where technical difficulties stood in the way of treaty-making, but also in cases where public opinion had not reached the point of decision necessary to making treaty-contracts, although apparently moving in that direction. As a means for accelerating public opinion, the recommendation would, therefore, be the first step toward a treaty, and would keep the matter alive ; whereas a rejected treaty would be difficult to recall. It was pointed out, in support of this point of view, that the history of labour treaties was a very slight one, that only two small matters already mentioned had been settled by general international contracts, namely, the prohibition of night work for women and the use of phosphorus in match making. If, therefore, the Labour Conferences were to be limited to this method of procedure—by treaty-making alone—they had no very large nor lasting history ahead of them. On the contrary, if their conclusions were to be submitted as recommendations for appropriate action by the different governments, they could be better adjusted to the variant conditions of law and custom, and so more sure of acceptance.

The American amendment to the British plan was, therefore, an addition to it rather than a limitation. This became apparent almost immediately when the question arose of the adhesion of Japan and the countries of newer or less industrial development. It will be unnecessary here to describe the further modifications in the plan which were made in order to secure the participation of those countries, but the point to be emphasised is that the difficulties presented by the United States Constitution carried the plan for the Labour Conference away from a somewhat narrow and legalistic conception of its possibilities, into an

adjustable instrument for world legislation.   The fact
that that legislation would be to a large degree simply
preliminary, and that it would have to overcome
various obstacles in the different countries before it
finally secured adoption, does not lessen the genuine
character as legislation.   The Labour Conference
becomes a sort of preliminary legislature in which
projects are shaped up for adoption, both immediate
and indirect.   This, after all, is all that can be accomplished in an international conference so long as
governments make their own laws.


V. THE CONFERENCE AND THE LEAGUE OF NATIONS

It is a perilous thing at best to attempt to erect an
international legislative body, even when the field in
which it works is one upon which there is practical
agreement and pressing need for international co-
operation.   But the International Labour Conference
deals with matters that have always been considered
the proper sphere of one's home government—except
by those whose creed is the " Internationale."   One
could not expect it to be a complete success and its
subsequent history may be far different from what was
in the mind of its creators.   Yet the experiment of an
international parliament in the sphere of industrial
democracy cannot help but clarify the supreme
problem of securing policies adaptable to variant
cultures, whether it really succeeds in securing the
adherence of participating states to all the definite

treaties which it prepares at the present time, or not.

It seems to the writer that a mistake was made in Paris in the method in which this Labour Conference was linked up to the League of Nations. One of the chief criticisms directed by Radicals against the League of Nations was that it lacked a proper representative body, and was simply a League of Governments. In the Labour Parliament there is an answer to that criticism in so far as one large field of interests was represented. The Commission which drafted the League of Nations could have silenced some of the criticism by the more definite and formal recognition of the principle of functional representation, for which the Labour Conference could furnish a model. In the Covenant of the League of Nations, the International Labour Office and a permanent administrative staff receives the prominence which should have been given to the recurring Labour Conference. On the other hand, in view of subsequent events, there is something to be said for the point of view discussed by the Italian delegation that it was risking a good deal to tie up the labour organisation closely with the League of Nations at all, for in it there is a possibility of an industrial league working internationally, no matter what happens to the larger scheme—a possibility which might prove a rallying point for other international action in case the League of Nations fails in the sphere of political action. This to many will seem like a strangely distorted perspective, but if as Baron Makino is reported

E

to have stated in Paris, the one great problem of the future is the labour problem, internationally as well as nationally, then the experiment of an International Labour Parliament is a major element of a League of Nations, and not a mere adjunct of it.

This conception of the work of the Commission in Paris was hardly shared by the leading statesmen there.  At the general session of the Conference in which the labour section of the Treaty was accepted, the perfunctory character of the proceedings, so far as those not on the Commission itself were concerned, was a matter of comment on the part of most of those present who had a real interest in what was being done.  But the forces which led the Peace Conference in the first place to recognise labour are not likely to be put off by any casual treatment of their demands ; and if the International Labour Conference fails, either through the lack of far-sighted statesmanship in its own councils, or through the unwillingness of governments to co-operate in the carrying out of its conclusions, the result will not be merely negative.  For the example of such a failure of the parliamentary " international " would not be lost upon the revolutionary " Internationale."

J. T. SHOTWELL.

# INTERNATIONAL TRADE UNIONISM

BY

## W. A. APPLETON, C.B.E.

General Secretary of the British General Federation of Trade Unions
President of the International Federation of Trade Unions

I. INDUSTRIAL AND POLITICAL ACTIVITIES

II. AIMS OF THE "TRADE UNION INTERNATIONAL"

# CHAPTER III

## INTERNATIONAL TRADE UNIONISM

### I. INDUSTRIAL AND POLITICAL ACTIVITIES

THE International Labour Movement has hitherto been regarded with suspicion and hostility. It has been looked upon not merely as a disturbing factor in industrial relationships, but as a political organisation having anti-national tendencies. Generally speaking, this trouble arises from the common failure to recognise in the International Labour Movement the existence of two distinct activities : the industrial activity, which is concerned with the evolutionary amelioration of evil labour conditions and the political activity, which frankly seeks to overthrow existing forms of society, and to substitute other forms in which the fact of a man's existence confers on him the right to maintenance, irrespective of industrial capacity or efficiency.

The inability of the general, and sometimes suffering, public, to differentiate between the industrial and the political activities of the international movement is pardonable, because in those European countries where industry is not highly developed, skilled workers are few and widely dispersed and the lines of demarcation between the two activities of the movement are never quite clear. In countries like America, Britain, France and Germany, the confusion of thought is maintained because in each there are always politicians who claim to possess the support of trade unionists for every political cause they espouse.

Confusion of thought and political exploitation have contributed to the misunderstandings which exist regarding the Trade Union International and have lent force to many charges preferred against those who aim at community of industrial action between the organised workers of different countries. Governments and capitalists, originally alarmed at the growth of national labour movements, became at one time tragically afraid of their international development, and where opposition to them with legal sanction was impossible, a campaign of unwise and dangerous misrepresentation has been instituted. In some cases this campaign was supported by calculated provocation. Social ostracism and industrial repudiation became the lot of many trade unionists who, finding themselves denied opportunities, even of stating their requirements or of arguing the justice of their position, gradually turned towards political as against industrial methods to attain their objects.

The common fears of various classes regarding the international labour movement should be dissipated, because they constitute an ever present bar to progress. They can be minimised by emphasising the fact that there are indeed two distinct activities in this movement, each of them claiming to promote a higher standard of human existence but differing in the character and extent of their aims and in the methods they adopt.

Taking the political activity first—not because it is necessarily more important or older than the industrial, but because it will be dismissed after an attempt to define its aims. It is perfectly clear that this political activity aims at the overthrow of existing forms of society. Its supporters regard this step as a necessary prelude to the establishment of a State in which all men shall be given equal means of subsistence and equal opportunities of happiness, irrespective of their natural or acquired capacity for service or of services actually rendered. The majority of the exponents of this theory advocate revolutionary methods for giving practical effect to it and profess their willingness to face all the consequences.

International Trade Unionism is less pretentious. It is more concerned with the present than with the future. Bread for to-day rather than an aureole for to-morrow aptly describes its mental attitude. It seeks neither the destruction of real wealth nor the overthrow of governments. It recognises that the former is essential to happiness and that the latter are necessary if ordered existence is desired. International Trade Unionism is by tradition and training a constructive force, and no community need fear its development if it can be defended against political exploitation.

It is concerned alike with the production and distribution of wealth, but its thoughtful leaders know that to perfect methods of distribution is futile if men fail to appreciate the need for production. It is with the vital problems of production and remuneration that the immediate tasks of International Trade Unionism lie. War has destroyed men and material. Reserves of food and other necessaries of life have disappeared. For five years men have been killing each other. Millions of efficient producers of wealth have died while the bulk of consumers survive and remain in numbers, though not in purchasing power, substantially as they were in 1914. To regain pre-war standards of comfort all nations must of necessity produce at least as much wealth as they produced under pre-war conditions. If they desire to raise their standards of comfort and well-being they must obviously produce more.

The conditions under which this increased production must take place, and the measure of remuneration given to workers, must necessarily be the concern of the Trade Union Movement and particularly of its International Federation. While more commodities must be produced, this need not necessarily entail an increased strain upon the human mind and body. With the aid of science and by the exercise of intelligence and goodwill the necessary increase in production may be obtained without involving dangers to health or curtailing leisure. The task of securing the aid of science is not so difficult as is the task of overcoming prejudices which lead men to look askance at new things and to regard the gifts of science in labour-saving or labour-accelerating devices—which are essential for large-scale production—as innovations to be opposed. A national labour organisation can face the problems incidental to combining increased production with increased benefits and a higher standard of life for workers with fewer fears than a local one, and an international organisation can face them best of all. The international organisation will concentrate upon general enterprises rather than upon local ambitions and it should be in a position to indicate and support broad lines of policy. Because of its size and ramifications it may sometimes succeed in avoiding strikes undertaken without knowledge of material factors and without chance of success. Equally, the greater organisation will be able, given intelligent support from its constituent parts, to wipe out of existence, if necessary, any firm of employers whose conduct, as regards the treatment of workers, deliberately offends against the standards required by the Trade Unions and supported by public opinion.

## II. AIMS OF THE " TRADE UNION INTERNATIONAL "

The International Federation has been in existence twenty years. Its earlier form was of German origin. It had its headquarters in Berlin and it was conducted by German Trade Unionists. It has been said that it was run in German interests. The evidence on this point would hardly satisfy an unbiassed judge, but even if the charge was proved the German could effectively retort by saying he worked and paid while others talked and speculated. Further than this, he was surrounded by cheap, unorganised and oppressed workers of various nationalities and languages. He was in industrial danger, and the instinct of self-preservation cramped and to some extent localised the German's conduct of affairs. He was compelled first to guard the interests of his own people, and if other nations were allowed to wait awhile, it was generally the fault of the other nations.

The new International Trade Unionism has wider interests and greater opportunities than the old. Its committee includes representatives of fifteen nations. The men who form its bureau are thoroughly experienced and animated with the spirit of achievement. They are also animated by a spirit of personal regard and loyalty towards each other which gives them advantages over many other committees or groups.

They know that progress may be slow and even painful, but are determined that there shall be progress. They hope to discover better means of measuring the value of a man's work than are provided by either the time or piece rates of to-day and, what is more, they believe that they can secure the power necessary to enable them to obtain general acceptance of such means.

Of necessity, the International Trade Union Federation must take cognisance, in defining its policy, of both general and labour conditions in all countries whether these are affiliated or not. It has neither the power nor the desire to impose rigidly uniform industrial conditions upon all countries, but it does desire that as far as possible relatively similar wages shall be paid for similar work in every country. Racial characteristics, climatic conditions, variations in temperature, and inequalities of soil, together with great differences in transport facilities and the proximity of both raw materials and markets make rigid uniformity of effort, conditions and results alike impossible and even undesirable. A uniform level might in more senses than one become a " dead " level. There can, however, be no valid objection to endeavours having as their object the securing to workers in every country, on a relatively uniform scale, of adequate recompense according to the value of their services, giving to each man the full value of his work after deducting his contribution to national charges and to national reserves.

This particular task of the International Trade Unions will be delicate and difficult. Different nations as well as governments may view with suspicion and hostility even well intentioned and obviously valuable intervention from an organisation international in character. It may never be possible for such an organisation to enforce acceptance of its ideals on the people of any country, but it will always be possible for it to offer advice in any quarter. Rigid honesty of purpose and perfect disinterestedness on the part of its administration will in time help it to win confidence. It may be that the work of International Trade Unionism will necessitate the education of public opinion in all countries with respect to its needs and its value. If this is so the task must be patiently undertaken and the results should benefit all peoples. For education, if it helps to develop good understanding and inspires a reverence for right because it is right among all peoples, will become a powerful instrument for modifying racial animosities and for making smooth the rough places in the path of progress.

It is in the settlement of international labour difficulties and in fostering labour interests universally that the Federation of Trade Unions hopes to succeed better than any political organisation. International Trade Unionism has a single object in view instead of the multiplicity of objects that pre-occupy politicians. It has at heart the interests of the people, not those of a party.

Before the International Federation of Trade Unions can commence its best work, the restrictions which prevent free communication between peoples must be removed and trade barriers modified. Ignorance of the personalities and ideals of others is the greatest obstacle to the good understanding essential to progress, and nothing so soon dispels this ignorance as association and intercourse. Transport facilities between nations must be improved ; not for the purpose of giving any one nation a preponderating advantage, but for the clear and intelligently postulated purpose of sharing among all nations all the fruits of the earth and all the products of human enterprise. The axiom, " each for all and all for each," must pass the limits imposed by arbitrary frontiers and diverse tongues if mankind is to make that moral and social advance which is clearly defined in its ideals.

Peace also is essential to the success of the International Federation of Trade Unions—peace within nations as well as peace between nations. Without peace there can be no development of mutual regard between nations, and no material basis for better conditions of life for any nation. Peace by negotiation was a phrase on many lips between 1914 and 1919. It is seldom heard to-day. Too many votaries of the ideal were insincere. They were not prepared to apply their formula to all circumstances. Yet peace by negotiation, based upon respect for right, is the only kind of peace that will last. The International Federation of Trade Unions will work for peace among nations, but it will concern itself hardly at all with treaties and covenants.  It will follow the example set by the founder of Christianity two thousand years ago, and appeal to the hearts of men for a peace based upon an appreciation of man's common origin, common functions, common needs and common end.

Apart from any political jealousies there are two great dangers ahead of the " Internationale." Those who are not members may obstruct too much, and those who are members may expect too much.  The former will be overcome, if possible, by reason and argument.  If these fail there are other means.  The latter will receive all the consideration which patient regard for them can devise, and they will learn, either by reasoning or by faith or by experience.  The first method is the most difficult, the last the most painful.  As they learn they will see that real progress is based upon work rather than rhetoric ;  that intelligent direction must be procured because it minimises the strain of work, and that capital, whoever controls it, is essential to the communal existence.  As they learn, the least intelligent will cease to waste, and the most intelligent will seek to serve, in the fullest manner, the general interests.

The tasks of the International Federation of Trade Unions are many and great ;  it has men and nations upon which to exercise its skill, and it has centuries from which to learn, and centuries in which to work.

Its success will be measured by the extent to which it can promote, throughout the world, unharmful production and proper remuneration of intelligence and of effort. As success can only be maintained on moral bases it will aim at securing universal adherence to the principle embodied in the phrase, " Right first, right always."

Under the conditions which the war has created, it is inevitable that International Trade Unionism will find itself in future more closely associated with the governments of various countries than all the labour movements which have preceded it. The Labour programme enunciated in the commitments of the League of Nations cannot be realised apart from co-operation with those who speak for the industrial worker. The International Labour Conference—full of good intentions and adumbrating ideals that but yesterday were regarded as the unrealisable hopes of the dreamer—will succeed only in proportion as it keeps in touch with sane Trade Unionism. The most unstable of all factors—the human factor—can never be controlled, even for its own advantage, by the machinery of Government. However perfect this machinery may be, it will always need the incentive of the forceful and less responsible demands which come from those whose interests in labour problems are less general than those which Governments are bound to take into account.

There must be no mistake about the position of

the International Federation of Trade Unions in relation to the International Labour Office. It may co-operate with the official international organisation, but it can never be in any way subordinate to it, and any attempt, either on the part of governments or on the part of those Trade Unionists who have secured election on the International Labour Conference, to dominate it, will at once arouse suspicion and antagonism. The millions of manual workers united in the International Federation of Trade Unions will repudiate all arrangements if they feel their independence is being jeopardised. They will see through subterfuge, should this be attempted, as children see through the sophistries of older folk and they will swing away from the present possibilities of orderly progress to a policy of a different kind— in a word they will swing away from evolution towards revolution.

Those who direct the policy of the International Federation of Trade Unions will have to adjust their relations with other organisations very carefully so as to guard their perfect independence as International Trade Unionists, or find that the organisation has alienated its membership.

Personally, I am in favour of co-operation between the International Federation of Trade Unions and the Labour Organisation of the League of Nations. But I see the dangers that may arise from attempts to manipulate the former body so as to influence its policy as a result of that co-operation, and I take this opportunity of warning both Governments and Nations that such attempts may result in disastrous consequences.

W. A. APPLETON.

# LABOUR LEGISLATION IN JAPAN

BY

## MINORU OKA, LL.D.

Japanese Delegate to the Paris Peace Conference
Formerly Director of the Bureau of Commerce and Industry of the
Japanese Government

I. INDUSTRIAL CONDITIONS IN JAPAN

II. THE JAPANESE FACTORY ACT

III. PROVISIONS OF FACTORY LEGISLATION

IV. ENFORCEMENT OF THE FACTORY ACT

V. FUTURE LABOUR LEGISLATION IN JAPAN

VI. INTERNATIONAL LABOUR CONVENTIONS :
    Japan's Relation to Labour Conventions
    Effect of Labour Conventions in Japan
    Special Treatment of Countries in Special Circumstances

VII. GENERAL CONSIDERATIONS

# CHAPTER IV

## THE PROTECTION OF LABOUR IN JAPAN

### I. INDUSTRIAL CONDITIONS

JAPAN, in spite of its small size and numerous mountains, has existed from time immemorial as a great agricultural country, thanks to the industry of the Japanese people. But the Japanese are specially noted for their manual skill in industrial occupations. As will easily be imagined, industries which existed in Japan before the time of the great political reconstruction were manual industries, but the number of people engaged in them was quite insignificant compared with that of people engaged in agricultural pursuits.

An industrial revolution was brought about in Japan through her intercourse with occidental countries about fifty years ago ; yet, strange though it may seem, the influence of this change on Japanese industries was not so far-reaching in its effect as was that of the political reconstruction. There are two reasons for this. Firstly, the habits of life in Japan still differ widely from those in Europe or America, and the manufactured goods daily demanded by people vary so much in style and workmanship according to the taste of individuals that European methods of manufacture have not as yet been applied to the production of these things. Secondly, as Japan is a densely populated country, the supply of manual labour is abundant and consequently there are many cases in which its employment is more profitable than the use of machinery, which is very expensive in view of the high rates of interest charged on the loan of capital required for its purchase.

A feature of Japanese industrial conditions to which attention must be called is that more than half the number of industrial workers are absorbed in what are termed " native " industries. Further, a majority of these workers are half agricultural and half industrial workers, and comparatively few of them are engaged wholly in industrial occupations all their lives or continuously for any length of time, while they are sometimes very slow and easy-going in their method of work. Almost all Japanese articles of common use such as clothes, géta (clogs), tabi (socks), paper, fudé (writing brushes), furniture, tatami (mattress), building materials, etc., are produced by the workers employed in native industries.

So far as the application of machinery and scientific appliances are concerned, the textile industries rank first among Japanese industries. The majority of textile workers are females and juveniles, though few of them are continuously engaged in the factories until they come of age. On the other hand, there are other industries in Japan, such as shipbuilding, engineering, munitions, smelting of iron and mining, in which adult male workers are engaged for comparatively long periods of time, and these men form a special class which may accurately be described as " labour " in the true meaning of the term. It is quite possible that Japanese labour will ultimately be organised systematically by these skilled industrial workers.

The mining industries of Japan cannot be said to be in a flourishing condition compared with other progressive industrial countries in view of the fact that she is not rich in mineral resources. In Japan, coal and copper are produced, but there is little iron. The scarcity of iron is a great handicap to the development of the Japanese iron smelting and engineering industries. With regard to transport, though Japanese shipping has made good progress, the mileage of railways in relation to population is far less than is the case in other progressive countries.

Finally, it must be remembered that Japanese industries should be studied under two distinct heads, namely, imported and native industries. If the industries introduced into the country from abroad are considered then it must be recognised that on the whole remarkable progress has been achieved in developing these branches of Japanese industrial activity. If, on the other hand, Japanese industries are considered as a whole, including all the native industries, it will be clear that a great difference exists between the relative position of the two heads of industrial activity which materially affects the position of the country when it is regarded as an industrial unit.

## II. THE JAPANESE FACTORY ACT

In view of the development of Japanese industry, due to the stimulus of the industries imported from abroad, the Government recognised the necessity of protecting workers by regulations applicable to both imported and native industries. The first step in this direction took the form of licenses issued by order of Local Government Authorities, which it was necessary to obtain before establishing factories and which regulated buildings, plant and equipment generally, so as to safeguard the workers' interests and health. Finally the Government developed its policy for the protection of workers by passing a comprehensive Factory Act through the national legislature.

Factory legislation in Japan dates back to 1882 when the Government first attempted to introduce it. At that time most of the Japanese industries were native industries and there was no public opinion in favour of legislation for the protection of workers, nor was there any demand for it from the workers themselves. In these circumstances the Japanese Government showed considerable foresight in anticipating future developments and in making wise provisions against possible dangers which otherwise

might have arisen in connection with them. The
labour policy of the Government, however, as might
have been expected, met with opposition from employers of both imported and native industries.
Their opposition was not aimed at the mere enactment
of factory legislation in itself, but at the introduction
of restrictions as far-reaching as those which have been
introduced in European countries. In some cases,
however, employers went so far as to declare that no
factory legislation was necessary in Japan under the
conditions existing at the time it was first introduced.

The Government, in these circumstances, realised
the necessity of bringing about a consensus of public
opinion on the subject of factory legislation in order
to facilitate the passage of their Bill through the
Imperial Diet. With this object they consulted the
Chambers of Commerce throughout the country by
circulating the draft proposals on factory legislation
among them for consideration, and they also consulted
the Special Commission of Agriculture, Commerce and
Industry, then established in the Department of
Agriculture and Commerce. It was found that a
majority of the members of this Commission recognised
the necessity of factory legislation. They submitted
to the Government, amendments and modifications
to their draft proposals for legislation, adding observations to the effect that, as adequate knowledge
regarding conditions generally affecting the workers
and the conditions under which they carried out their
duties in factories was absolutely essential for proper

consideration of the problem of labour legislation, the Government should institute a thorough investigation of these matters.

The Government gave effect to this recommendation and appointed temporary staffs in 1899 to carry out a thorough investigation of industrial conditions. As a result a fresh Bill was drafted in November of 1901, and was on the point of being introduced in the Diet, when the dark clouds which had been gathering over Manchuria burst into flame on the declaration of war between Japan and Russia. The war delayed the introduction of the Bill, and it was not until 1908 that it was again brought before the Diet. It was then found that opposition against the clauses prohibiting night work was still very strong in the Diet, and as the Bill in consequence was in imminent danger of being rejected, the Government withdrew it on the ground that further investigation into industrial conditions was necessary. The Government, nevertheless, was firmly determined to fight the Bill through and to embody its provisions in the national laws. Accordingly, in the succeeding year, a fresh Bill was submitted to the Diet after further consultations with the Chambers of Commerce throughout the country and with the Economic Investigation Commission of the Department of Agriculture and Commerce. Finally, in February, 1909, the Factory Act was passed through both Houses of the national legislature, and became law. It was, however, found necessary to postpone the application of the provisions prohibiting night work for a period of fifteen years.

It must be observed that although the Japanese Factory Laws met with opposition similar to that encountered by early factory legislation in European countries, its provisions are more advanced in details than those of earlier European factory laws, and, as a matter of fact, they will be found to compare very favourably with the present factory legislation of some European countries.

### III. PROVISIONS OF FACTORY LEGISLATION

Roughly speaking, Factory Regulations provide amongst other matters for the following :—

1. Age limits and working hours.
2. Provisions concerning factory buildings, plant and equipment.
3. Welfare assistance for workers.
4. The regulation of apprenticeships.
5. Provisions regarding the employment and dismissal of employees.

Provisions regarding age limits and working hours at present apply to women and juvenile workers only. The limit of age for industrial employment is twelve years, and the working day may not exceed eleven hours[1]. Arrangements concerning factory buildings, plant and equipment can only be made subject to approval by the Government.

[1] Appendix III. Article 5, p. 330.

With regard to welfare assistance for workers, the treatment of injuries and illness is a charge on employers, so far as such injuries and illness are due to the work upon which employees are actually engaged when they are injured or become ill. The regulations relative to apprenticeship make it necessary for employers to obtain a license from the local authorities permitting them to engage and train apprentices. This precaution has been provided in view of the " man traffic " which existed a long time ago in certain branches of industry. Finally, with regard to the provisions controlling the employment and discharge of workers, a number of definite and necessary obligations are imposed upon employers for the benefit of workers.

It is clear that the Japanese Factory Act at its inception contained certain unsatisfactory elements of which the following among others are examples. The eleven hours working day, although in itself too long, became an aggravated evil through a provision allowing its extension in special cases. Instead of a weekly rest of a day, only two holidays a month are provided for. A period of fifteen years is allowed after the passing of the Factory Act, that is, twelve years from the present time, for the application of regulations prohibiting night work. With regard to the compensation for injuries and illness to be paid by employers, the liability of employers is limited under the Act to cases where injuries and illness are directly due to work at which employees are engaged at the time, instead of being made to cover all cases of illness and injury arising in any way in the course of the workers' employment. Further, the amount of compensation provided by the Act is in any case small.

Thus, taken as a whole, the Japanese Factory Act leaves much to be desired. It is perhaps unavoidable in attempting to frame laws for the control of two classes of factories which differ so greatly in conditions and working efficiency as the native and imported Japanese industries, that such laws should tend towards laxity in details, especially in view of the fact that the majority of Japanese workers are not even yet alive as to the advantages of shorter working hours coupled with the concentrated efforts of intensive methods of manufacture. The fact that the original Factory Regulations contemplated by the Government which were comparatively rigid instead of lax in their details, did not meet with an approval of the general public may fairly be attributed to these circumstances.

## IV. ENFORCEMENT OF THE FACTORY ACT

The Japanese Government, after duly investigating the methods of enforcing Factory Acts in Europe and America, came to the conclusion that in the whole field of legislation factory laws are the most difficult to enforce. Consequently they decided that the state should defray the expense of appointing factory inspectors in sufficient numbers to enforce the law. In all, two hundred factory inspectors, including specialists in law, political economy, engineering, chemistry, and medical science, among other qualifications, have been appointed throughout the country. It is satisfactory to note that these factory inspectors are systematically co-operating to discharge their administrative duties, assisted by policemen who undertake additional duty as factory inspectors, under the able direction of local authorities, who are invested with strong powers with regard to civil as well as judicial administration. Unlike some countries in Europe the control of factory buildings and plant in Japan is entrusted to one and the same local authority, which also supervises the conditions under which workers are employed. Thus the supervision of both the material and moral conditions of industrial life in factories is carried out in Japan in a satisfactory manner under unified control. The Japanese Government can also fairly claim credit for the efficient manner in which its Factory Act is enforced, which compares most favourably with the practical application of industrial legislation in other progressive countries.

## V. FUTURE LABOUR LEGISLATION IN JAPAN

With regard to the future of Japanese labour legislation, the first thing to be done is to try to perfect the existing provisions governing the protection of workers under the following heads :—

1. The protection of workers should not be confined

to the particular factories provided for in the Japanese Factory Act, but be extended to all factories. Further, due protection should be assured for all the workers employed outside factories.

2. The present conditions under which workers are employed should be improved, and their properly constituted Trade Unions should be accorded public recognition with a view to stimulating a healthy development of their aspirations.

3. Existing working hours should be curtailed[1].

4. Definite methods of paying wages should be established.

5. Sunday rest should be enforced.

6. Child labour should be abolished.

7. A compulsory system of insurance for the benefit of workers should be established.

8. Industrial Councils for the solution of industrial difficulties should be established.

9. Generally speaking, not only the material but also the moral conditions of industrial life should be improved and raised to a higher plane.

Japan, standing as she does in special and peculiar circumstances, should endeavour to secure good practical results from labour legislation by carefully adapting it to suit her special circumstances rather than by directing the efforts of her legislature towards elaborating regulations of which the form rather than the practical worth is the primary consideration.

[1] Appendix III. Article 9, p. 330.

## VI. INTERNATIONAL LABOUR CONVENTIONS

### 1. *The Relation of Japan to Labour Conventions.*

It must be remembered that the readiness of Japan to approve of the International Labour Organisation set up in Paris in 1919 in connection with the Peace Treaty with Germany was not impelled by any labour unrest at home, from which indeed she was almost free at the time. It was impelled by the same strong inherent love of progress which led her statesmen to establish their modern constitution fifty years ago in the absence of any revolutionary menace. Just as Japan desires the League of Nations to be established as a means of securing universal peace in the field of international politics, so she desires the International Labour Organisation to secure stability and peaceful progress in the fields of international economics and industry. Japan upholds the principle of fair play in international trade. She upholds principles of justice in relation to social organisations. She is proud that she endeavoured in the past to initiate laws for the protection of her own workers, and glad to be one of the pioneers in a great international effort to bring about the improvement of labour conditions throughout the world in co-operation with other countries.

### 2. *The Effect of Labour Conventions in Japan.*

The existence of two different kinds of industries in Japan has already been mentioned, namely, imported industries which, so far as their external aspect is concerned, are similar to those of Europe or America; and native industries, which in both form and substance are entirely different from those of western countries. It has also been stated that the majority of workers engaged in both kinds of industries are on the whole content at present with existing conditions, although some signs of discontent are looming on the horizon of the field of labour.

Japan, however, is not yet troubled with any class war, in the strict sense of the word, and agricultural occupations are so commonly combined with industrial that it is even difficult to find among the Japanese that sharp dividing line which in western countries separates masses of workers into industrial and agricultural classes. Moreover, in Japan, most happily, there is no enmity or even antipathy between capital and labour, consequently, the relations between them are good and are not complicated or rendered critical by elements of suspicion and passion. Bearing these facts in mind, it is interesting to note the probable effect of the inclusion of Japan as a member state of the International Labour Organisation under the League of Nations, which carries with it an obligation upon her Government, for the first time in Japanese history, to place Japanese workers on an equal footing with Japanese employers and capitalists by giving the former the same voting power as the latter in shaping the policy of the International Labour Organisation. Japanese labour and capital will thus be brought suddenly into close and friendly co-operation in settling labour problems which are not only national but international in scope. It may be, in this way, that the international labour conventions will have the effect of enabling Japanese capital and labour to reach at one peaceful stride an advanced stage of progress in co-operation, and so to establish firm guarantees for industrial peace without first experiencing the throes of the bitter class wars which unhappily characterise the present domestic affairs of western nations. Whether this happy solution of problems which would inevitably arise in future from the relations of Japanese capital and labour can be realised, will depend mainly upon a wise and sympathetic policy on the part of the Japanese Government and Japanese capitalists and employers towards the Japanese workers. At any rate the International Labour Organisation offers Japan a great and favourable opportunity for solving many dangerous domestic problems through the friendly co-operation of employers and workers. It is highly desirable, therefore, that the Government, legislative bodies and capitalists of Japan should all act on the basis of a broad national policy with regard to the adoption of the conventions and recommendations of the International Labour Conference.

### 3. *Special Treatment of Countries under Special Circumstances.*

The League of Nations will probably include as many as fifty different countries. These countries must of course differ very greatly with regard to their respective stages of industrial development. They may roughly be divided into the following three classes :

(i) Countries in an advanced stage of industrial development regulated by comparatively complete codes of labour legislation.

(ii) Countries in a less advanced stage of industrial development with an imperfect system of labour legislation.

(iii) Countries in a primitive stage of industrial development which lack labour legislation.

It may be that the great differences in both industrial development and legislation which characterise these countries will make it impossible to establish anything like uniformity in labour conditions in all of them. Moreover, there are other difficulties in the way of achieving strict uniformity of these conditions, due to the differences of climate, of habits and customs, of economic opportunities and of industrial traditions as mentioned in Article 427 of the Convention. The writer of this article is by no means opposed to attempts to achieve relative uniformity in the conditions of labour as far as possible throughout the world, but he desires that the international labour conventions or recommendations should be considered carefully with a view to making them adaptable to the special circumstances of different countries in which way alone can they be made practicable for all countries.

## VII. GENERAL CONSIDERATIONS

When Japan was aroused from her unbroken slumber of centuries about sixty years ago, her people, who had lived in perfect seclusion from the outside world in their small islands of the far East, suddenly found themselves faced with a menace to their national existence. To defend her national rights and independence Japan was twice forced within a comparatively short period of time to take up arms against neighbouring powers. These two wars cost Japan dear in treasure and she had scarcely recovered from their heavy financial drain on her resources, when she was again compelled to go to war to save humanity from the menace of German militarism. Indeed, the history of Japan for the past fifty years is a record of one continuous life and death struggle for her national rights and independence. It is most unfortunate that their strenuous efforts to defend themselves against unprovoked aggression has given rise to an entirely mistaken idea that the Japanese are a restless and warlike people.

It is a blessing for Japan that, as a result of the European War, a League of Nations has been set up in the hope of securing the peace of the world. Japan welcomes a League of Nations for two reasons : firstly, because it gives her an opportunity to disprove the charge of militarism wrongly made against her, and secondly because it enables her to concentrate her energies on the task of carrying out

much needed domestic reforms, amongst which labour
legislation is of first importance. The writer of this
article expresses his sincere hope that the Japanese
Government will see its way to carry out labour
reforms, based on the suggestions outlined in the
preceding pages. Further, he expresses his desire
that the member states attending the deliberations of
the International Labour Conferences will not confine
their efforts simply to effecting a systematic and
relatively uniform progress in the industrial conditions
of every country, through the instruments of international legislation, but that they will go further and
aim at international co-operation with regard to the
distribution of raw materials and the supply of labour,
so that workers throughout the world may enjoy
equal opportunities of employment in their own
particular spheres of activity. For instance, it is well
to attempt to solve the problem of unemployment
and to establish the principle of a minimum wage
systematically throughout the world, but equally
systematic efforts should also be made through
international conventions to give workers throughout
the world equal opportunities of employment in all
countries on the condition of equal or relatively equal
rates of wages for similar tasks.

Critics may denounce the writer's desires as vague
international ideals and inopportune at a moment
when every country is devoting its whole attention and
energy to the solution of many difficult domestic
problems arising from conflicts between its own

classes of capital and labour. Nevertheless the writer firmly believes that governments, capitalists, and workers, who are now co-operating for the first time systematically in an international endeavour to build a new foundation for society upon principles of true democracy, humanity and social justice, will regard these problems not as vague ideals, but as practical business questions which await a final solution at their hands.

MINORU OKA.

# LABOUR REFORMS IN BELGIUM

BY HIS EXCELLENCY

## EMILE VANDERVELDE

Minister of Justice and State
Belgian Delegate to the Commission on International Labour
Legislation, Paris Peace Conference

I. SPECIAL CIRCUMSTANCES IN BELGIUM

II. THE PROBLEM OF UNEMPLOYMENT

III. THE COST OF LIVING AND RATE OF WAGES

IV. THE ECONOMIC EFFECTS OF EIGHT-HOUR DAY

V. THE NEED OF ECONOMIC FREEDOM

# CHAPTER V

## LABOUR REFORMS IN BELGIUM

### I. SPECIAL CIRCUMSTANCES IN BELGIUM

THE labour clauses of the Peace Treaty define certain general principles as underlying the policy of the International Labour Conference.[1] No obligations, however, are imposed regarding the observance of these principles. In other words, the High Contracting Parties declared certain reforms to be desirable, but they did not undertake to enforce them in their respective territories. Moreover, they made a formal reservation with respect to special circumstances which might make it difficult or impossible to give effect to these reforms on uniform lines, or simultaneously in all countries. Among these special circumstances, some are of a permanent nature such as climate, customs and difference in degrees of industrial development, while others are exceptional and temporary, such as the damage and disorganisation occasioned by the war.

Belgium has the misfortune to be afflicted with the special circumstances caused by the war. During over

---

[1] Appendix I. Article 427, p. 273.

four years of hostilities, ninety-eight per cent. of her territory was in hostile occupation. The narrow strip which remained free—in the inundated district of the Yser—was continuously under fire. The ravages of invasion, together with the exactions imposed by the enemy and the Allies' blockade, completely paralysed the productive activities of Belgium during the war. To-day the want of machinery, of raw material and transport facilities, all beset the resumption of Belgian industry with innumerable difficulties. Under these conditions is it possible to expect in a country so ravaged, the rapid realisation of all the reforms embodied in the labour clauses of the Peace Treaty ?

It must be understood, however, that this question does not arise, so far as Belgium is concerned, as regards the greater number of these reforms. Before the war, for instance, Sunday rest was legally established in Belgium, and the industrial employment of children under the age of fourteen was forbidden. No discrimination was made against foreign labour by the Belgian laws, which further allowed industrial workers full freedom to form combinations and associations. Since the war this liberty to form unions has been extended to workers employed by the state and the communal and provincial authorities, who have formed strong associations among themselves. Speaking generally, the number of the members of these bodies has more than trebled and is still increasing. But apart from these matters there are two reforms mentioned in the labour clauses of the Peace Treaty, which are not in force in Belgium and which the special circumstances in that country at the present time serve to render both extremely desirable and very difficult to attain.

In the words of the Peace Treaty these reforms are firstly, the payment to work-people of a wage which shall ensure them a fair standard of living, and secondly, the general adoption of an eight hour day or a forty-eight hour week. Since the war these two questions have ranked among the most pressing reforms. In the remotest Belgian village it would be hard to find an agricultural labourer, however humble, who is willing to work except for the standard rate of wages for a shortened working day. However unanimously the Belgian workers as a whole make these just demands, there is one great difficulty in satisfying them—namely, the impossibility of finding enough work for them. The urgent problem in Belgium at the present time is not that of the restriction of hours of work nor of the question of wages, but that of the resumption of work—the resumption, that is to say, of all the activities of peaceful national existence in a highly organised industrial community which have been almost wholly paralysed during the war. It is interesting as well as necessary to consider the present state of industry in Belgium, before considering to what extent these conditions render difficult or impossible reforms concerning the length of the working day and the fixing of adequate rates of wages.

## II. THE PROBLEM OF UNEMPLOYMENT

Generally speaking, at the time when the German troops evacuated Belgium, unemployment was prevalent in all branches of industry. During the war agriculture alone flourished. Collieries worked only three or four days a week. In November, 1918, however, the Germans took away the pit ponies, and the miners remained unemployed for more than two months. As regards other industries, all except those which had supplied enemy government requirements were obliged to suspend operations from various causes, but chiefly through lack of machinery, raw materials and foreign markets. For over four months after the Armistice, this state of affairs continued. At the end of March, 1919, the Belgian National Relief Committee which was responsible for granting aid to the unemployed issued a tabular statement concerning the assistance given (see page 109).

These figures show that three months after the Armistice, more than 700,000 families were in receipt of relief grants. This, if the number of individuals is taken, means that a third of the entire population of Belgium, including the majority of industrial workers, were being supported by the state at a cost of over 40,000,000 francs per month. Of course, among those included in the above statistics were some who were not industrial workers in the strict sense. A certain number of small shopkeepers and clerks were also assisted. Nevertheless, excluding

persons employed in agriculture, mining, quarrying,
public works and railways, almost the whole of the
industrial workers of Belgium, including the large
number usually employed in the great iron, steel,
cotton and wool industries, were without work of any

FAMILIES AND INDIVIDUALS IN RECEIPT OF RELIEF GRANTS
DURING THE SECOND FORTNIGHT OF FEBRUARY 1919.

| Province. | Families Assisted. | Individuals Assisted. | Cost (in Francs). |
|---|---|---|---|
| Greater Brussels - | 91,272 | 244,618 | 2,617,548 |
| Antwerp - - | 100,478 | 345,564 | 2,808,656 |
| Brabant - - - | 41,664 | 147,896 | 981,028 |
| East Flanders [1] - | 158,275 | 580,017 | 6,496,003 |
| West Flanders [1] - | 18,822 | 68,512 | 281,852 |
| Hainault - - | 164,286 | 489,794 | 4,148,187 |
| Liège - - - | 120,873 | 350,392 | 3,053,251 |
| Limburg - - - | 14,233 | 63,399 | 270,972 |
| Luxemburg [1] - - | 3,947 | 13,418 | 46,380 |
| Namur - - - | 27,742 | 86,845 | 508,803 |
| Total - | 741,592 | 2,390,455 | 21,212,680 |

[1] Provisional figures.

kind. Some idea of the extent to which the mass of
Belgian industrial workers were left almost completely unemployed after the German evacuation of
their country, may be gathered from certain additional
figures, relating to the principal industrial centres.
In Brussels, out of a total of 120,000 workpeople,
only 28,000 were employed. In the whole of Flanders,

out of 47,134 textile operatives, 1215 only were at work.
At Verviers out of 19,750 wool workers, 733 alone
were employed at repairs. In the Hainault metal
industry, 10,000 people were at work out of 95,000.
In the province of Liège, where the Germans had
carried off all machinery, the situation was even worse.
At Antwerp, nine-tenths of the dock workers were
suffering from enforced idleness. Nothing shows in a
more striking manner the state of things prevailing
in Belgium just after her deliverance than the figures
relating to her principal port before and after the war.
In February, 1914, the number of vessels arriving
was 509 with a total tonnage of 966,378, the vessels
leaving being in proportion; in February, 1919, 160
vessels entered the port, their total tonnage being
244,250, of which eighty per cent. was in ballast.

Since that date it is true there has been a per-
ceptible general improvement, and by July, 1919,
the prospects on the whole were somewhat better.
Work was being resumed little by little, railway
communication was being restored at a speed which
reflects great credit upon the state railway administration; the highroads were being repaired and there
were hopes that in a few weeks the canals which the
Germans had obstructed in their retreat, would again
be in use. At Antwerp, the volume of shipping was
increasing, owing partly to the Allies having installed
their naval bases there. In spite of these and subsequent improvements, however, the difficulties which
complicate the task of reconstruction in Belgium are

still very great. To appreciate their extent one has only to consider how varied and numerous were the causes which led to unemployment during the war, and which still tend to prolong its effects.

It was thought by many that peace would bring a revival of business activity, similar to that which occurred almost immediately after the Franco-Prussian War of 1870. Those who held this opinion must have ignored or underestimated the effects of the deliberate and systematic efforts made by the Germans during the four years of war to destroy the whole industrial organisation of Belgium, as well as the profound dislocation of industry and commerce caused by the war throughout the world. The causes which at present retard the revival of Belgian industry in many trades are at the same time general and local in their nature. Among local causes are those incidental to warfare, such as the destruction of property, pillage, fires and bombardments, which have transformed certain towns into masses of ruins, especially in West Flanders and on the French frontier, where the first and last fighting of the war took place. Surprising though it may seem, the total destruction of buildings used for industrial purposes took place on the whole in comparatively few cases. This tends to give a wrong impression, as it makes it appear that Belgium has not suffered much damage from the war. Almost all the front walls of factories everywhere are intact, and the devastated regions of Nieuport and Ypres are small, compared with the large areas of desolation about the Somme and the Aisne.

Unfortunately for Belgium, this apparent immunity is far from being a reality. Although the number of factories totally destroyed by the Germans was small, they carried out a wholesale removal of raw materials and machinery from factories throughout the country, including accessories indispensable for the use of machinery. There are very large manufacturing establishments in Hainault and Liège for instance, of which scarcely anything remains except the four walls. Elsewhere, although the removal of machinery and materials may not be complete, it makes very little difference as regards the possibility of resuming work any sooner. The following extracts from the *Revue de Travail* serve to illustrate the conditions in which Belgian factories were left when the Germans evacuated the country. " At Mons apart from the cylinders and other materials removed from the iron manufacturing plant during the war, the Germans, in their retreat, carried off all the driving-belts, all the stocks of leather, oil, lubricants, hard steel and various other articles." Similar conditions prevail in the textile industry of Flanders. " In 1916, 1917, and 1918, requisitions and forced deliveries were constantly carried out by the Germans ; driving-belts, cotton yarn, cables, waste, copper, indiarubber, rope, packing materials, bronze bearings, foundry tools, driving rods—all were taken." Factories generally were also stripped of materials, manufactured articles, horses,

wagons and motor-vehicles. Added to these depriva-
tions were the removal of stocks of coal; the destruction of bridges, canal, locks and railways by the
German army in its retreat, and the loss occasioned
by the Germans failing to pay for their vast expro-
priations. Such instances serve to give some idea
of the state of Belgian industries when hostilities
ceased.

These veritable catastrophies constitute some of
the local causes which give rise to, and tend to per-
petuate unemployment in Belgium on a scale so
widespread and complete that it may even be termed
national as compared with the fractional unemployment of normal times. As already explained the
effects of local causes are considerably aggravated by
certain general causes which would even in normal
times exercise a profoundly depressing influence upon
industry. Among these general causes are the
shortage of mercantile shipping, together with a
shortage or entire lack of various essential kinds of
inland transport by land and water; the lack of new
machinery to replace lost, damaged, or worn out
plant, and the need of stocks of raw material of every
sort. All these direct causes of unemployment can
only be remedied very gradually. Finally, the
cumulative effect of all these general causes is seriously
increased by the unfavourable state of the foreign
exchanges—as, for example, in relation to the dollar.
The exchange seriously handicaps Belgian industry
in competing with other countries in exports to foreign

markets, by increasing the cost of things which it is necessary to purchase in the great manufacturing countries that hold the advantage of exchange. The financial situation further results in delays by the Belgian Treasury in paying sums advanced to manufacturers on account of the indemnities to be paid by Germany. The human factor also comes into play in the reduced energy and productive power of workers, whose physique and moral has been enfeebled by four years of anxiety and privation. In short, the period of industrial paralysis caused by the war is not yet at an end. Meanwhile, the new spirit born of the war incites workers to demand benefits greater than those which they sought under settled and prosperous industrial conditions in the past, including a shorter working day and higher rates of wages.

### III. THE COST OF LIVING AND RATE OF WAGES

A characteristic feature of the situation in Belgium some months after the Armistice was that manual workers preferred to remain idle rather than work for an insufficient wage, and subsisted on the relief granted by the National Committee, distributed since June 1919 by the Department of Industry and Labour. The total sum distributed in relief grants as shown by the statistics quoted, exceeded 40,000,000 francs a month, but this vast sum only represents a weekly grant of 10.50 francs for an individual and 21.50 francs for a family of five persons. It is true that in nearly every industrial centre, the communal and provincial authorities granted supplementary allowances. It is also true that the majority of the unemployed were able to supplement their relief grants by cultivating a garden plot; by finding employment in public works, and by doing work other than their normal occupation. Nevertheless the great difference between the cost of the necessities of life and the purchasing power of the working classes in Belgium in 1919, can be realized by comparing the cost of living to-day, with the cost in 1914. In Brussels, for example, if the cost of living in April 1914 be taken as 100, the cost in January 1919 would be represented by the following figures :

1. Prime necessities - - - - 699
2. Less necessary articles - - - 615
3. Clothing, boots and shoes, heating, lighting 516

Total - - 639

Thus, directly after the signing of the Armistice, the cost of living in the capital was more than six times greater than before the war. Since that date there has been some improvement in the situation, as will be seen from the following table taken from the *Revue du Travail*.

|                              | Index numbers 1919. | | | | |
| ---------------------------- | ---- | ---- | ---- | ----- | ---- |
|                              | Jan. | Feb. | Mar. | April. | May. |
| 1. Prime necessities      - | 100  | 81   | 58   | 49    | 48   |
| 2. Less necessary articles  | 100  | 85   | 78   | 74    | 66   |
| 3. Clothing, boots and shoes,      heating,      lighting      -      - | 100 | 91 | 83 | 74 | 68 |
| Total -      - | 100 | 84 | 66 | 59 | 55 |

The two tables taken together show that the cost of
living in 1919 was still three times as high as before
the war. Consequently when the industrial workers
limit their demands to an increase of 100 per cent. in
their nominal wages—as is done by their Trade Union
Federation—they are in point of fact agreeing to
submit to a standard of living greatly lower than that
which they formerly enjoyed. Yet, this increase has
not been granted them without great opposition,
which is due to the exceptional conditions prevailing
in the leading industries. To overcome this opposition,
the Trade Unions have had to exert all their power.
They have been assisted to some extent by the
Public Authorities, who have temporarily suspended
the collection of local taxes and other deductions from
unemployment allowances on certain conditions which
are not without influence in regard to the fixing of
rates of wages. Thus the rules of the Employment
Exchanges, drawn up by the Department of Labour,
lay down that deductions may in no case be made

from the relief grants when the employment offered exceeds nine hours of work per day, and when the wage is below the following minimum rates.

(1) *Men.* 1 franc per hour in industrial districts and 0.85 franc in semi-urban.

(2) *Women.* (When not doing same work as men) 0.75 franc per hour in industrial districts and 0.65 franc in semi-urban.

(3) *Lads or Girls.* 0.50 franc per hour in industrial districts and 0.40 franc in semi-urban.

(4) *Agricultural Workers.* 5 francs per day.

When these minimum rates are not paid, or when the workers strike in order to obtain them, the relief grant can be claimed or continued. Needless to say, this method of state intervention for stabilising wages will disappear when the unemployment relief ceases to be granted, and industrial conditions again become normal. At the present time, however, the principle of the minimum wage is widely accepted and there is no doubt that little objection will be raised against legislation giving effect to it in certain trades.

IV. THE ECONOMIC EFFECTS OF EIGHT-HOUR DAY

The Belgian workers did not wait for the principle of the eight hour day to be approved by the Peace Conference for general application before demanding that reform themselves, and effect has already been given to it in a number of cases. In all public services, as for instance the state railways, which employ over 100,000 workers, the eight-hour day is in force. In other occupations, notably the mining and metal industries, the government has formed mixed committees consisting of employers and workers in equal numbers, to consider the adoption of an eight-hour day. The Metal Trades employers' representatives after long deliberations have drawn up the following statement : " The representatives of the employers in the metal trades express their doubts as to the advisability of reduction in the length of the working day—at any rate so long as protective customs duties discriminate against Belgian manufactures in foreign markets. They note that the question of the introduction of the eight-hour day is placed on the agenda of the International Labour Conference at Washington. They declare, however, that they are willing to adopt an eight-hour day—with modifications rendered necessary by conditions under which workers are employed at furnaces in continuous operation—as soon as those manufacturers whose output is large, take the initiative."

In the coal-mining industry, the mixed committee has adopted the following rule to meet the case of underground workers. The length of the working day as defined by the law of 31st December, 1909, is reduced to eight and a half hours, as from June 1st, 1919, and to eight hours as from 1st December, 1920. The surface workers have their day already fixed at nine hours. In the textile industry again, the workers have only agreed to resume work on condition that their hours are limited to fifty-four per week. This limit, however, they merely regard as a stage towards further progress. The parliamentary socialist group has prepared a Bill which purposes to introduce a general working day of eight hours. The government meanwhile in view of the Washington Labour Conference, has authorised its delegates to vote at the Conference in favour of the legal eight-hour day or forty-eight hour week.

It is clear, therefore, that in the near future, effect will be given to the reform in Belgium as elsewhere. What will be the consequences as regards the output of labour ? Will it be possible in the special circumstances which now prevail in Belgium to reduce the hours of labour without retarding the revival of industry and adversely affecting the power of her people to compete for the sale of their products in the markets of the world ? This is the all important question upon which the very existence of Belgian industry depends, and I propose to consider it in connection with a short summary of the conditions prevailing in certain leading industries.

(a) *Mining.* The eight-hour day would appear to involve a decrease in output at least for a time. Technical improvements which it is hoped will in future more than compensate for reduced output cannot at once be put into operation. The supply of the necessary machinery, the making of new roads, and the repair of those in existence in order to adapt

them for motor transport, will all take time to effect.
Further, for instance, it must be remembered that
production in the Belgian coal-mines presents a
problem radically different from that of coal-mines
in the United States. We have no rich veins firmly
embedded, which permit of hewing by machinery.
The mechanical hammer is the only tool which can
be used in the majority of Belgian coal-mines, and
even then its employment involves drawbacks. The
development of underground haulage, coupled with
more systematic and uniform methods of work, will
probably prove to be the most effective measures for
increasing output.

It is significant that recognition of the men's unions
by employers, has resulted in an increased output.
The miners in one of the principal Belgian coalfields
had refused to work more than five days a week, so
long as negotiations were carried on directly between
employers and the groups of workers concerned, but
when the employers consented to treat with their
union—the National Federation of Miners—their
leaders had little difficulty in persuading the men to
work full time. The miner's leaders themselves
acknowledge that the energies of even the extremists
among them became concentrated on increasing production with good results. This is remarkable because
the miner knows by experience, that as soon as coal
begins to accumulate at the pit-head, it is likely that
his earnings may decrease, because as soon as stocks
accumulate there is a tendency to reduce production.

Yet when the men agreed to increase production the yards of our collieries were congested with reserve stocks of coal awaiting transport. It was clear, of course, that these reserves would be quite insufficient to meet the demand in a few months' time, and that they must be increased as much as possible. The Miner's Federation, however, was the only body which could convince the men of the absolute necessity for doing this, as they would not listen to or obey any other authority.

In Belgium, as in other countries of the Old World, the lack of coal may precipitate a serious economic crisis, which can only be avoided if the miners realise that their interests are bound up with the interests of the whole nation. It is only by friendly consultation between the miners and those representing the great mass of consumers, that a mutually satisfactory arrangement can be made. If the Miners' Trade Union took part in these consultations, and impressed upon the men the need of increased production as an essential condition of any sound arrangement in their own as well as in the national interests, it would greatly facilitate the task of making such an arrangement. Moreover, once the public realised that the miners, while considering their own interests were also alive to the interests of the nation as a whole, and that they would carry out the agreements made on their behalf by their Trade Union, a feeling of confidence would be engendered which would materially assist in the settlement of trade disputes generally.

(b) *Iron and Steel Trades*.  In this industry, the establishment of the eight-hour day will necessitate the reorganisation of work in three shifts.  To keep down the cost of production as much as possible, the blast furnaces will have to be provided with up-to-date charging apparatus and made as large as possible, and, since all but two have been destroyed, it will be easy to construct them with all modern improvements.  Even then, the Belgian iron and steel industries can only compete successfully in foreign markets if they can obtain raw material in the shape of iron-ore on generous terms from the Allies, and if their finished products are not subjected to prohibitive tariff charges abroad.  The Belgian rolling-mills were as a rule well equipped, but the majority have been destroyed during the war.  The eight-hour day in the iron and steel trades will undoubtedly necessitate the installation of automatic machinery, and this in turn will involve a system of combination through which the rolling-mills will co-operate in regard to their output in order to economise transport.  To effect this, a plan is under consideration by which the factories existing before the war would share out work on the different standard sizes of steel and iron products, each mill rolling one or a few standard sizes only.  All the mills would thus be kept in operation and a valuable economy in transport would be effected.

(c) *Glass Making Trade*.  Among labour reforms to be discussed at the Washington Conference, those which specially affect glass manufacturers are the prohibition of the employment of children, and the prohibition of night-work for boys under the age of sixteen. As regards the former reform, glass-manufacturers contend that a lad to attain efficiency in their trade must commence to learn it when quite young as an apprentice in a factory, where he does the work of second helper. They contend, further, that if the boy-helpers—who at present carry out the simplest operations in each shift or gang of workers— are abolished, it will be difficult to find men to perform these easy tasks which at their age can lead to nothing in the future. The result will disorganise the whole shift, and in time put an end to the supply of glass-blowers. The prohibition of night-work they contend will disorganise one shift out of every three, unless the manufacturer shuts down his furnaces during the hours in which child labour is prohibited, and this means extending his plant by one-third to maintain his normal output.

These are, of course, the arguments of employers, and particularly those of the bottle-makers. They appear to exaggerate difficulties. It will not be impossible to replace child workers with adult male labour, and a youth of sixteen, who has had a good technical training will soon learn to be a glass-blower. If effect is given to the reforms in question, they will probably result in appreciably augmenting the use of machinery in bottle-making on the system adopted by the Germans before the war. This will necessitate large scale production in standard sizes, and at the same time render the question of exports to foreign markets a vital problem in the revival of the Belgian glass bottle trade—the solution of which depends upon the possibility of favourable treatment for the Belgian industry in foreign markets.

The Belgian window-glass trade, for the same reason, will have to adopt an extended use of machinery for glass rolling in preference to blowing—as in the Fourcaux process which was discovered in Belgium—and similar improved processes adopted in the United States during the war. Unfortunately, these methods do not as yet produce sheets of better quality, except on a small scale, and it is good quality glass upon which Belgium must depend for her export trade to foreign markets. The revival of these important industries in Belgium is thus complicated, not only by possible developments of international labour legislation, but by the tariff policy of the countries in which lie her best export markets.

(d) *The Textile Industry.* The prohibition of night-work for women was at one time very strongly opposed by wool manufacturers, while cotton and linen factories on the other hand, would rarely adopt the two-shift system. Conditions, of course, have changed since the war. Moreover, the stocks of raw materials now available are scarcely sufficient to ensure full employment even for one shift. But once the materials are available, the demand for textile goods will be so great that work in a large number of factories is likely to be carried on day and night to satisfy it. Another factor that tends to make the adoption of the two-shift system almost inevitable, more particularly in the linen industry, is the destruction of a large quantity of machinery, which will involve utilising that available to its utmost capacity before it will be possible to equal the normal output before the war.

It might certainly be possible to meet the situation by authorising two shifts of eight hours, or of seven and a half hours each, as provided for in the Ghent collective agreement and also, in special cases, by permitting work to be carried on at night for a limited period by manufacturers who have not been able to procure machinery to replace plant lost during the war. In any case, a working day of eight hours must entail a diminution of output in the immediate future. But it is to be hoped that it will speedily lead in the majority of mills to the workers agreeing to put a larger number of looms in operation by reducing the number of men at present working on each loom. In the spinning processes it will perhaps be more difficult in any case to maintain the rate of production per head at the same level. Still, by increasing the number of machines in use as suggested, through modifying the present system of work by making general double shifts of eight hours and allowing night work only where necessary, it will ultimately be possible not only to make good the loss of output due to reduced hours, but even to increase output.

(e) *Engineering Trades.* The majority of employers in this branch of industry are attempting to make up for the reduction in the length of the working day by the use of automatic machinery. Their experience during the war has doubtless taught them to adopt this method on its merits, irrespective of the length of the working day. As the use of automatic machinery is specially suited to standardised products, the engineering trades seem to be tending towards the policy of mass production, the success of which again depends on the favourable treatment of Belgian industries under the tariffs of foreign countries. The demand of the Belgian home market cannot justify large scale production, nor will favourable customs treaties with a few countries only, justify this innovation.

Modern methods of manufacture in fact, are not practicable where the market for goods is restricted to any great degree. For this reason, it is difficult to conceive how countries with a small restricted home market are to secure complete political and economic independence and maintain prosperous conditions for their working class populations, unless they are able to secure markets for their industries outside their home markets. If, therefore, the League of Nations after having guaranteed small countries their political liberty fails to secure for them full economic liberty through free access to the markets of the world, it will fail to give practical effect to the great international ideals which it has been established to uphold.

(*f*) *Transport*. It was perhaps in Belgian harbours where excessive overtime was most practised. Sometimes a gang of dockers would work twenty-four to thirty-six hours on end, to complete the loading and discharging of a ship in a specified time. It would be difficult to prohibit overtime for dock labour altogether, but the Trade Unions are not inclined to tolerate it, except in so far as it may be unavoidable, and then only within reasonable limits. Here, again, the solution of the problem of shorter hours of work must be found in extended use of machinery for loading and discharging ships, and perhaps also in a gradually developed specialisation of ships for carrying particular classes of cargo, which will make possible more systematic, regular and rapid loading and discharging of freight. The extended use of mechanical appliances for handling cargoes on specialised shipping will, however, only provide a satisfactory solution of the problem raised by shorter hours of work in the case of ports employed for a large volume of general traffic, like Antwerp before the war. The question whether Antwerp will regain its former volume of trade, therefore, becomes a vital one for the Belgian people, and invests the problem of labour reforms with peculiar anxiety for them. Whether these reforms, however desirable, can be reconciled with the necessary measures for re-establishing national prosperity on a sound basis in all its peaceful activities, seems to depend upon the extent to which the great nations can assist Belgium by the grant of concessions which will enable her principal port to compete with its rivals.

For instance, the trade of Alsace Lorraine and Luxemburg is of vital importance to Antwerp. Will this trade now be diverted gradually to Boulogne or Dunkirk through the instrumentality of harbour and warehouse dues ? At one time it was feared that Great Britain would use Rotterdam as the gate of her commerce with Germany in preference to Antwerp, but public opinion in Belgium is now reassured on this point, although it is not certain that Rotterdam will not again reassert her claims. This example suffices to illustrate clearly the fact that the attitude of our late Allies in the League of Nations towards Belgium will determine to a great extent, if not wholly, how far it will be possible for her to introduce the labour reforms urged by the Imperial Labour Conference, without making the task of re-establishing her industries infinitely difficult and perhaps incurring the risk of grave disaster.

## V. THE NEED FOR ECONOMIC FREEDOM

This short and general consideration of the special circumstances which must be taken into account in the case of Belgium in connection with the labour reforms outlined in the Peace Treaty, leads to certain definite conclusions. These reforms need not necessarily inflict upon Belgian industry a permanent loss of the power of production. Although the eight-hour

day will on the one hand certainly result in an
initial diminution of output, it will on the other hand
necessitate considerable mechanical improvements
calculated to increase output, which will be facilitated
by the fact that plant lost or damaged during the
war can be replaced by the best and latest patterns
of automatic and other machinery of all kinds. Thus
re-established as an industrial nation, Belgium will
stand equipped with modern plant for that large scale
production which characterizes the new era of commercial development, and which, because it involves
an output far in excess of the normal demand of her
home market, will make free access for her industries
to the great foreign markets, an essential condition
of Belgian prosperity in future.

If the new Belgium is forced to depend for her
development even mainly upon her home market,
she will scarcely be able to exist. If, on the other hand,
the energy of her manufacturers and her workers is
given scope in the markets of the world under fair
conditions, her future is full of hope. Belgium has
done her share in the making of the new world. In
that world she demands neither favours nor privileges.
What she needs and what she asks, with justifiable
emphasis, is that the great neighbouring nations and
more especially her allies shall not deny her full
opportunities in their markets, to enable her to regain
the prosperity she did not hesitate to sacrifice in
defence of her liberties and those of her allies.

For small countries like Belgium, the policy of

making social legislation international in scope
carries with it, as an essential condition of success, the
policy of bringing the markets of the world within
reach of their industries. Small nations can only
prosper if great nations buy their products. For
great nations to proclaim the political freedom of
small nations, and at the same time to deprive them
of commercial freedom, would be a vain and meaning-
less policy. For in time small nations would inevitably become first economically and then politically
dependent on some great nation or group of nations,
the markets of which absorbed their products. Moreover, to shut small nations out from the great markets
of the world through custom's barriers, would condemn
them to a cramped and narrow life which would check
the development of their industry in every branch,
and stifle progress towards the attainment of labour
reforms and the high standard of living for workers
which it is the object of the International
Labour Organisation under the League of Nations to
achieve.

This would not only beset labour reforms in small
countries with great difficulties, but would react
prejudicially upon the whole movement to make
labour legislation international in scope. Even if
this question did not effect the welfare of their own
workers, it is impossible to conceive that the great
nations—with whom Belgium, among other small
nations, fought so long and indomitably as their
ally—should hesitate to adopt an economic policy

which is necessary to secure to the workers in small countries, the just fruits of their past sacrifices in the new world that is being reshaped with the return of peace.

EMILE VANDERVELDE.

# PRACTICAL PROBLEMS

OF

# INTERNATIONAL LABOUR LEGISLATION

BY

## SOPHY SANGER

Formerly Secretary of the British Section, International Association for
Labour Legislation

I. INITIAL DIFFICULTIES

II. PREVENTIVE MEASURES IN UNHEALTHY PROCESSES

III. PREVENTIVE MEASURES AGAINST ACCIDENTS

IV. REDUCTION OF HOURS AND NIGHT WORK

V. CHILD LABOUR

VI. THE PROTECTION OF MOTHERS

VII. THE BERNE "LABOUR CHARTER"

VIII. CONCLUSION

# CHAPTER VI

## PRACTICAL PROBLEMS OF INTERNATIONAL LABOUR LEGISLATION

### I. INITIAL DIFFICULTIES

IT will be seen from the historical review written by Mr. Arthur Fontaine, that the attempts at international labour legislation in the decade preceding the war were in a large measure unsuccessful. The movement towards international regulation of industrial matters was, indeed, still in its infancy in 1914. But even in its early stages it had encountered difficulties of a very serious nature. Two main obstacles had made their appearance. The first was the lack of any regular machinery for bringing international labour conventions into being and the second, a lack of consecutive policy.

The conventions concluded in 1906 were brought into being by official and diplomatic conferences between the governments of different states at which no representatives, either of employers or workers, were present. The two conventions concluded as a result of these conferences were a splendid achievement for a first step, but no means existed for maintaining progress in the movement thus started. The International Association for Labour Legislation, with its biennial meetings of delegates, did not lack initiative. It was the originator of the Conventions of 1906, and was ready with recommendations for further conventions almost at once, but it was 1913 before the next official conference met to consider further measures of international legislation. Even then the results were disappointing.

The International Association for Labour Legislation had studied, with as much care and detail as is possible for an Association of that kind, the two subjects brought forward for discussion. A special committee of the Association had drawn up concrete proposals for two conventions. But no representative could be present at the conference of government delegates to urge the considered views of that organisation. Nor could that Association, or any other non-government organisation, by deputation or other means, bring influence to bear on the delegates who merely assembled for a few weeks to consider as quickly as possible the matters placed before them. These two defects will now disappear under the new scheme of a permanent International Labour Organisation under the League of Nations. We may thus hope for steady progress in the international regulation of industry, and it is interesting to consider on what lines it should be developed, and what practical problems in particular are ripe and suitable for international legislation.

## II. PREVENTIVE MEASURES IN UNHEALTHY PROCESSES

Perhaps the most obvious subject for immediate action is the prevention of the use of poisonous ingredients in certain manufacturing processes, and of diseases which the workers in certain industries are liable to contract. The Convention of 1906, which prohibited the use of white phosphorus in the manufacture of matches, is an excellent example of practical international legislation. It has a double advantage. It not only checks the use of the poison in the factories of every signatory state, but also carries its penalty with it, for each state agrees likewise to prohibit the importation of white phosphorus matches. Thus even those outside the Convention are penalised for their use of the poisonous material by losing their markets for phosphorus matches. For example, the adhesion of India to the Convention was of the greatest importance, not only in the interests of the few workers in the infant Indian match industry but because it closed this important market to phosphorus matches, so that it was not long before Belgium and Norway took steps to conform to the Convention while in Japan the use of white phosphorus is said to be dying out, and to exist now only for purposes of trade with China.

There is no reason why the model of the white phosphorus convention should not be followed in respect of other industrial poisons.[1] The British

[1] Appendix III. p. 332 (white phosphorus) and p. 320 (lead poisoning).

Section of the International Association for Labour Legislation, for example, had drafted just before the war an international convention to prohibit the use of lead in the manufacture of earthenware and china, on the same lines as the convention respecting white phosphorus, except that owing to the great complexity of the pottery industry, provision had to be made for temporary exceptions, or rather extensions of time for applying the terms of the convention. These extensions were to be allowed for particular works on the authority of an international technical commission.

Since that convention was drafted, the successful effects of the British regulations for the pottery industry and of the increased use of lead in less harmful forms, have indicated the possibility of going a very long way towards the elimination of lead-poisoning in this trade, without absolutely prohibiting the use of lead. In any case, however, the draft convention is an interesting example of the lines on which international action might be taken to prohibit the use of poisonous ingredients in processes of manufacture which are more difficult to deal with by legislation than the relatively simple case of the match industry. Through the new International Labour Organisation it should in any case be possible, as technical knowledge advances, to eliminate at once from all industries in all countries the use of poisonous ingredients for which chemical research succeeds in providing effective substitutes, and research to discover substitutes for poisonous substances used in manufacture should be encouraged by the new international body as one direct practical method of combating a great evil.[1]

The protection of workers in industries which involve danger to their health from the use of poisons or other causes is mentioned specifically in the report of the Commission of the Peace Conference on International Labour Legislation as one of the subjects to be dealt with by the first International Labour Conference. The matter is to be considered especially from the point of view of the protection of women and young persons. Naturally this aspect of the question makes a special appeal, but in practice it is impossible to deal with the protection of women workers in unhealthy trades without affecting conditions as a whole. Nor is it desirable that the employment of women should be singled out for special prohibition or restriction, where it proves possible by means of suitable regulations, well enforced, to render an industry healthy for all workers alike.

Lead, in certain forms is the most common of industrial poisons. It is used in the manufacture of pottery and electric accumulators, in tinning metal pots and pans, and in numbers of other industries. Workers in india-rubber factories are exposed to the injurious effects of bi-sulphide of carbon ; in certain other trades they are in danger of injury from chrome ; in others again from arsenic. Even where no specific poison is a cause of loss of

[1] See p. 257 (Health Section).

health, a trade may still be excessively injurious to workers owing to other causes. Dust, for instance, in its many forms—from metal, from stone, from slag— has disastrous effects upon the lungs when inhaled continuously day by day. Compulsory preventive measures, based upon scientific knowledge, are needed to ensure a proper standard of safety in all such trades.

Where the risk arises from dust, whether toxic or not, or where it arises from poisonous fumes, it can be avoided in some cases by the use of specially constructed machines from which no dust or fumes can escape, or by systems of exhaust ventilation attached to powerful fans which draw the dust or fumes away from the worker. Persons whose work involves contact with poisonous materials, need to be provided with proper facilities for washing their hands and faces before taking meals, and in some cases the provision of baths for the workers may be necessary. The standard of general cleanliness is of great importance in specially injurious occupations. The floors of factories where they are carried on need to be capable of thorough washing, and ought to be constructed without cracks or spaces in which poisonous elements can accumulate and afterwards escape in the form of dust.

All these, and many other matters, are already the subject of special regulations governing unhealthy industries in a number of countries. In some cases these regulations were preceded by the exclusion of women and young workers from long lists of dangerous trades and processes. But there is a tendency to develop specific regulations governing the conditions of employment for all workers in injurious trades in addition. For example, in France, by the side of the schedules of processes prohibited to women workers, we find regulations for the protection of all workers in trades involving risk of lead-poisoning, and in several other unhealthy industries. Regulations of this kind show a remarkable degree of similarity in the different countries.

It is clear that in this matter—encouraged by the International Association for Labour Legislation—nations have been influenced by good example and have not been slow to benefit by the experience of others which took the lead in these reforms. With the more powerful stimulus of the new International Labour Organisation, we may well hope to see a uniform international code of regulations in force in all countries governing employment in unhealthy industries, accompanied by provisions dealing with compensation for workers who suffer loss of health through their occupation—the effect of which would be to stimulate preventive measures.

One of the most useful duties of the International Labour Office, in connection with the collection of information, will be to furnish reliable statistics of disease among workers in any country due to specific injurious occupations.[1] Statistics are essential in order to enable the risks of an occupation

---

[1] See p. 253 (Scientific or Intelligence Section).

to be rightly estimated, as well as to call attention to the need for preventive measures. They also serve to show whether preventive measures are efficacious, and to what extent their modification is necessary. The British system of medical examination of workers in certain regulated trades, and of the compulsory notification of what are known as "occupational" diseases, has made it possible to keep a close check upon ill-health from certain causes and to observe accurately the effect of the preventive measures.

Here is an instance where the result of British experience, through the medium of the new International Labour Office, can be spread throughout the world. An immense field of work lies before the Labour Office in preparing comparative statistics concerning the health of workers in all countries engaged in injurious occupations, and in collecting complete information regarding the various methods employed in different countries for the elimination of dangerous conditions. This information will be essential to the International Labour Conferences as a basis for conventions and recommendations.

### III. PREVENTIVE MEASURES AGAINST ACCIDENTS

An equally useful field for the work of the International Labour Office lies in collecting data regarding the provisions in force in different countries for the prevention of accidents. Mechanical safeguards for the prevention of accidents, such as the fencing of machinery, the effect of the hours of labour, the age and sex of workers and the conditions of life and work generally in relation to the number of accidents, and the effect of legislation to provide compensation for accidents in minimising and preventing accidents, are all questions which should be studied from an international point of view. For instance, the experience of the United States of America should be more widely known, and their methods for preventing accidents promoted by the "Safety first" movement should be studied and applied universally.

These methods have resulted in a remarkable decrease in the number of accidents in many works where it was already low by comparison with accidents in less well-managed firms. A committee of workers co-operates in the prevention of accidents, by inspecting machines and investigating the causes of every accident that occurs. The workers are encouraged to make suggestions regarding measures to prevent the occurrence of accidents. Their attention is continually drawn to danger points by conspicuous notices, and to the question of preventing accidents generally by periodical notices giving, for example, figures of accidents in the different departments. By these and other means the workers are trained to guard against accidents, and the number of those caused by ignorance or inattention are reduced to a minimum. Knowledge of the efficacy of such methods and of the latest devices for the prevention

of accidents, as, for example, those which guard the danger points of engines and machine tools, can be spread abroad in every country by the International Labour Office, and brought by suitable means to the notice of governments, employers, and workers.

## IV. REDUCTION OF HOURS AND NIGHT WORK

Another urgent task before the International Labour Office and Conference is to bring to full fruition the ideas underlying the attempted Conventions of 1913. One of these was to reduce the hours of labour of women and boys to ten a day. Since then we have advanced, and the programme for the first International Labour Conference at Washington includes the general introduction of an eight hour day for all workers, men and women alike.[1] Perhaps the Conference will go further and consider the possibility of reducing the hours of boys and girls to a still lower limit. The adoption of an eight hour day or forty-eight hour week no longer needs to be argued. It is an accomplished fact in a large number of countries already.

Czecho Slovakia, France, Germany, German-Austria, the Netherlands, Norway, Poland, Portugal, Spain, Switzerland, have all adopted laws to establish an eight hour day for industrial workers during the past few months,[1] whereas before 1918 such laws were in force only in Australia, in certain of the South American

[1] Appendix III. p. 294.

Republics, and for particular trades such as mining, in a number of other countries. This interesting development has entirely changed the aspect of affairs as far as women workers are concerned. Only a short time ago, women were endeavouring to secure a ten hour working day. They now suddenly find themselves benefiting with their men-folk in the new standard of eight hours work. The eight hour day, or forty-eight hour week, whichever may eventually be taken as the basis, needs now only to be consolidated by international legislation.

The other convention under consideration in 1913 was the prohibition of night employment for boys. This matter is also to be considered at the Washington Labour Conference.[1] The International Trade Union and Socialist Conferences held at Berne in February, 1919, went further and demanded the general prohibition of night work, with exceptions in the case of men only where the conditions of manufacture or other reasons made night work essential. Thus the movement for prohibiting night work for women,[2] adopted by the Berne Convention of 1906, has now developed into a movement to prohibit night work as far as possible for all workers, which will doubtless result in the matter being considered at an International Labour Conference in future.

The question is of great interest from the point of view of international competition. A country

[1] Appendix III. p. 327. (Night Work for Young Persons.)
[2] Appendix III. p. 315. (Night Work for Women.)

K

where machinery is utilised continuously for the whole or the greater part of the twenty-four hours might gain a competitive advantage over rivals whose work was confined to eight or sixteen hours in the day.  If the human interests of the worker were ignored no doubt it would be to the nation's advantage to keep its men at work in shifts all night, but the evils of night work for men are only less in degree than those resulting from the employment of women at night.   Night work for all workers should be reduced to an absolutely necessary minimum, and allowed only where unavoidable or in the public interest, as in the case of blast-furnace workers, newspaper printers, and transport workers and post office officials engaged in the transmission of night mails.   If the International Labour Office after due investigation could schedule the industries and occupations in which night work in the general interest was unavoidable, the Labour Conference could consider at some future time how far night work might be universally limited by international convention.

### V. CHILD LABOUR

A question of vital importance, upon which international action is to be considered at the forth-coming Labour Conference at Washington, is the age at which children shall first be employed in industrial or other employment.[1]   Wide diversity exists both in the age limits fixed, and in the occupations affected in

[1] Appendix III. p. 323.

different countries. An international standard is
urgently needed. The problem, however, is not so
simple as may appear at first sight. It is intimately
connected with the question of education. Countries
with no system of compulsory education, or where
the age limit for school attendance is very low, would
no doubt feel unable to raise the age for employment
suddenly, thereby launching their children into a period
of several years occupied with neither education nor
work. Although education may in theory be regarded
as outside the scope of industrial regulation, it is, in
practice, so closely connected with the question of
child labour that the two matters cannot be
divorced. It is an interesting fact that the " Labour
Charter " adopted simultaneously by the two International Conferences of Socialists and of Trade
Unionists respectively assembled at Berne in February,
1919, begins with education. The first sections read
as follows :—

" Primary education shall be compulsory in all
countries, and a system of vocational and general
technical education shall be established.

" Higher education shall be free and accessible
to all. It is not right that the capacities and
aspirations of young persons should be thwarted
by the material conditions in which they happen
to live.

" Children under 15 years of age shall not be
employed in industrial occupations. Young

persons between 15 and 18 years of age shall not be employed for more than 6 hours a day, with a break of one and a half hours.

"At least two hours instruction in technical and continuation classes shall be given to young persons of both sexes, daily, between the hours of 8 a.m. and 6 p.m. Young persons should be allowed 'time off' to attend the classes."

It is to be hoped that the International Labour Conference will deal with the matter boldly and work for an international standard of primary education as being the necessary complement to the regulation of children's wage-earning work.[1] As a first step, no doubt, the possibility of raising the age of leaving school and for entering employment to 14 will be considered. This is a lower limit than exists in some American states, in parts of Canada, and in Victoria, but it is above the standard in many other countries. Owing to the diversity of practice regarding this question in different countries, it might be necessary to allow an extension of time for some countries before they are required to conform to the international age limit agreed upon. In tropical countries it might be unreasonable to enforce the same age limit as that approved for colder countries where the human physique develops more slowly. All such points will have to be investigated and considered carefully by the International Labour Office. On the basis of their

[1] See p. 259 (Education Section).

reports, the Labour Conference should encounter no insuperable difficulty in establishing a relatively fair minimum age for the employment of children.

### VI. THE PROTECTION OF MOTHERS

Another important item on the agenda of the first Labour Conference concerns women workers alone. This is the question of employment shortly before and after childbirth.[1] To allow women to be employed in arduous work or for very long hours in the factory up to the date of confinement, and again almost immediately after the child is born, would be clearly contrary to the interests of mother and child and, indeed, of the nation itself. But the mere prohibition of employment in all or any specific work such as is found in most of the older industrial codes in existence, fails entirely to meet the case. It is only the poorest women—those who cannot possibly dispense with a few weeks' wages—who will voluntarily continue working till the last moment, and return to factory work within a month of confinement.

Such women will necessarily return to work by hook or crook in defiance of any legal decree to the contrary as soon as they can. If the employer asks no questions, no harm will be done if a breach of the law is committed, for he cannot be prosecuted unless he "knowingly" allowed a woman to return to his employment within the prohibited term. Practically all laws on

[1] Appendix III. p. 310.

this subject protect the employers by some such phrase. Even if the employer conscientiously observes the law, there is nothing to prevent a woman from seeking work in another factory where her family history will be quite unknown, or she may be driven to undertake irregular work, often of a heavy nature such as charring, which is not subject to regulation, or to enter upon some sweated home industry.

Clearly, then, the prohibition of women's employment in industry about the time of childbirth needs to be supplemented where necessary by pecuniary grants, to save the mother from want or absolute destitution during her enforced absence from work. It might be argued that a suitable scheme of adequate maternity allowances and benefits for working women immediately before and after childbirth would remove the necessity of prohibiting employment at all, as no woman relieved from the necessity of working for her living would choose to do so at such times. Be that as it may, these two questions — namely, the exclusion of women from employment for a certain period about the time of confinement, and the benefits to be paid her in compensation for loss of earnings— are to be considered at Washington. It is perhaps not a matter in which diversity among nations affects their position as regards competition in international trade, but it is of such importance to women and to their children at a critical time in their lives, that it is properly included in the programme of the first Labour Conference, and much good will be done if the period of compulsory exclusion from employment and the question of adequate compensation for consequent loss of wages, become the subjects of an international convention.

In some countries, insurance benefit is provided for women at the time of confinement, but this benefit is usually singularly inadequate. It is strange that maternity benefits should so commonly be the same as benefits allowed for ordinary sickness. Considering that sickness benefit usually takes the form of some percentage of wages (50 or 60%) in order that the sick person may not be too greatly encouraged to remain on the sick list, it seems the reverse of logical to provide a like sum for maternity benefit, one of the main objects of which is to encourage a woman to refrain from work during a reasonable period before and after the birth of a child.

Maternity benefit, or maternity allowances — where direct grants without insurance are adopted, as in France — should certainly be equivalent to the worker's whole wages or even more, in view of the extra household expenditure arising from the incapacity of a working man's wife and her need of extra nourishment and attendance about the time of childbirth. Money benefits should, moreover, be supplemented by free medical treatment, both before and after as well as at the time of confinement, and by the institution of free advice and help where necessary for pregnant women. It would be a piece of highly valuable work within the scope of the new International Labour Office, to collate the experience of different countries on this matter. A report and detailed recommendations on this subject would form a necessary supplement to an international convention fixing a legal period of exclusion from employment, and providing that suitable benefits should be granted during exclusion.


## VII. THE BERNE " LABOUR CHARTER "

Most of the subjects mentioned above are included on the agenda for the Washington Conference of 1919. It is of interest to see what other matters are included, as needing international regulation, in the " Labour Charter " adopted at the International Conferences at Berne, to which reference has already been made. These may be assumed to be the questions which will be dealt with *seriatim* as the annual International Labour Conferences and the International Labour Office can dispose of them.

One of the most urgent reforms which figures in the Berne charter, is the general introduction of the Saturday half-holiday. This arrangement, customary for years in Great Britain, was until recently almost unknown in foreign countries. The movement in favour of what is known on the continent as the " English week " is a comparatively recent development. In some countries, it is true, the Factory Acts provide that women with households to attend to shall be released from work

an hour or two earlier than the normal time on
Saturdays.    But the object of this provision is
merely to ensure the comfort of the family by giving
the woman a little time for domestic shopping.   A
free hour, devoted to domestic instead of factory
work, hardly partakes of the nature of a holiday.
It was only recently that the French dressmakers and
milliners, after a successful strike, secured by law a
short day on Saturday.

This question, of course, is intimately connected
with the question of hours of work, and is bound
to be considered in connection with the suggested
international agreement on the eight hour day.
Will the eight hour day be a rigid rule, or will it
be permissible to extend the hours on other
days of the week in order to procure a Saturday
half-holiday, or will the eight hour day be coupled
with a short day on Saturday, making a forty-four hour
working week ?   These questions must be answered
in due course and the solution embodied in an international convention.   The weekly whole holiday is
another question dealt with in the Berne Labour
Charter, where a minimum rest of thirty-six hours
taken between Saturday and Monday morning is laid
down as the standard.

The question of wages is touched upon in several
sections of the Berne Labour Charter.   It arises in
connection with Sunday work and night work.
Where such work is essential it should be paid for
at a rate higher than that paid for normal hours.

The principle of equal pay for equal work is laid down somewhat vaguely. Vaguely, again, the Charter demands that where the average earnings of any workers are found to be insufficient to provide a proper standard of living and no trade union rates can be secured, Wages Boards, equally representative of workers and employers, shall be set up to fix minimum rates of wages. The Berne Labour Charter does not give a clear lead to the International Labour Conference as regards the possibilities of regulating wages by international convention. No doubt in time the International Labour Office will collect data upon which it may be possible in future to base a scheme for ensuring at least a relative equality of wages in some if not in all industries so as to prevent low wages in any one country from exercising a retarding influence upon the movement for higher wages and better conditions in others.[1]

The right of combination and freedom of immigration have an important place in the Berne Labour Charter, and should receive attention from the Annual Labour Conferences as soon as other matters more urgent or more ripe for solution are settled.

The immigration question very closely affects that of unemployment, which figures on the agenda of the first Conference.[2] It will be interesting to see what recommendations of an international nature the Conference feels able to make in connection with this very difficult problem. The Berne Labour Charter

[1] See p. 259 (Wages Section).   [2] Appendix III. pp. 305-308.

also demands, without entering into details, a special code of regulations for the protection of seamen, and deals with the risks to which railway workers are exposed in coupling and uncoupling waggons, by demanding international regulations to enforce the use of automatic couplers.

The regulation of home-work also figures in the Berne Labour Charter.[1] This is a matter of vital importance to women and children—to women, because the ranks of home-workers are filled largely by women, and to children because their health and happiness are at stake when injurious or dirty processes are carried on in the home, or when they are pressed into the service of their parents to help to swell the low earnings that so often prevail in home industries. To take an example. Enquiries into the Hungarian pottery industry some years ago, revealed terrible cases of young children suffering from lead poisoning in acute forms contracted from contact with the lead used in their parents' trade, carried on without any precautions or understanding of its dangerous nature, in the very rooms where they played, slept and ate. Whatever the advantages or disadvantages of home-work may be from a general point of view, it is clear that such conditions should not be allowed. The Labour Charter expressed this view in a clause demanding the prohibition of home-work, " in the case of work liable to give rise to poisoning or to serious injury to health."

[1] See p. 258 (Home Work Section).

The most efficacious method of protecting children from overwork in home industries is clearly to secure proper and adequate remuneration for the parents. The Berne Labour Charter accordingly contemplated the establishment of wages boards for home industries to fix legal rates of wages. The new International Labour Office when it takes up this question will, it is to be hoped, take the broader view indicated in another section of the Charter to which reference has already been made, and which demands the introduction of authorities for fixing minimum rates of pay for all workers in " sweated " trades, whether carried on in the home or in workshops.

This is the method adopted under the Trade Boards Act of Great Britain, where a measure to regulate wages of home-workers alone would not have found favour and would not have been effectual. In France, however, where home-work is very common, and where home-workers were well known to receive less pay than workshop employees, the power to fix minimum rates applies only to women home-workers in certain trades, and was created with the specific object of raising home-workers' wages to the level of those paid in factories and workshops. Probably in a matter of this kind, different methods may be found necessary to suit the differing national conditions. Here lies another useful field of work for the International Labour Office—the investigation of conditions of home-work in all countries, the scheduling of trades which should be prohibited in dwelling places, and the determination of methods best suited to prevent sweating and other abuses found in home-work.

## CONCLUSION

Such, in brief outline, are some of the tasks which will occupy the International Labour Office and the Annual Labour Conferences under the League of Nations in the next few years. Courage and determination will be needed to overcome innumerable difficulties in building up a great code of international labour legislation, with the object of promoting the true welfare of millions of workers throughout the world. But by the united efforts and goodwill of workers, employers and governments in all countries, this task, however difficult, can in time be achieved successfully, to add immeasurably to the sum of human happiness.

SOPHY SANGER.

# A REVIEW

OF

# INTERNATIONAL LABOUR LEGISLATION

BY

## ARTHUR FONTAINE

Councillor of State
Director of Labour to the Ministry of Labour in France
Chairman of the Governing Body of the International Labour Office

I. DEFINITION OF INTERNATIONAL LABOUR LEGISLATION

II. CAUSES THAT LED TO INTERNATIONAL LABOUR LEGIS-
LATION

III. THE BIRTH OF INTERNATIONAL LABOUR LEGISLATION

IV. FIRST EXPERIMENTS IN INTERNATIONAL LABOUR LEGIS-
LATION

V. THE BERNE CONVENTIONS

VI. A PROGRAMME OF INTERNATIONAL LABOUR LEGISLATION

VII. GENERAL CONCLUSIONS

# CHAPTER VII

## A REVIEW OF INTERNATIONAL LABOUR LEGISLATION

### I. DEFINITION OF INTERNATIONAL LABOUR LEGISLATION

BEFORE dealing with the history of international labour legislation, it is necessary to define the sense in which the words " international legislation " are used. Strictly speaking, there is as yet no such thing as international labour legislation, but there has been a series of endeavours and enactments, which are tending to establish it and make it a reality. I briefly set forth the history of the ideas that inspired these endeavours and enactments, with a view to showing what was the general situation regarding international legislation on labour questions up to the time of the Paris Peace Conference in 1919.

It must be understood clearly that the Paris Conference has not created an international authority to make and enforce laws on labour questions generally. It may, however, be said to have anticipated this development to some extent by its resolutions. In the literal sense of the words, international legislation would imply a uniform code of laws adopted and enforced

L                                    161

by different nations united in a league.  It would pre-suppose the existence of an international parliament or conference empowered to draw up such a code, together with some simple method of procedure which would enable the member states of the League to apply its laws, as passed by the votes of a certain majority of the states represented at this conference or parliament.  It would further pre-suppose the exist-ence of a supervisory body, organised to ensure that these international laws were enforced.  Nor would international legislation, in its literal meaning, exclude provision for appeals from the decisions of this parlia-ment to a supreme court, an upper house or a council of states which would exercise functions analogous to those of a higher legislative body in a national constitution.  Once laws received the sanction of both international legislatures, they would be binding alike on all the nations in the League.

The Paris Conference has not brought us to this stage of development.  This is clear from the labour clauses of the Peace Treaty.  Yet, though each member state is free to accept or decline the conventions and recommendations of the International Labour Con-ference, when these are submitted for approval to its national parliament—thus preserving fully the prin-ciple of the political independence of each member state—nevertheless distinct progress towards effective international legislation has been made.  Every member state is pledged to submit the conventions and recommendations of the International Labour

Conference to its national legislation for adoption as national laws. Should they be ratified it follows that the member state admits the right of international enquiries and obligations with respect to them, under the League of Nations and the International Labour Office, in case of its failure to give effect to conventions and recommendations.

Thus the principle of international co-operation in the making of labour laws is definitely established. However tentative the first efforts at co-operation may be, and however elastic the obligations which result from them may seem, it is clear beyond all doubt that *the principle of international labour legislation has at last been established.* Whatever modifications may be made as the result of future experience in the International Labour Organisation as originally constituted, it marks a development of great importance, and it defines at the present time the whole position and meaning of international legislation. Moreover, it prepares the way for the next great step in progress, which the Commission on International Labour Legislation somewhat timidly advocated by the following resolution :—The Commission expresses the hope that, as soon as it may be possible, an agreement will be arrived at between the High Contracting Parties with a view to endowing the International Labour Conference, under the auspices of the League of Nations, with power to make, under conditions to be determined, resolutions possessing the force of international law.

Mr. Barnes and Dr. Shotwell, in other chapters of this book, have explained the principles and methods applied by the Paris Convention of 1919 in establishing the International Labour Organisation.  I can therefore confine myself to discussing the conditions which form the basis of international labour legislation.  It is advisable, however, to define the limits of the subject with which I deal, to preserve the necessary balance between the various chapters of this book.

Thus I propose to set out the causes which have given rise to the need for international legislation on labour questions, and indicate the different bodies which have been formed from time to time in order to satisfy this need.  I will also deal with the nature of the first measures taken with this object, and the results attained.  My review of developments will end with the Paris Conference of 1919, and as I commence by indicating characteristic features of the new International Labour Organisation set up by the Conference, I will conclude by considering briefly certain results of its work in the light of the labour clauses of the Peace Treaty.

## II. CAUSES THAT LED TO INTERNATIONAL LABOUR LEGISLATION

The civilised nations of the western world in Europe and America have similar needs and habits of life which do not differ greatly. They share a common mental outlook and culture. Their national life follows the same trend of democratic development, inspired by those ideals of welfare, justice and freedom for all workers which dignify labour. There is nothing strange in these similarities among human beings whose industrial methods, manufactures and even pleasures are relatively uniform, and who are further drawn together by the influence of printing and railways. How closely industrial conditions, in particular, tend towards uniformity in these countries is illustrated by statistics concerning accidents arising from certain classes of employment, which show that the average death rate arising from such accidents, whether due to chance or carelessness, is relatively the same irrespective of the nationality of the workers. Uniformity in characteristic features of dress, furniture, dwellings and towns among western peoples, are of course clearly apparent. It is easy to understand that this general uniformity of occupation, habit and culture has given rise among the workers of this great human group to common sentiments, aspirations and ideals, especially with regard to reforms which will secure for them better conditions of life.

Each successive step towards the realisation of these reforms, however, becomes more difficult in proportion as the agitation of workers for higher wages and better conditions, together with competition in selling the commodities they produce in the markets of the world, tend on the one hand to increase the cost of production and on the other to reduce profits. The cumulative effects of these upward and downward tendencies naturally complicate the whole system of manufacture and commerce which they concern, and call for increased efforts and greatly improved organisation on the part of the manufacturers and merchants to cope with them effectively. For example, if an employer considers the question of reducing his workmen's hours, he must take into account the advantage his rivals may reap, during some perhaps lengthy transitory period, through their men working for longer hours. Again, if he contemplates suppressing night work, he has to remember that plant, such as wool combing, spinning and glass making machinery, will become relatively more costly, because it will take longer for him to recover the purchase price from earnings. Such considerations gradually convinced men that the labour reforms they desired, based on ideals of justice and democratic progress, could only be attained through the co-operation of all civilised nations not only in Europe and America but also in the Far East, and that these reforms must be agreed upon and confirmed by international conventions formulating precise regulations making progress in all countries as far as possible simultaneous and relatively uniform.

### III. THE BIRTH OF INTERNATIONAL LABOUR LEGISLATION

If, what—for want of a more accurate term—we may already call international labour legislation, were to embrace all the existing legal principles concerning workers upon which civilised peoples are agreed and which they have embodied in their codes of law, then this branch of legislation would cover to-day a considerable field, and its interesting history would comprise a systematic survey of the national labour laws at present in force in different countries. A lengthy analysis of this kind, however, would lie outside the scope of this chapter, for in tracing shortly the growth of international labour legislation, I am not concerned with the fortuitous enactments of the different nations and the extent to which they are more or less identical. I am concerned only with formal treaties guaranteed by international conventions which, moreover, are not confined to treaties between neighbouring peoples with regard to commercial intercourse, but which include general conventions binding large groups of nations to adopt definite principles, and to enforce them as international laws.

In connection with these general international conventions, it is useful to recall briefly the nature and object of certain stipulations relating to labour as set out in direct agreements made between two contracting nations. The need for the stipulations in question arose through the emigration and temporary movements of citizens of one country to become workers in another country.  The mother country was, of course, responsible for  protecting her people in the foreign country to which they went, and would have to take action if necessary to secure for them the rights of free men, if not the actual rights of citizens.  Such intervention would include measures to facilitate the accumulation and remittance home of money saved by its citizens, and arrangements for their freedom of movement.  These measures would fall under the head of stipulations embodied in what are known as " establishment " treaties, as distinct from stipulations analogous to those embodied in commercial treaties.  Many examples could be given of such stipulations, but as they lie outside the scope of my subject I need not refer to them beyond mentioning a few which serve to illustrate the difference between direct treaties between nations and international legislation in its true sense.

In principle, the citizens of different countries in Western Europe mingle freely as workers.  This practice, however, is not based on any recognised political right.  Speaking generally, public opinion recognizes the moral right of manual workers of all countries to intermingle freely in seeking employment in civilized countries.[1]  In consequence, we find this moral right the subject of an important clause in the Franco-Swiss Convention of 23rd February, 1882 :—

" Every kind of industry or commerce permitted to

---

[1] See Append. III. p. 310 (Recommendation concerning Reciprocity of Treatment for Foreign Workers).

be carried on by Frenchmen in France will be allowed also to Swiss subjects, without the imposition of any more onerous conditions, whether pecuniary or other." This is an example of a stipulation which the " most favoured nation " clause commonly included in treaties prior to 1914, had rendered of fairly general application.

Many direct treaties and conventions between peoples relate to difficulties connected with the employment of Chinese or Japanese labour. Others cover a wide field in dealing with emigration and immigration; the right to work; business connected with workmen's savings banks deposits, and compensation for injuries due to accidents in the course of employment, and the payment of old age pensions. The treaties concerning compensation for accidental injuries are particularly numerous, and have given rise between pairs of nations to a complex network of stipulations and guarantees which could without difficulty be superseded by comprehensive international conventions.

All these direct treaties between two nations carry mutual obligations. Belgium protects her subjects in France, France protects hers in Belgium; similar advantages being conceded by both parties. Where identical mutual concessions cannot be made, or are considered insufficient as fair compensation for the advantages conceded by one side or the other, then the difficulty has been adjusted by suitable commercial or other concessions, arranged perhaps in a more general treaty. The Franco-Italian agreement of 15th April,

1904, which I had myself the honour of drawing up at Rome in conjunction with the great statesman, Luzatti, was a typical example of a direct treaty between two nations dealing with labour problems which contains features that certainly characterise international labour legislation in its true sense, and has led to its being considered the first labour treaty properly so called.

Luzatti wished to obtain for Italians working in France certain advantages, such as equitable treatment in case of industrial accidents, and old age pensions, and a special protection or guidance for the young Italian workers in France. Recognising that neither commercial concessions nor reciprocal measures would provide adequate compensation for France, we hit upon a new and fruitful solution of the problem. We decided to lay down principles dealing on the one hand with the insurance and protection of foreign workers, and on the other with national laws regulating the conditions of labour. These principles commended themselves to both parties. The development of the regulation of labour in Italy, however, was from the standpoint of commercial relations more advantageous to France, where such regulation was well advanced, while the principles relating to workmen's insurance were most particularly advantageous to Italy, a large number of whose population had emigrated.

Thus the Franco-Italian Treaty of 1904 contained clauses regulating the general conditions of labour and benefiting alike Italians in Italy and Frenchmen in France. This is the characteristic feature of true international legislation, then in its origin. By Article 3 of this convention the two peoples bind themselves to encourage international legislation, as will be seen by its wording—" In cases where the initiative is taken by one state to convoke various other states to an international conference with a view to unifying, by common agreement, certain laws for the protection of workpeople, the adhesion of one of the two contracting states to the proposed conference shall entail in principle a favourable reply from the other contracting state."

## IV. FIRST EXPERIMENTS IN INTERNATIONAL LABOUR LEGISLATION

The idea of an international convention to regulate labour conditions is closely bound up with the development of industry and the means of transport. As long ago as 1818, Robert Owen addressed a memorial on the international regulation of labour conditions to the plenipotentiaries of the Holy Alliance.[1] In France the earliest Factory Acts were passed in the middle of the nineteenth century, at a time when machinery universally applied to industry together with the first railways was stimulating commercial competition. The causes which tended to make

[1] *Vide* Ch. Mahaim, *Le Droit International Ouvrier*, p. 186.   Larose & Tenin, publisher, Paris, 1913.

national legislation regulating labour conditions inevitable, also tended to make international labour regulations inevitable. The economist Blanqui suggested the idea first in 1839, but did not press it. The Alsatian manufacturer Le Grand, from 1839 to 1859, whenever a new Factory Act was passed in France, England, or Germany, insisted on the need of such legislation, and held that it should be international in scope.[1]

The repeated efforts of Le Grand to advocate international labour legislation were unsuccessful. The first industrial evils to be remedied were so grave—as, for instance, the employment of children from eight to twelve years of age in factories for more than twelve hours per day—that the public conscience would not tolerate the postponement of national legislation to abolish them to await international action. Industrial abuses, moreover, were so terrible that improvements in labour conditions could not adversely affect national industry. Later, however, from 1870 to 1890, when less serious abuses arose, the utility and the need of international labour legislation became clearer. Economists of all opinions advocated international action for the solution of labour problems. I am unable to trace the development of this idea in detail, but will quote examples which mark its progress. Thus as early as 1855, the Swiss canton of Glaris in making a proposal for an international agreement suggested the utility of general international stipulations, which,

[1] Cf. Bauer, *Vierteljahrscrift für Social und Wirschaftsgeschichte*, 1903.

however, it referred to as " vain desires." In 1866, the Working men's International Association at the congress of Geneva declared in favour of international stipulations—and maintained this position at every congress afterwards. In 1876, the President of the Swiss Confederation, Colonel Frey, proposed to the Swiss National Council " to conclude international treaties tending to regulate labour questions on uniform lines in all industrial states."

In 1881, the Swiss Federal Council, in pursuance of a resolution moved by Colonel Frey, approached the governments of Germany, Austria, Belgium, France, Great Britain and Italy, with a proposal to regulate employment in factories by international legislation. This proposal was not accepted. From 1880 to 1890, an increasing number of proposals regarding international legislation were brought before various parliaments and congresses, among others by Caesar de Paepe, de Mun, Edouard Vaillant, the Catholic Socialist Party, with the Prince of Loewenstein, Decurtins, Favon, and Millerand. That is to say, the present day Socialists, Radicals, and Catholic Socialists, advocated international labour laws, while among others, Prince Bismarck and Karl Bucher opposed this legislative development. In 1885, Bismarck declared the protection of workers by international agreement impossible and impracticable. Four years later, however, it appeared that this development would presently become both practicable and possible.

In 1889, the Swiss Federal Council, which had before

taken the initiative in this matter, invited the governments of other countries to a preliminary conference on the subject of international labour legislation. The agenda comprised six points, namely : the age of admission of children to industrial employment ; Sunday rest ; the length of the working day for juvenile labour ; (adolescent workers) night work for juvenile labour and women ; the employment of women and juvenile labour on dangerous and potentially injurious trades ; and the nature of obligations under international agreements, together with the methods of enforcing such obligations. Favourable replies were received by the Swiss Federal Council, and preliminary discussions had commenced when the Emperor William II. of Germany suddenly intervened, inviting the governments concerned to a labour conference in Berlin.

It was in Berlin then in 1890, that the first international conference upon labour legislation was held. A great variety of questions were discussed, including the protection of child workers, women workers and miners, and the hygienic problems of industry, but this conference proved abortive. The governments represented were not willing to pledge themselves to introduce the proposed reforms in their respective countries, therefore no international convention was signed. Resolutions and recommendations dealing with these reforms were, however, proposed by the delegates of Germany, Austria-Hungary, Belgium, Denmark, France, Great Britain, Italy, Luxemburg,

Holland, Portugal, Sweden, Norway and Switzerland. This check to the progress of international legislation proved to be apparent rather than actual, because it resulted in giving a great impetus to labour legislation generally and did not put an end to efforts to bring it within the scope of international law. Fifteen years, however, elapsed before the Conference of 1905 really laid the foundation of international labour legislation in the two Berne conventions of 26th September, 1906.

The International Association for Labour Legislation—a body formed in Paris in July, 1900—deserves credit and gratitude for its efforts, which largely contributed to these results. The work of this Association formed the basis of the discussions of 1905 and 1906 ; it furnished memoranda to the Swiss Federal Council, and it suggested that the Swiss Government should take steps to summon an international conference. In 1913, again, the deliberations of this Association resulted in the passing of resolutions, on the strength of which the Swiss Federal Council invited the governments of Europe to a conference upon international labour legislation.

## V. THE BERNE CONVENTIONS

The Berne Conventions marked a definite stage of progress. They initiated a period of practical results. They inaugurated methods upon which the Peace Treaty of Versailles of 1919 is based, with regard to the international organisation of labour. Special

importance, therefore, attaches to the history of the
Berne Conventions, and it is desirable to record
the definite results of the 1905 Conference embodied
in the 1906 Berne Convention, which future conventions will confirm and extend. It is also convenient to record certain results, attained solely
" *ad referendum* " by the 1913 Berne Conference,
which the war prevented the High Contracting
Parties from embodying in a definite Convention,
in 1914. The last mentioned results will have to be
revised to harmonise with the principles laid down
by the Paris Peace Treaty of 1919, and will in this
form be included in the conventions agreed upon by
the first International Labour Conference which
assembles at Washington in October, 1919.

(*a*) *The Berne Convention of* 1906. The International Association for Labour Legislation found
the choice of subjects to be dealt with by the
first Berne Convention to be a difficult task. On
the one hand, it was necessary to avoid subjects
involving elements of sharp controversy—which pre-
cluded the hope of agreement—in favour of subjects
upon which, in principle, different nations were already
in agreement, as being more likely to give results.
On the other hand, the proposed reforms had to be
truly important if public opinion was to be impressed,
and if the international machinery to be provided for
dealing with them was to justify itself.

The two subjects ultimately decided upon were
those which the Swiss Government desired strongly

to adopt as the subject of the 1905 Conference, namely:
the prohibition of industrial employment for women
at night, and the prohibition of the manufacture and
sale of matches made with white phosphorus. As
regards the former reform, certain countries had already
forbidden the industrial employment of women at
night. Apart from general hygienic reasons which
make night work undesirable for all workers, there
were additional reasons against women being so
employed. As a rule the woman who works at night
at a factory is in a sense employed both day and night,
owing to the fact that certain domestic duties must
be performed by her during the day which seriously
curtail the time she needs for rest. Night work,
moreover, is seldom essential in factories except where
furnaces are kept burning continuously, and this work
is unsuitable for women owing to its physical strain.
Finally, the prohibition of night work seemed on
general grounds to be more necessary for women than
for men.

Setting aside the argument that social evolution has made women's proper place the home
rather than the factory, it is clear that women have
failed to unite and organise themselves to further
their interests as men have done, either because they
are unable to do so, or because they lack the necessary
knowledge. It is clear also that for physical causes
women are unable to withstand the strain of work
such as that involved by night employment as well
as men, and that for this reason work which involves

M

excessive or special strain tends through women to react prejudicially upon the younger and future generations. The employment of women further tends to affect unfavourably the conditions of labour for men, as for example through competition, because women are content to work for lower rates of wages.

These were and are sound reasons upon which to base labour reforms affecting women—providing of course that they do not aim at eliminating the employment of women altogether. Accordingly it was felt that the reform in question, if submitted to the Berne Conference of 1906, stood a good chance of becoming the subject of international agreement, and that if this proved to be the case a reform of great social importance might be achieved, which would at the same time tend to equalise in more than one respect the conditions of international industrial competition.

With respect to white phosphorus, France, Germany, Holland and Switzerland had before 1906 prohibited its use in the manufacture of matches, owing to its harmful effect on workers through phosphorus necrosis. Doubtless this evil might have been prevented through improvements in machinery and methods of manufacture and the protection of workers from contact with phosphorus. These measures might have proved effective except in case of carelessness. But the conditions of the industry would still have been undesirable while the terrible white phosphorous was used instead of other harmless substances. Consequently, this industry provided the subject for a reform to which effect might well be given by international agreement. Nevertheless, the difficulties involved were considerably greater and more complex than in the case of night work for women. France and Germany which had already forbidden the use of white phosphorus, did not export matches, and the former country, by its government monoply of the sale of matches, was not subject to foreign competition in this trade. The exporting countries, England, Austria, Sweden, and Norway, were confronted with the objections of Japan and other Asiatic countries to introduce this reform, and as a simple European convention would therefore be insufficient to protect them against Asiatic competition in the match trade, strong opposition to reform might be expected on their part.

The first conventions which had been originated between 1902 and 1904 by the International Association for Labour Legislation, resulted in two official conferences which, in effect, were one and the same. The first was a technical conference in May, 1905, at which delegates with expert knowledge drew up proposals for reference to the governments concerned. The second was a diplomatic conference in 1906, at which these proposals were formerly dealt with. Fifteen states were represented at the two Conferences of 1905 and 1906, namely, Germany, Austria, Hungary, Belgium, Denmark, Spain, France, Great Britain, Italy, Luxemburg, Norway, Holland, Portugal, Sweden and Switzerland. The United

States had not been invited because questions of labour legislation could not constitutionally be dealt with by the Federal Government.[1]   Greece, Roumania, and Serbia did not reply to the invitation issued by the Swiss Government.  Fourteen states—Norway alone excepted—signed the convention relating to the prohibition of night work for women in industrial establishments.  This convention did not merely stipulate that women must not be employed between the hours of 10 p.m. and 5 a.m., but it also guaranteed to every woman engaged in an industrial occupation a night's rest of not less than eleven consecutive hours. The importance of these provisions was not lessened by certain indispensable reservations which permitted the night rest for women to be reduced to ten hours on sixty occasions in any year under exceptional circumstances in any undertaking, more particularly (i) in unforeseen emergencies when work had been interrupted by causes not recurrent in character ;  (ii) in cases where raw materials or articles in some process of manufacture were subject to such rapid changes that loss would inevitably result if work was suspended before the process was completed ;  (iii) in case of industries affected by seasonal influences.

As regards the prohibition of the manufacture, importation and sale of matches made of white phosphorus, the refusal of Japan to sign the convention resulted in several other countries also refusing.  Six states only signed the convention, namely, Germany,

[1] See page 58.

Holland, Switzerland and France—two of which already had such prohibitions in force—together with Luxemburg, which had no match industry, and Italy. This was to some extent a check. Yet such was the moral force of these provisions upon public opinion, that first England, then Austria, Spain, Hungary, United States, and finally Finland, forbade the use of white phosphorus—England and Spain by joining the Convention, and the other countries by giving effect to its provisions in their national laws. Since then, the Danish colonies, the French colonies, Tunis, the Dutch Indies and the British Dominions have also prohibited the manufacture and sale of matches made from red phosphorus, so that the market for this commodity has become very restricted, and M. Mahain in his book on international labour legislation,[1] states that within a short time the phosphorus match industry of Belgium will die out for want of markets.

Certain additional clauses inserted in the first conventions signed should be embodied in later agreements. These relate to arrangements for enabling countries to join a convention subsequently to its completion, and also to enable colonies and protectorates to do so in cases where their inclusion does not automatically follow by the act of the motherland in joining a convention. The clauses in question further comprise special provisions applicable to states and colonies outside Europe, with a view to

[1] *Le Droit International Ouvrier.*

facilitate their joining a convention despite difficulties connected with special circumstances relating to climatic or industrial conditions ; the question of delays before giving effect to conventions, and for dealing with defaults in giving effect to conventions. Thus a definite type of convention was created by the agreement under discussion, which will certainly influence the form of subsequent conventions in spite of certain differences which characterise the regulations of the new International Labour Organisation. Let me say in passing, that these regulations comprise measures analogous to those just mentioned relating to the inclusion of colonies, protectorates, and countries in which special circumstances have to be taken into account.

It is desirable to go more fully into the question of supervision and guarantees for giving effect to the provisions of the conventions under discussion. As regards the former point, each contracting state was directly responsible for carrying out the terms of the convention strictly within its frontiers. It was under obligation to communicate to each of the other contracting states the laws and regulations through which effect was given to particular measures, together with periodical reports upon the application of these regulations. There was no provision for any international supervision either of a permanent or occasional nature.

In 1906, Great Britain attempted to bring about a stricter control by means of a Permanent Commission. This body would have been composed of delegates of the contracting states, whose duty would be to investigate matters of dispute and complaints submitted to them and report on them by simple statements of fact. As a final resort, these constitutional questions would be submitted to arbitration for settlement. No proposal of this kind, however, had been submitted to the Technical Conference of 1905. Germany, Austria, Hungary, and Belguim opposed it strongly. On the other hand, France, Italy, Spain and the other states represented approved it. It was not, therefore, adopted, and was never carried beyond the stage of a resolution.[1] It is satisfactory to record that this important resolution in the history of international legislation is now the basis of regulations defining the functions of the International Labour Organisation which are inserted in the Paris Peace Treaty of 1919 and which have already been referred to by Mr. Barnes.

It is interesting to consider here, what guarantee there was for giving effect to the Berne Conventions by the contracting states. In a treaty between two parties, as for example, the Franco-Italian Treaty referred to in preceding pages, in which arrangements regarding international labour legislation are closely intermingled with the guarantees offered to foreign workers, the mutual obligations are clearly indicated and easily rendered effective. For instance, France said to Italy in 1904 : " I will grant such and such advantages to Italian workpeople employed in France, on condition that my industrial rival will put into

[1] Appendix II. p. 291.

force in her own land certain measures regulating labour conditions." The two undertakings are correlative. In the Berne Conventions between several nations, what exactly are the obligations? Each contracting state undertakes simply to introduce a certain reform in its laws. Clearly, if one of these states fails to carry out its obligation, the others are no longer bound to fulfil theirs. If, on the other hand, a state after introducing a reform, should abolish it or should commit other breaches of faith, what would happen? Should the Convention be denounced under the forms prescribed for this purpose? These points are not clear. Perhaps a country injured as regards its industry by the act of a defaulting state, would take commercial reprisals. It is especially in the direction of economic measures that writers on this subject have sought to find suitable guarantees for the performance of international contractual obligations.[1]

Fortunately, each of the reforms proposed in the agreement under discussion is based upon justice, and upon progress in the general well-being of mankind, and therefore a departure from them could not be anticipated. What the contracting states had in view in making these international agreements is to assist one another in realising certain reforms which all hold to be desirable. This being so, public opinion in the states concerned would tend to oppose any de-

[1] In a very interesting series of studies a socialist writer, Edgard Miland, professor at the University of Geneva, has set forth the whole system of economic measures of enforcement which are implied, in his opinion, by the functional activities of a League of Nations.

parture from co-operation for progress. All that has happened since 1906, when the two Berne Conventions were signed, supports this view. Although the Paris Peace Treaty of 1919 and the rules of the International Labour Organisation make due provision for economic measures, moral considerations have been given full weight, and those responsible for drafting the rules when discussing them, attached as much importance to moral factors as to definite measures of enforcement.

(b) *The Proposed Convention of* 1913. Scarcely had the invitations to the first Berne Conference been issued by the Swiss Government, when the International Association for Labour Legislation set to work to consider new reforms, and brought them forward for discussion at its Congress at Geneva, Lucerne, Lugano, Zurich, and then laid them before the Federal Council in 1912. On this occasion, the Swiss Government invited nineteen European states. Sixteen accepted—those that is to say, who had already been present at the 1905 and 1906 Conferences—together with Russia, but fourteen only took part in the discussions, as the delegates of Denmark and Luxemburg did not attend. The Russian delegate announced at the first session that he was not empowered to attach his signature to the final resolutions, even though these should be signed solely *ad referendum* by the technical delegates of the states represented.

Regulations of two kinds were submitted to the deliberations of the Berne Conference of 1913. Two draft proposals had been prepared by the delegates of the various states which were to be submitted in September 1914, for the consideration of a Diplomatic Conference which the Swiss Government proposed to arrange with European governments. The outbreak of war, of course, prevented this plan from being realised. The two draft proposals dealt with the following reforms:—

(1) The general standardisation of a ten hour day for women and children under 16 years of age.
(2) The prohibition of the employment at night of juveniles under 16 years of age.

The first was agreed to by delegates of twelve states, viz., Germany, Austria, Hungary, Belgium, Spain, France, Great Britain, Italy, Holland, Portugal, Sweden and Switzerland. The second was agreed to by the same states with the addition of Norway.

The ten hour day for women and young persons had already been instituted in England, Germany, France, Holland, Serbia, Bulgaria and Roumania. There was among all nations a tendency to adopt this reform, at least for women and children. The making of a ten hour day general for all workers, including men of adult age, was one of the objects which the Leeds Labour Conference of 1916 had in view. The prolongation of the war, however, has given rise throughout the whole world to a demand from industrial populations for an extension of this reform. The Paris Peace Treaty advocated the principle of an eight hour day for all workers, while many nations have already adopted an eight hour day as a general rule for industrial workers. Nevertheless, the proposal for a *universal* eight hour day which will be discussed at the first International Labour Conference, will afford useful indications as to necessary exemptions from this rule for seasonal trades, as well as permanent exemptions which may be found unavoidable in connection with the general application of an eight hour working day, or any other normal day which may in future be adopted.[1]

It had not been possible to make an international regulation prohibiting industrial work under 18 years of age—as has been done by the national legislature in several countries. At the Washington Labour Conference of 1919, the question is to be discussed in connection with a lower minimum age limit than 18.[2] The Conference of 1913 was strongly united upon 16 years, and considered it impracticable to make provision in an international convention for the exemptions, numerous as it considered these would be, that would be necessary in the case of young persons between 16 and 18 years of age. Even the French delegates, in advocating an 18 years limit, proposed to make it encumbent on national legislatures to provide for the necessary exemptions for workers between 16 and 18 years of age.

On the other hand, no exemptions whatever for industrial employment under 14 years of age were

[1] Appendix III. Articles 2-6, pp. 296-8, Articles 9-11, pp. 299-301, and Article 16, p. 303.

[2] Appendix III. p. 323.

proposed, and an extremely strict view was taken of
the infrequent exemptions accorded to youths and
girls of 14 to 16 years, either in case of unforeseen
emergencies or in the interests of the state. A
long discussion took place concerning three groups
of trades in respect of certain occupations for
which it was desired to grant permanent exemptions,
permitting the employment of young workers from
14 to 16 years of age. In the case of mining, exemption was made conditional upon the eight hour working
day being adopted for underground workers. This
was proposed by Great Britain and Germany in respect
of mines where two eight hour shifts are worked daily,
while Belgium urged exemption for workers from 14
to 16 in surface mines, and works of maintenance and
road making, which are clearly not more strenuous
than coal mining. In the case of the glass manufacturing industry, Austria proposed, provisorily, permanent
exemptions in the case of lads of 14 to 16 ; Belgium
proposed to allow the same exemptions as were
granted in the case of coal-mining, and Germany asked
simply for a delay of five years before the proposed
regulations prohibiting industrial work under 16 years
of age should come into force. France upheld certain
amendments in the nature of a compromise based on
the fact that eight hour shifts had already been introduced generally into glass works which were operated
at night. To arrive at a general agreement the German
proposal to postpone the reform was accepted—the
postponement being prolonged to ten years.

It is to be hoped that the modern machinery now used in this industry, which gives satisfactory results, will bring about a revival in glass manufacture, doing away with the necessity of employing so many furnace workers and at the same time solving the problem of an adequate supply of labour. It should be remembered that the adoption of the three-shift system of eight hours each in all industries where furnaces are kept burning continuously—which was proposed in 1913 as a solution of this question—will make the present day problem less acute, and will facilitate prohibition of night work for juvenile workers.

A similar measure to that adopted for the glass-making industry was adopted in the use of metal manufactures. The representatives of the French and Belgian metallurgical trades considered that a permanent exemption for workers from 14 to 16 might be made for the lighter class of rolling mills. This proposal was not supported by any other state, and was not brought forward for discussion. It was therefore agreed to postpone this reform for ten years in the case of iron works and rolling mills. At the time the draft of the convention *ad referendum* was being signed, the Belgian and Austrian delegates made it clear that they would find it difficult to justify the reform even with a delay of ten years in the case of the glass making industry. Their attitude, however, did not preclude the hope that a general agreement on this point might be reached.

VI. A PROGRAMME OF INTERNATIONAL LABOUR
LEGISLATION

We have seen that the Berne Conferences had initiated successfully a series of international conventions
on labour legislation.  The length of time required
to achieve results was due to the difficulties involved.
Nothing less than a new procedure, necessarily complex
in nature, was being inaugurated.  Still, apart from
the Conventions of 1906 and the proposals of 1913,
a large number of reforms were prepared by
the International Association for Labour Legislation,
and these might have been carried out comparatively quickly.  The reforms in question, for example, comprised among others a weekly rest day ;
an eight hour working day in factories continuously
operated ; minimum wages for workers engaged in
home industries, and the protection of workers in the
unhealthy lead and mercury trades.  It is to be
hoped that through the more powerful and elastic
International Labour Organisation created by the
Paris Peace Treaty of 1919, better results will be
obtained in a shorter time.

The field of operations in labour reforms is very
wide.  Its bounds, which are marked by the preamble
to the regulations for the International Labour Organisation, embraces the regulation of hours of labour ;
a maximum length for the working day and week;
the supply of labour measures dealing with unemployment ; the question of a fixed wage sufficient

to ensure proper conditions of living; the protection
of workpeople against illness, whether of a general kind
or arising from employment, and against accidents
incurred through their occupation; the protection
of children, young persons and women; the age
and infirmity pensions; the protection of workpeople
employed in foreign countries; the right of combination, the organisation of trade and technical instruction, and other similar measures.

In this extensive programme, all items are not to the
same degree proper subjects for international action.
When reforms result even temporarily in increasing
the cost of production, it is especially necessary for
the leading industrial nations to deal with this
problem by international action. Whether the
problem is dealt with by conventions or recommendations, or by enquiry and the collection of data,
there will certainly be ample opportunity for useful
work by the International Labour Organisation.

### VII. GENERAL CONCLUSIONS

From this brief review of its developments, it is clear
that international labour legislation is in the process
of elaboration, and that such legislation was made
necessary by common national aspirations towards
social progress and the growth of international
relations among civilised peoples, and by the nature
of modern democracy and the modern technical
processes of international commerce. The first

result of international labour legislation was seen
at Berne ; its form being based upon that of earlier
treaties, but with this form enlarged to include
almost all the industrial nations.

A great step forward was made at the Paris Peace
Treaty in 1919, as regards both the organisation through
which international labour legislation is to be evolved
and carried into effect by successive conferences, and
also as regards the programme of international labour
legislation contained in the labour clauses of the Treaty
—which will probably become a veritable Labour
Charter.   Labour legislation is now firmly established
upon international, social, and political collaboration.
It is one of the corner stones of the League of Nations
which must be founded and built upon separate
national organisms, each of which reacts to a common
impulse born of common interests.

In conclusion, I desire to recall the words of Vandervelde at the Peace Congress, when speaking upon the
labour clauses which constitute the last act accomplished in the domain of international labour legislation : " Some may have wished that it (the Labour
Charter) were richer in promise, and may have compared
its wording—which one must admit is rather bare—
with the text of the resolutions recently adopted by the
Labour Conference at Berne.   One need hardly point
out that this is not a fair comparison.   The Berne
Conference expressed the desires of the working
classes, and made clear their aspirations.   What we
ask of the International Labour Conference is at once

more and less than this. We ask it to transform some
of the aspirations of the industrial populations into
principles of policy affirmed by their governments.
It would be a great step forward if the governments
of the whole world were to declare, as a matter of
principle, that they considered the minimum wage ;
equal wages for both sexes ; the protection of night
workers and of child workers ; freedom of combination, and finally, the eight hour day, to be essential
conditions for a just peace."

We can say with Vandervelde that the history, still
too short, of international labour legislation, has closed
upon a chapter full of hope, and that the organised
workers by their propaganda, and the democrats by
their love for social progress, will be able to turn
this hope into realities. This task was defined in
these splendid words by Professor Mahaim of Liege
in February, 1912, in an address at the University of
Paris : " Labour treaties endeavour to define a minimum of needs below which the modern workman must
not be allowed to descend. And with that innate
force which draws nations more and more to unite
themselves into one society, they help to fasten more
closely those bonds which bind them one to another
in every land by raising the level of the working class,
until it becomes more cultured, more powerful and
more free."

With these remarks I associate myself by words used
at Ghent in 1913 : " By our long and patient effort
to harmonise the interest which aims in all civilised

N

lands at improving the life of the working classes, by creating an international organisation to combine them, we shall perhaps move forward to a far-off end which will be fruitful in peace and unity among the nations." It is surely significant that on the very morrow of a war which convulsed humanity with the most awful storm of death and hatred in all history, we find clearly manifested in the Peace Treaty of Paris, the revival of vigorous efforts for international unity and welfare through the instrumentality of international labour legislation.

ARTHUR FONTAINE.

# THE WASHINGTON CONFERENCE—1919

BY

## H. B. BUTLER, C.B.

Secretary General of the Washington International Labour Conference
Deputy Director of the International Labour Office


I. COMPOSITION OF THE CONFERENCE
II. ORGANISATION
III. THE WORK OF THE CONFERENCE
IV. FUTURE PROBLEMS

# CHAPTER VIII

## THE WASHINGTON CONFERENCE—1919

THE task of giving some account of the first International Labour Conference held under the Peace Treaty at Washington is no easy one. On the one hand, simply to record the plain facts of the Conference, such as the number of States represented, the number of delegates, the findings of the Commissions appointed, and the Draft Conventions and Recommendations adopted, would be to give a very inadequate and colourless idea of the nature of the Conference and of its actual achievement. On the other hand, to attempt any estimate of the extent to which it represents a break with the past, or foreshadows a great and fruitful development for the future, would be to court the errors and pitfalls which the historian writing of events which he has just witnessed cannot hope to avoid. However tempting, therefore, it might be to draw speculative inferences and conclusions, I propose to confine myself as nearly as possible to an appreciation of the Conference as it was, and to eschew any more ambitious notion of estimating its ultimate place in the history of industrial development or of international co-operation.

I. COMPOSITION OF THE CONFERENCE

The circumstances surrounding the meeting of the Conference at Washington were peculiarly unfavourable. Indeed, they might themselves have been sufficient to destroy at the outset an organisation which had not contained in itself the germs of a vigorous life. In the first place, the United States had not yet ratified the Treaty of Peace. The long struggle in the Senate actually reached its climax during the sittings of the Conference. Under these conditions it was inevitable that the interest of Americans should largely be diverted from the doings of the Conference itself, and that they should feel some hesitancy in regard to an organisation created by a document which had not been accepted by the United States, but which was, on the contrary, the subject of the most acute contemporary controversy.

Secondly, the Industrial Conference convened by the President in Washington in order to establish new and better relations between capital and labour in America had broken down shortly before the International Conference met. American industrial politics were left in a state of bitterness and confusion, which could not fail to infect the atmosphere surrounding the Conference, and which was aggravated by an extensive strike in the steel trade and later by a national strike among the miners, which broke out while it was in session. Lastly, and most unfortunate of all, President Wilson had fallen seriously ill about a fortnight before the opening sitting. He had taken a keen personal interest in the Conference, and was particularly anxious that its first meeting should take place in the United States. What the Conference lost through the absence of his encouragement and support is difficult to compute. The resolution of deep regret at his illness which was adopted on the opening day was no mere pious expression of condolence, but represented the universal feeling of the delegates that the inability of the President to assist their deliberations was a misfortune of the first magnitude.

Any fears that the world was not ready and willing to try the experiment in international labour legislation provided in the Peace Treaty were certainly dispelled when the Conference met for the first time on October 29th in the hall of the beautiful Pan-American Building. The representatives of no less than thirty-five nations took their seats at the opening sitting, and before the close of the meeting the number had risen to thirty-nine. In the case of every country in which labour is effectively organised, there was an employers' and a workers' delegate, selected by the employers' associations and the trade unions, in addition to one or two Government representatives. With the exception of the enemy countries and Russia, every European country was present.[1] There was almost a full representation from South America; there were delegates from China, Persia and Siam,

---

[1] Canada, India and South Africa took their places as separate units for the first time in an official international assembly.

labour delegates from India in their turbans, ambassadors, cabinet ministers, great captains of industry and well-known labour leaders from every part of the globe. Altogether there were 123 delegates present at the meeting, of whom 73 were Government delegates, 25 employers, and 25 workers, and they were assisted by a body of advisers about 150 in number, of whom 23 were women. One of the most prominent delegations was that of Japan. In that country the Conference had aroused the most extraordinary interest, and the Japanese Government had determined to pay great attention to its results. Consequently all sections of the Japanese delegation came fully prepared to deal with every point under discussion. They were, moreover, attended by a large party of journalists, whose presence was sufficient proof of the interest which was being taken in Japan in the proceedings of the Conference. The most prominent absentee was of course the United States, whose Government felt they could not participate, until the Treaty had been approved by the Senate. At its opening sitting the Conference passed a resolution inviting the American employers and trade unions to appoint representatives to take part in the proceedings in an unofficial capacity. The American Federation of Labour accepted this invitation, and appointed its President, Mr. Samuel Gompers ; but his position was necessarily a difficult one, and he only attended one sitting.

One of the first duties which the Conference

undertook was to deal with its own composition. On the second day it decided by a majority of 71 votes to 1 to admit Germany and Austria into the International Organisation. The reasons in favour of this decision were cogently put forward by Mr. Jouhaux, the Secretary General of the Confédération Générale du Travail, who said that to admit the enemy countries was not only in the spirit of the League of Nations, upon which the reconstruction of the world so largely depended, but was also practically necessary, since without their co-operation no system of international labour legislation could be really effective in Europe.   Both the German and Austrian Governments accepted the invitation, but owing to the shortage of shipping and the delays caused in sailings from Europe as a result of the American strikes and other causes, the German and Austrian delegations were unable to sail in time to reach Washington before the close of the meeting.   The Conference further appointed a Commission on Credentials to deal with any objections raised to the appointment of the delegates present, and another Commission on the admission of new members. The only serious objection was that against the Japanese Labour delegate on the ground that he had not been chosen in agreement with the Japanese Trade Unions.   The Credentials Commission, however, accepted the explanation of the Japanese Government delegates that in view of the small extent of Trade Union organisation in Japan the Government had decided to adopt a special method for electing its Labour delegate, in order that he might be regarded as thoroughly representative of the workers. At the same time Mr. Oudegeest, the workers' member of the Commission, expressed the opinion that in future it would be preferable if the Japanese Government chose a Labour delegate in agreement with the Trade Unions.

The principal question before the Commission on applications for admission related to Finland. Her claim raised a difficult point of law, inasmuch as she was neither a signatory to the Treaty nor one of the countries mentioned in the Annex to the Covenant as entitled to become a member of the League of Nations immediately. The majority of the Commission took the view that these facts did not prevent the Conference admitting Finland at once to the Labour Organisation; but this opinion was strongly contested by a Minority Report submitted by Mr. Rowell of Canada. Eventually the Conference agreed upon a compromise, which avoided giving any ruling on the question of principle, but admitted the Finnish delegates to take part in the Washington Conference on the same conditions as other countries which had not yet adhered to the Covenant of the League of Nations. Luxemburg was subsequently admitted on the same terms. The vigorous debate which took place on this subject indicated a strong feeling in the Conference that the Labour Organisation should be as far as possible autonomous, and should not necessarily be guided by political considerations. In fact, the whole action of the Conference in regard to its composition showed the determination of the delegates to throw open the Labour Organisation as widely as possible, so that its decisions might benefit the workers of all countries without exception.

## II. ORGANISATION

As its principal officers the Conference elected the Hon. W. B. Wilson, Secretary for Labour in the United States Government, as its President, and the Right Hon. G. N. Barnes, M.P. (Great Britain), Mr. Jules Carlier (Belgium), and Mr. Léon Jouhaux (France), as Vice-Presidents. It then proceeded to appoint a Commission of Selection to nominate the members of Commissions and Committees for the approval of the Conference, and generally to regulate the course of its business. This Commission was constituted in the same manner as the Governing Body provided in the Treaty, and consisted of 12 Government members, 6 employers and 6 workers, the Chairman being Mr. Arthur Fontaine of the French Ministry of Labour. Commissions were then set up to deal with the various subjects on the agenda, and in every case the principle was adopted of appointing an equal number of Government, employers' and workers' representatives. This principle was accepted without discussion by the Government delegates, for it was felt that, although by the constitution the Governments had been given a double representation, for the reasons which have been

explained by Mr. Barnes in the opening chapter
of this book, there was no reason why on the
Commissions the representation of the three groups
should not be equal.

There is no doubt that this arrangement tended to
promote mutual confidence between the groups; but
at the same time it must be recognised that it involved
a considerable sacrifice on the part of those countries
who could not obtain representation on commissions
in which they were particularly interested. In order
to facilitate the transaction of business, it was unavoidable that the number of members on the commissions should be limited. This necessarily implied
that the majority of Governments could not be represented on any particular commission, although they
had full opportunity to place any evidence which they
pleased before it. Some doubts were expressed as to
the wisdom of such an arrangement. It was feared
that so many points of view would be left unrepre-
sented that when the reports of the commissions were
received, there would be considerable criticism of
them in full conference by those who had not been
allotted representatives on the commissions. The
fact that these fears proved groundless suggests two
considerations. In the first place, it emphasises a point
which became constantly clearer as the Conference
proceeded, namely, that industrial problems and the
possible solutions of them are surprisingly similar in
all countries. Secondly, it illustrates the extent to
which international co-operation was found possible

in the industrial field, inasmuch as representatives of the Governments of five or seven countries were often able to represent more or less adequately the points of view and the interests of thirty-nine. At the same time, it must be remembered that, although the selection of members was not made on any strict basis of nationality, in cases where there was no Government representative from a particular country there was often a representative of its employers or workers, who was able to speak with full knowledge of its industrial conditions and to put forward any special circumstances which might affect it.

Commissions were set up in the first instance to deal with the questions of unemployment, women's employment, the employment of children and un- healthy processes.[1] The question of the 48 hours' week, which was generally recognised as the most

---

[1] The full agenda of the Conference as fixed by the Peace Treaty was as follows :

1. Application of principle of the 8-hour day or of the 48-hour week.

2. Question of preventing or providing against unemployment.

3. Women's employment—
    (a) Before and after child-birth, including the question of maternity benefit.
    (b) During the night.
    (c) In unhealthy processes.

4. Employment of children.
    (a) Minimum age of employment.
    (b) During the night.
    (c) In unhealthy processes.

5. Extension and application of the International Conventions adopted at Berne in 1906 on the prohibition of night work for women employed in industry and the prohibition of the use of white phosphorus in the manufacture of matches.

important and most difficult before the Conference, was not referred to a commission immediately. A debate lasting two days took place on the general question, which brought out clearly the divergences between the employers' and workers' groups on the matter, and in particular made it evident that the workers were not disposed to accept a 48 hours' week, unless it was also accompanied by a limitation of the normal daily hours of work to 8. It was eventually decided to refer the whole question to two commissions, one consisting of 15 members to deal with the general problem of the hours of work, the other to deal with it as it affected the tropical countries and other countries in which special climatic or other conditions exist. In order that these countries might be fully heard, and that their case, which was realised as being one of exceptional difficulty and importance, might be throughly discussed, this commission was composed of one Government, one employers' and one workers' representative for India, Japan, South Africa and tropical America, one representative for China, Persia and Siam, together with three Government, three employers' and three workers' delegates from the non-tropical countries, making 24 in all. Mr. Tom Shaw, M.P., one of the British Labour advisers, was chosen Chairman of the General Commission, and Mr. G. N. Barnes, M.P., of the Special Commission.

The results of the work of the Commissions will be dealt with later. All of them sat continuously for more than a week, some of them twice daily, and it was interesting to notice how much close contact round a table did towards breaking down the barriers of language and nationality, and towards promoting understanding of each other's views among the members of the different groups. In some cases, and especially on the question of the hours of labour, there was a strong divergence of view between employers and workers, between whom the Government delegates acted as mediators. In other cases, however, difference of view was determined by national custom and habit of mind rather than by group interests. It was not at all uncommon to find employers siding with workers, or workers with Government delegates, on questions of principle, on which each delegate had to make up his own mind, and which did not fall within any of the usual cadres of economic theory.

Before passing from the subject of organization, it may be interesting to say a few words on the language difficulty, which is always a thorn in the side of international gatherings. The official languages of the Conference were English and French, and every utterance in the full Conference was promptly translated into the other language by a corps of interpreters. This inevitably made the proceedings somewhat slow, and when speeches were long, not a little wearisome. The fact of interpretation being necessary, however, undoubtedly tended to reduce the length of the delegates' remarks, and to induce them to put their points as succinctly and clearly as possible.  In fact, so far did they become inured to this habit, that towards the end of the Conference they accepted without demur the proposal made by the Committee on Rules that speeches should be limited to 15 minutes in length, exclusive of the interpretation. Those who were unable to speak either English or French, and their number was surprisingly small, could speak in their own tongue, provided that they had an interpreter of their own present competent to translate their remarks into one of the official languages.  In point of fact the only other languages in which speeches were made were Spanish, Italian and Dutch, and the number of such speeches was inconsiderable.

On the whole, the language difficulty was far less serious than might have been expected.  On the Commissions especially the members became largely accustomed to conducting their debates in English and French indifferently, without formal interpretation in every case.  By this means discussions were greatly shortened.  The understanding of the course of the proceedings was also greatly assisted by the issue each morning, in accordance with parliamentary practice, of the full report of the previous day's debate printed in English, French, and also in Spanish.  By this means the delegates had no difficulty in keeping abreast of everything which went on in the Conference, and as all motions and resolutions had to be circulated in print before they could be discussed, the debates proceeded in a regular and orderly manner.

In view of the novelty of the experiment of an International Parliament, it may safely be said that the difficulties of procedure were found to have been greatly exaggerated in anticipation. Writing of the Assembly of the League, Mr. Keynes has told us that it " must become . . . an unwieldy polyglot Debating Society," [1] incapable of transacting business or of reaching important decisions. In the light of the Labour Conference such premonitory pessimism seems altogether misplaced. If the experience of the Conference proves anything, it proves that with adequate arrangements the most polyglot assembly can discuss subjects of the most difficult and technical character, and arrive at conclusions in a form lacking little of the precision or the completeness of parliamentary legislation.

In addition to the Commissions, mention should be made of the work of the different groups. The employers' and workers' groups used to meet with considerable regularity to discuss the principal questions before they came up. Inasmuch as these groups were largely founded on a community of interest, they acted for the most part as concerted wholes with selected spokesmen, a practice which undoubtedly tended to simplify the issues and to shorten debate. Even when the group meetings did not reach unanimous decisions, they served to bring into relief the main points for discussion, and to render them

[1] *The Economic Consequences of the Peace*, by J. M. Keynes, C.B., p. 243.

capable of adequate presentation by a few speakers.
The Government delegates, having less identity of
interest, met much less frequently and seldom acted
in unison. This again was by no means disadvan-
tageous. It gave a reality to the debates which would
have been lacking had the three groups all worked
as more or less disciplined units. The fact that the
Government group was the largest and the most open
to conviction offered its members considerable opportunities for effective conciliation, and often left the
outcome of the discussion in doubt until the vote was
actually taken.

One other point deserves some emphasis. As
Professor Shotwell has mentioned, there was a good
deal of opposition on the Labour Commission in Paris
to giving to the Governments twice the representation
accorded to the employers and the workers. The fear
was expressed that this arrangement would often leave
the workers in a hopeless minority against the employers and the bulk of the Government delegates,
a fear which was re-echoed by the International
Federation of Trade Unions at Amsterdam. Experience showed at Washington that in practice these
fears were hardly justified. In the first place, there
was far more cross voting among the Governments
than might have been expected, and there were
even examples of the two Government delegates
from the same country voted on different sides.
There were of course a few occasions when the
bulk of the Government delegates voted against the

workers' group, but in these cases the majority would have been decisive, whether the official representation had been single or double.  On the other hand, there were some instances in which the workers' group won with the aid of the double Government vote, whereas they would probably have lost had it been single. While it cannot be said generally that the size of the Government group had any very marked effect one way or the other, owing to the differences of view which appeared among the official representatives on almost all the questions on which there were important divisions, it is nevertheless the case that the double Government vote was on the whole more favourable to the workers than otherwise.

### III. THE WORK OF THE CONFERENCE

Each of the Commissions presented a careful report to the Conference embodying the decisions at which they had arrived in the form of Draft Conventions, Recommendations and Resolutions accompanied by an explanation of the difficulties which they had to meet, and the reasons which led them to adopt the solutions put forward.  The most important reports were those dealing with the hours of work.  Anyone who has given any study to the question will be aware of the immense difficulty of regulating the hours of labour on any uniform system, even within a single country.  The variety of the work and of the customs governing it in different industries

is so great that to supply a rigid eight hours' day or 48
hours' week to them all is manifestly impossible.   In
every country where the general principle of the eight
hour day has been adopted, it has been found
necessary to make exceptions and qualifications to
meet the peculiar requirements of different trades.
If this has been the experience of countries taken
singly, the application of the eight hours' principle on
an international scale might seem at first sight practically impossible.   The variety and complexity of
the problems presented become infinitely greater,
when account has to be taken of the differences
created by the varieties of climate, national habit and
other peculiarities, all over the world.   Nevertheless,
the General Commission succeeded in producing a
Draft Convention to which all the countries in which
normal industrial conditions operate could adhere
without reservation.   This result was only achieved
after long and often sharp debates.   On a number of
important points there were marked cleavages between
the employers and the workers, which were only got
over by the mediation of the Government delegates.
But even their efforts might have proved fruitless without the tactful and impartial chairmanship of Mr. Shaw.

The Commission had before it a Draft prepared by
the Organising Committee, which had been appointed
after the Peace Conference to collect the necessary
information and to prepare a basis for the discussions
of the Conference.   That Draft confined itself to
affirming the principle of the 48 hour week without

dealing with the daily period of work.    As was stated above, the workers' delegates objected strongly to this omission, and after considerable discussion, it was agreed that the normal day's work should be limited to eight hours, but that in cases where less than eight hours was worked on one or more days of the week, the time so lost might be made up on the remaining days, provided that in no case should the day's work exceed nine hours. This means that where the weekly half holiday is customary, the weekly period of work need not necessarily be reduced to 44 or 45 hours, but the Commission was careful to add a resolution emphasising that the Draft Convention should not interfere with cases in which the workers already enjoyed more favourable conditions as regards hours of work than were provided in the Draft Convention.

As will be seen from Article 1 of the Draft Convention,[1] the principles thus agreed upon were applied to industry in the widest sense of the term, not excluding the transport of passengers or goods " by road, rail, sea, or inland waterway." As regards maritime and water traffic, it was agreed that the practical application of the principle would have to be worked out by a " special conference competent to deal with the peculiar difficulties involved in maritime employment." This Seamen's Conference is due to be held in the course of the present year (1920).

This is not the place in which to comment in detail on the provisions of the remaining Articles of the

[1] Appendix III. p. 295, Article 1 (d).

Draft Convention, which deal with the various cases
in which exceptions to the general rule are unavoidable
on account of unusual circumstances, but one or two
points of special interest are worth noticing.   In the
case of work such as that connected with blast furnaces,
which under present conditions has to be carried on
without interruption by successive shifts, the Convention provides that the normal week may be one of
56 hours.   The Commission recognised the force of the
workers' claim to a 48 hours' week in this case also, but
inasmuch as its introduction would necessitate a considerable increase in the number of skilled employees,
they regarded it as impracticable in many countries
at the present time.   They pointed out that, in any
case, the Convention would necessitate the reduction
of the daily shift from 12 hours to 8, entailing the
employment of a complete extra shift of workers,
and that even where this reduction had already been
made, the change was so recent in most cases as to
make it impossible to find immediately the number of
additional workers who would be required, if the working week were further reduced from 56 hours to 48.
The Organising Committee had attempted to draw up
a schedule of processes which might be considered
as continuous for the purpose of this exception.
They also proposed a further schedule of processes
in which the normal limit of 48 hours might be extended, e.g. in the case of men not engaged in continuous work throughout the day, or whose attendance
before or after the normal hours was necessary for

the starting or maintenance of the plant ; and a third schedule of industries in which, owing to special conditions, overtime might be permitted, provided that it was limited to a maximum of 150 hours in the year. The Commission decided, however, no doubt wisely, that to attempt to deal with these questions in detail was impossible without the most careful preliminary investigation in all the countries affected, which neither they nor the Organising Committee had been able to undertake. They therefore adopted two methods of ensuring that, where such exceptions might prove indispensable, they should not be abused.

In the first place, they laid it down that all such exceptions should only be allowed after consultation with the organisations of employers and workers concerned. That is to say, the principle of collective agreements between employers' associations and trade unions was given the fullest recognition, and was adopted as the most practical method of regulating modern industrial conditions. Secondly, the duty was imposed on the International Labour Office of making an annual report to the Conference, containing a list of the processes classed as continuous in the various countries, and giving full information as to the working of collective agreements permitting occasional extensions of the daily period of work, and as to the regulations allowing overtime. The Draft Convention also adopted the principle that for all overtime worked not less than 25% should be added to the normal rate of wages. This represented a compromise between the employers' view, which was strongly opposed to any overtime rate being fixed, and the workers' claim that it should be 50% higher than the ordinary rate. In order further to ensure the proper enforcement of the Convention, requirements were added as to the steps which employers should be required to take by law, in order to make known to the workers the hours of work, and the Governments were placed under the obligation to furnish all the information required by the International Labour Office for the purpose of its annual report. It will, therefore, be seen that the Convention on the hours of work was conceived in a thoroughly practical and businesslike spirit. It was an instrument so framed as to ensure that its principles should not be merely pious aspirations, but should be carried out to the letter in all countries which undertook to apply them.

The recommendations of the Special Commission in regard to countries in which abnormal industrial conditions existed, were embodied in a separate report and considered at a special sitting of the Conference. It is scarcely necessary to point out the enormous importance of the work entrusted to this Commission. No attempt had ever been made before to bring the conditions of labour in oriental and tropical countries into any relation with those existing in Europe and Northern America. Dr. Oka has already explained in his chapter the peculiar situation of Japan, which is in a state of rapid transition from domestic to large-scale industry. The same is true of India, though in a much lesser degree, and the most important question before the Commission was how far it was practical and desirable to bring these countries into line with countries of a more mature industrial development. A comparison of the provisions of the Draft Convention with the legislation previously existing in India and Japan affords sufficient evidence of the great advance which the Commission's work represents. At the present time the Factory Act of Japan permits employment in factories for 13 hours a day, including Sundays, and also allows 120 hours of overtime to be worked during the year. In the silk industry, in which some 900,000 persons are employed, these hours are actually worked, so that in that industry the present working week averages 93 hours, and even this limitation only applies to 47% of the workers, who are employed in large factories. In other industries the usual working day is about 12 hours, including overtime, so that the working week may be regarded as about 84 hours. The change in these conditions which is represented by the proposals of the Draft Convention is little less than revolutionary. For all factory industries the hours of work are reduced to 57 in the week for persons over 15, except in the case of the silk industry, where the limit is extended to 60. For miners and for persons under 15 years of age the working week is fixed at 48 hours. Any exceptions from these provisions may only be made under the same conditions as those provided in the general clauses of the Convention.

These proposals were embodied in the Majority
Report of the Commission, but a Minority Report was
presented by Mr. Shichiro Muto, the Japanese Labour
member of the Commission, denying that there was
any justification to be found in the climatic conditions
of Japan for its exceptional treatment, and claiming
that the rapid development of Japanese industry on
modern lines made it necessary to adopt modern
conditions of labour without any delay whatever.
When the report of the Special Commission came
before the full Conference a lively debate took place
on this Minority Report.   Mr. Oudegeest advocated
the view of the Japanese workers' delegate, and
proposed an amendment to the effect that the industrial situation of Japan warranted the application of
the eight hour day and the 48 hours' week, with a
delay of two years, and that the general Convention
should accordingly be applied in Japan without
modification not later than January 1st, 1922.   This
amendment was strongly supported by Mr. Mertens
(Belgium), Mr. Jouhaux, and Mr. Baldesi (Italy), to
whom Mr. Kamada and Dr. Oka, the Japanese Government delegates, and Mr. Barnes, the Chairman of
the Commission, replied.   Mr. Kamada stated that
there were already unmistakable signs in Japan
indicating that the people were determined to treat
labour problems seriously, and to co-operate with
Europe and America in the improvement of working
conditions.   All that they asked was that they might
not be requested to make at one blow a transition

which had required a hundred years of industrial evolution to bring about in other countries. Moreover, the Majority Report had pointed out " that the Japanese Government had given expression to its intention to make every effort to accelerate the unqualified adoption of the rule (as to the 48 hours' week) in harmony with the general trend of the world." On this ground it recommended to the Conference that the Japanese Government might be requested to consider the possibility of applying the provisions of the general Convention within five years of effect being given to the special provisions relating to Japan. The real gist of the argument against pressing Japan to go farther than she felt it possible to do at the moment was put to the Conference by Mr. Barnes in these words :

" We have met in the Special Commission, and we have regarded this matter from the viewpoint of making treaties with Japan and the other countries concerned ; and here let me say that in my judgment Mr. Oka and his colleague have met us fairly. The employers' delegates have also been induced to go a long way in the direction of all those who have spoken this morning, and what we have done is really to make treaties with the Governments, including Japan. We have made these bargains, and I think if they are endorsed, we go away with the perfect understanding that these bargains will be carried out. They have all the force of treaties. But what

happens if you turn them down ? Can you
impose your will upon Japan ? Can you impose
your will upon India ? Not at all. If you turn
these treaties down, and you do not put in their
place something else to which you as a full Conference might induce these Governments to agree,
then those Government delegates go back relieved
of the moral obligation. At present they are
under a moral obligation to put into effect these
bargains that we have made with them."

After a very interesting and picturesque debate the
amendment was finally lost on a record vote by 42
votes to 45, and the Majority recommendations of the
Commission were accordingly adopted.

In the case of India, the Commission found that the
number of persons employed in ordinary industrial
undertakings constituted "but an insignificant proportion of the whole population," but that the existing
Factory Acts had been effective and well administered
as far as they went. They thought that in the absence
of fuller information about the small industries the
Conference could only usefully legislate in regard to the
large industrial undertakings which already came
within the scope of those Acts. They, therefore,
recommended the reduction of the working week from
72 hours to 60 in all industries covered by the Factory
Acts, in mines, and in railway work. The Commission
thought, however, that it should be possible further
to limit the hours of work underground in mines to

54 or even lower, and recommended the favourable consideration of this proposal to the Government of India. They also suggested that the definition of the term " factory," which at present applies only to establishments employing at least 50 persons, should be revised with a view to applying it to smaller undertakings. The Conference adopted these recommendations, and agreed that further provisions limiting the hours of work in India should be considered at a future meeting of the Conference. As regards China, Persia, and Siam, the Commission did not think that they were sufficiently developed, from the industrial point of view, to make it possible to apply the Convention to them, but suggested that the Governments of these countries should be requested to adopt the principle of the protection of labour by factory legislation. In the case of China, they further proposed that the Government should consider the adoption of a ten hour day or 60 hours' week for adult workers in factories, and of an eight hour day or 48 hours' week for persons under 15 years of age, together with the principle of a weekly rest day. The Draft Convention provides that the hours of work in these countries should be considered at a future conference. Delays of two or three years were agreed upon in the case of various industries in Greece and Rumania, but it was not found necessary to make any specific exceptions in the Convention to meet the special conditions existing in South Africa and tropical America.

When the reports of the General and Special Commissions on hours of work had been adopted by the Conference, their recommendations were put into the form of a single Draft Convention by the Drafting Committee. After a few minor amendments had been inserted on the presentation of the Convention to the Conference, it was adopted in its final form by 82 votes to 2, with one abstention, amidst the applause of the delegates, who rightly felt that this result represented a solid achievement in the field of international labour legislation.

The second item on the Agenda of the Conference was "the question of preventing and providing against unemployment." The Commission appointed to consider it had a vast field before it, and the remarkable work which it accomplished was largely due to the energy and enthusiasm of its Chairman, Mr. Max Lazard, of France. Its findings may conveniently be considered in two parts, inasmuch as the problems of preventing and alleviating unemployment are largely distinct. The former reaches down to the foundations of the present industrial system and of the existing fabric of international commerce and exchange. The latter is rather a palliation of an admitted evil than a remedy for it. To take the second question first as being the more immediate and the less fundamental, the Commission proposed a Draft Convention for the establishment of a system of free, public employment agencies under central control and assisted by committees including representatives of employers and workers. It further provided that States which already had systems of insurance against unemployment should agree between themselves upon arrangements whereby workers moving from one country to another might continue to enjoy the benefits to which they would be entitled in their native land, if they were out of work. The Commission added a recommendation that effective systems of insurance, either provided by the Government or by Associations assisted by Government subventions should be created in all countries.

These measures were all accepted by the Conference. If put into practice, they would constitute a considerable step in the direction of alleviating the distress caused by want of work, and would also ensure as far as possible that workers should be able to obtain work if it was available. It was recognised, however, that if the evil of unemployment was to be really eliminated, further and more radical measures were necessary. At this point the want of adequate information as to the deeper causes of unemployment made itself felt. The Report presented by the Organising Committee contained a table giving examples of the fluctuations of unemployment so far as they could be traced from the figures hitherto available, but, as the Committee had pointed out, the data were altogether insufficient to enable any really trustworthy conclusions to be drawn from them. The Commission therefore proposed that the first Article in the Draft Convention should require each Government to communicate to the International Labour Office, at intervals not exceeding three months, all available information, statistical or other, concerning unemployment. Obviously a great deal of work will be required on the part of the International Labour Office before the figures, which it obtains in this way, will be sufficiently comparable to enable the movements of employment to be followed with certainty and precision ; but until a thoroughly scientific study of the whole problem is undertaken in this way, the right method of solution can hardly be expected. A further recommendation of the Commission was that in every country the execution of all work undertaken under public authority should be co-ordinated, in order to ensure as far as possible that such work should be undertaken during periods of unemployment, and in the districts most affected by it. This again, however, can at best be but a partial remedy. The amount of public work undertaken in most countries is not likely to be sufficient to meet the unemployment caused by severe trade depression, and it could hardly be so variegated in character as to provide employment for all the different kinds of craftsmen who might be thrown out of work by general financial stringency and slackness of trade.

With the inadequate information at their disposal the majority of the Commission felt that it was impossible to go further at that stage ; but there was a strong feeling voiced by a Minority Report presented by Mr. Baldesi, the Italian Workers' delegate, and supported by a large section of the Conference, that some more drastic action was immediately necessary in view of the tremendous crisis of unemployment which existed in many European countries at the moment, as the result of the wholesale devastations and economic disturbances produced by the war. This Report proposed that the League of Nations should be asked to study at once the question of the proper distribution of raw materials. " Broadly speaking, we have," it stated, " on the one hand, vast quantities of raw materials awaiting the work of man to convert them to profitable use, and on the other hand, we have nations with abundant supplies of labour anxiously seeking for those same raw materials in order to make them of value to themselves and others." This question produced one of the most interesting debates which occurred during the meeting. Mr. Baldesi was strongly supported by the Polish Delegation, Mr. Ilg of Switzerland, Mr. Jouhaux, and others, who, from their personal experience, were in a position to realise the acuteness of the distress in Central Europe. Their argument was summed up by Mr. Jouhaux in the following words :  " It is not possible that the working-classes in some countries should be condemned to perpetual idleness, while other countries prevent the exportation of the raw materials which are necessary to give work to the workers in countries which do not possess

P

them.   It is not possible that the privileged situation
of one country should be artificially safeguarded
in defiance of the general interest. . . .   There cannot
be any true economic equality ;  there cannot be
any real possibility of reconstruction for the exhausted
countries ;  there cannot be any adequate solution
of the problem of unemployment, unless this question
has first been solved."   On the other hand, the
proposal that raw materials should be controlled
internationally was strongly opposed by other delegates, who maintained that it was outside the jurisdiction of the Conference to deal with the question
at all.   To quote Mr. Rowell of Canada, " I say, with
great respect, this conference has no more jurisdiction
over the question of the distribution of raw materials,
which the delegate from Italy referred to, than it
has over the question of discovering a way of navigating
from the earth to the moon.   It might just as well
be clearly understood that the nations which have
raw materials will deal with them as they believe
fair and in the national interest, but they will deal
with them by their own parliaments, their own
legislatures, and they will not accept international
regulations with reference to the control of their
own property."

Mr. Baldesi's motion was eventually lost by 40 votes
to 43.   Though it may not have been practical
politics, as Mr. Blomjous of Holland pointed out in
a forcible criticism, and though it may have sought to
impose on the League of Nations a burden heavier

than its youthful shoulders could bear, the debate and the vote voiced clearly enough the evils from which large parts of Europe are now suffering and the kind of solution for which many are looking. In doing so they served a useful purpose, but they also served to bring out the divergence of interest between the New World and the Old, which emerged more than once during the Conference and was perhaps one of its most significant features.

This same divergence became again apparent in connection with the proposals of the Unemployment Commission in regard to emigration. On this head the Commission had agreed with considerable difficulty upon a Draft Convention, which would bind the States ratifying it to admit immigrants from other ratifying States to the same rights of lawful organisation and of labour protection as their own citizens. It soon became evident, however, that the Draft Convention stood little chance of adoption. Dr. Rüfenacht of Switzerland opposed it in a closely reasoned speech, pointing out that the Commission had not the time nor the information at their disposal to enable them to estimate the precise effects of such a proposal on the legislation of each country, and that in some cases the results would be altogether unexpected. Though not himself opposed to the principle of reciprocity, he proposed an amendment referring the whole question back to the Governing Body for further examination. Eventually this proposal was defeated, but only after there was substituted for the Draft Convention, a simple Recommendation to the Governments in favour of special agreements between the various States in regard to the reciprocal treatment of immigrants. The Latin American countries declared their acceptance of this Recommendation, as they welcomed immigrants and made no distinction between the treatment of aliens and nationals. The Canadian delegates also pronounced in favour of it, though Mr. Rowell uttered a warning that the American countries " would not accept any international determination as to who should compose their own population, or be entitled to the right of citizenship, or the rights that citizens should enjoy within their own territory." The interest of the non-European countries in this question was further demonstrated in connection with a resolution to appoint a Commission to consider, " having due regard to the sovereign right of each State, what measures can be adopted to regulate the migration of workers out of their own States and to protect the interests of wage earners residing in States other than their own." This resolution would probably have been defeated, if a proviso moved by Mr. Gemmill of South Africa had not been accepted, requiring that the representation of European States on the Commission should be limited to one half of the total membership. It is evident that the whole subject of emigration involves many difficult and delicate questions, but in its treatment of them the Conference showed that its truly international composition ensured that the interests and standpoints of all countries would be carefully safeguarded and that no hasty or ill-considered action need be feared from it. In fact, for these reasons it proved itself a very competent body to handle a problem of perennial difficulty, which can only be successfully solved on lines of international cooperation.

The Commission on the employment of women, which was presided over by Miss Constance Smith and which largely consisted of women, presented two reports. The first recommended the re-adoption of the Berne Convention of 1906 prohibiting the employment of women between 10 p.m. and 5 a.m. with certain modifications, which tended to strengthen it. Important amendments were moved by Mr. Baldesi and by Mr. Guérin, the French Employers' delegate, the first extending the hours of rest to 6 a.m., the second permitting women to be employed between the hours of 4 a.m. and 10 p.m. or 5 a.m. and 11 p.m. where two shifts were worked, with an interval of an hour in each shift. Both these proposals were defeated. The Draft Convention was finally adopted by 94 votes to 1, and it is noticeable that it was accepted by the Japanese Government delegates, although, as Mrs. Tanaka, one of their advisers, complained with great force to the Commission, women have hitherto been regularly employed for long hours during the night in Japan.

The second report of the Women's Commission dealt with the much more difficult question of the employment of women in industry before and after childbirth. There was no disagreement on two fundamental principles, first, that no woman should be permitted to do any industrial work for a certain time after her confinement, and that while so resting she should be given a sufficient benefit to maintain herself and her child in good health ; and secondly, that a woman should have the right to leave her work on production of a medical certificate during a certain period before childbirth, during which she would be likewise entitled to benefit. In all cases she would have the right to reinstatement when she resumed work. When it came to the application of these principles, however, there were marked differences of opinion on various points, which gave rise to a lively discussion in the full conference. The majority of the Commission recommended that the period of rest allowed before confinement should be six weeks, but a strong minority, consisting chiefly of employers, proposed to reduce the period to four weeks on the ground that medical opinion favoured the shorter period. This amendment was vigorously resisted by Miss Macarthur of Great Britain, and though supported by Miss Hesselgren of Sweden and others, was eventually lost. On the question as to the source from which benefit should be paid there was another division of opinion. A substantial minority was opposed to any system of insurance, and demanded that in all cases the entire cost should be borne by the State. The great majority were, however, in favour of allowing a system of insurance as an alternative to direct payment by the State. The discussion of this report was unfortunately rather curtailed, because it could not be taken until the last two days of the Conference. It certainly merited longer and more careful consideration. The Draft Convention was eventually carried by 67 votes to 10, but the Government delegates from several countries, including Great Britain, abstained from voting. The establishment of the right of women to be relieved of the need for earning their living, and to be properly maintained during the critical weeks before and after childbirth, is none the less a real achievement, and it is one upon which the men and women who worked so hard to bring it about at Washington may well be proud.

The Commission, which dealt with the employment of children, and which also contained a number of women, presented two reports through its chairman, Sir Malcolm Delevingne. The first, and most important, proposed a Draft Convention prohibiting the employment of children in industry under the age of 14. It is remarkable that this was a unanimous proposal, and that it was accepted by the Japanese Delegation, subject to a proviso that in Japan, where the leaving age varies between 12 and 14, children who had completed their education might be employed when they reached the age of 12. The great importance of this convention for the improvement of the mental and physical development of the race needs no emphasis. For many countries it marks a great and notable advance, and it may be expected to produce as a collateral result the extending and deepening of popular education. Indeed, the difficulties involved in forbidding the employment of children, when they were no longer at school but were still under 14, was one which met the Commission constantly. In Japan an exception was allowed to meet the point, as already mentioned. In Italy, Spain, and Belgium, where the school leaving age is at present 13, relaxation of the convention so as to permit employment of children between 13 and 14, was suggested as a temporary measure, until the age for leaving school was raised to 14. The Commission decided against allowing any exception in these cases. It drew the attention of the International Labour Office to the difficulty, however, and suggested that it should approach the Governments concerned with a view to finding a solution.

The hardest problem was that of India, where as yet there is no universal compulsory education. In view of this fact and of the earlier maturity of children in the Indian climate, the Commission recommended the postponement of any definite decision for a year, in order to allow the Indian Government to submit proposals in the light of the scheme for general education which was understood to be under consideration. There were many who felt, however, that some immediate steps should be taken to limit the employment of children in factories working under western conditions. This feeling was voiced by Miss Margaret Bondfield, who moved an amendment on behalf of Mr. Stuart-Bunning, the British Workers' delegate, to the effect that children under 12 should not be employed in India in factories employing more than ten persons, in mines, on railways and on docks. Her argument was concisely summed up in the formula that " where western methods of industry are being introduced into eastern countries, they should be simultaneously accompanied by western safeguards." Her powerful speech, which was strongly seconded by Mr. Joshi, the Indian Workers' delegate, made a considerable impression on the Conference. Mr. Chatterjee made an eloquent reply on behalf of the Indian Government, in which he depicted the difficulty of propagating the idea of education among the masses of the people who as yet had no desire for it, and of obtaining sufficient teachers even to staff the schools which were being set up. " Until there are adequate educational facilities available for children in India," he declared, " and until such children can be compelled to avail themselves of the facilities, the raising of the age of employment will only throw the children on the street. In a country where children develop much earlier than in the north and in the west, and where the customs of the country do not enable the mothers to look after their children with the same freedom and capacity as they could do in the west, the result would be more disastrous to the children than otherwise."

Despite these arguments the majority of the Conference were convinced by Miss Bondfield's plea for some immediate action instead of further delay, and carried her motion by 39 votes to 21. With this important amendment the Commission's report was adopted together with a rider requesting the International Labour Office to study the question of limiting the age of employment of children in commercial and agricultural occupations.

The second report of the Children's Commission dealt with the employment of young persons in industry during the night. The principle of prohibiting their employment under the age of 16 between 10 p.m. and 5 a.m. had been agreed to by the Berne Conference of 1913, but owing to the war had not been adopted in the form of a convention. The Washington Conference unanimously agreed to increase the general age of prohibition to 18 with a reduction to 16 in the case of certain continuous processes. In the case of Japan, the age was fixed at 15 for three years and 16 thereafter, and in that of India at 18 for girls and 14 for boys. Moreover, in regard to the hours between which work is allowed, some modifications were inserted to meet special cases, such as that of tropical countries in which a period of rest is allowed during the heat of day.

This brief summary of the provisions of the two conventions relating to children can hardly do justice to the great social reforms which they embody.

If it had achieved nothing else, the Washington Conference would have justified itself by adopting these two measures alone for the protection of the coming generation ; and yet they were only two among a number of agreements of equal or even greater moment to the life of the industrial workers throughout the world.

Finally, the Commission on Unhealthy Processes, containing a number of famous medical experts under Dr. T. M. Legge, Chief Medical Inspector of Factories in Great Britain, presented its report. The Commission was hampered by the large field comprised in the term "unhealthy processes." Each dangerous process needs careful and prolonged study before any international agreement as to the right method of eliminating its dangers can be expected. There had been no opportunity for such study before the Conference, and the Commission had not sufficient time or facilities at their disposal for detailed and scientific investigation. They therefore confined themselves to clearing the ground for the treatment of three of the most dangerous of industrial diseases, namely, carbonic oxide poisoning, plumbism, and anthrax. In regard to the first, resolutions were adopted laying down certain general principles and recommending further study of them to the International Labour Office with a view to the preparation of a draft convention for a future Conference. On the subject of anthrax the Commission went rather further, and proposed a Recommendation which was adopted by the Confer-

ence to the effect that arrangements should be made
for disinfecting wool infected by anthrax spores,
either in the exporting country or, failing that, at
the port of entry of the importing country. In
regard to lead-poisoning, a further Recommendation
was adopted. It proposes the total exclusion of
women and young persons under 18 from certain
processes connected with the handling of zinc and
lead, which endanger the function of maternity and
the physical development of young persons through
the risk of plumbism. The Recommendation further
suggests certain precautions where women and young
persons are employed in processes involving the use
of lead compounds, and the compulsory substitution
of non-toxic substances for the latter, wherever
practicable.

To make the record of the Conference's work
in matters of health complete, it should be added
that a Recommendation was adopted in favour of the
adoption in all countries of a system of medical
inspection of factories working in co-operation with the
International Labour Office, when its Health Section
is established, and another Recommendation urging
the adherence to the Berne Convention of 1906
prohibiting the use of white phosphorus in the manufacture of matches, of those countries which had not
already ratified the Convention. To the layman all
these provisions may seem dry, technical and un-
interesting, but if properly carried out, they are
fraught with great possibilities for the elimination of

needless suffering and the improvement of the health of the industrial population, on which the recruiting statistics of all the belligerent countries have thrown such a lurid light.

Such was the work of the first International Labour Conference. It is indeed only a beginning, but it was certainly no slight accomplishment for an assembly unique in its composition, speaking many tongues, and working under untried rules of procedure, to have achieved in the space of a single month. And if its work is carefully examined, it bears few signs of being hasty or slipshod. Every Convention and Recommendation is the product of close discussion by experts chosen by their trade unions or their employers' organisations or their national administrations for their knowledge of the subjects before the Conference. They did not overlook or avoid the difficult points, but faced them and tried to hammer out practical solutions. The secretarial staff supplied each Commission with a secretary who knew its subject matter thoroughly, and the reports when adopted by the Conference were put into treaty form by a small drafting committee with juristic experience, who had to assure both legal precision and absolute identity of meaning between the French and English texts, the latter a far more difficult task than some might think. The work had all to be done at very high pressure, but every one brought an energy and an enthusiasm to bear upon it, which have produced results capable of facing the test of leisured criticism.

IV. FUTURE PROBLEMS

AND what will be the outcome of it all ?   International Conferences have met frequently in the past, and have adopted manifold resolutions which have done little but increase the quantity of printed matter in the world. Will the decisions of the Washington Conference be translated into action, or will they meet a similar fate ? The answer will, I believe, be found to lie in three elements of the International Labour Organisation : first, its official character ; secondly, its basis of popular representation ; and thirdly, its administrative organ, the International Labour Office.

The presence of two delegates from each country directly appointed by its Government and directly responsible to it, ensures that the Draft Conventions and Recommendations for which they voted cannot be ignored. The votes of the official representatives were not merely the expression of their personal opinions. They were the acceptance on behalf of their Governments of agreements entered into with the representatives of the other nations present, agreements which had been arrived at after free discussion and detailed negotiation. Whether or not the Government Delegates were plenipotentiaries in the strict diplomatic sense of the term, need not be disputed. Under no democratic constitution, whether of a nation or of a trade union, is the representative appointed to negotiate an agreement ever fully plenipotentiary. His work has always to be endorsed and finally accepted by the community which he represents. But there is no doubt that every official delegate at Washington regarded himself as committing his Government in a greater or lesser degree, and that, as Mr. Barnes emphasized in the passage quoted above,[1] he was so regarded by his colleagues.

And even if there were a disposition on the part of the Governments to " turn down " their delegates when they got home and to consign the Washington Convention to the wastepaper basket,—which is unlikely—there are several considerations which would prevent them from doing so. In the first place, the Peace Treaty itself makes it impossible. Every Government is bound to submit the findings of the Conference to its Parliament or other competent authority within a year, or, at most, eighteen months. But this is not all. The popular element in the composition of the Conference makes it certain that in every democratic country its decisions will receive the most careful attention. For they were accepted not only by the Government delegates as agreements between each other and the nations which they represented, but also by the employers and workers as bargains between capital and labour for the better conduct of industry. The workers will naturally insist on these bargains being put into effect by their

[1] See pp. 219-220.

Governments, in order that the level of industrial life may be raised, and the employers are scarcely less interested, because any failure to do so would necessarily react disastrously on their relations with their employees. In other words, there is a great mass of public opinion in each country which will press for legislative sanction to be given to the Washington agreements. It is true that owing to the exceptional difficulty of transmitting news of the Conference to Europe owing to the pressure on the cables at the time, its results and their importance are not yet fully realised ; but as they become better understood, public opinion will become more pronounced. Moreover, that opinion will be not only national, but international. At the next annual meeting of the Conference the steps taken in the various countries to ratify and give effect to the Conventions and Recommendations adopted at Washington will be reviewed. The delegates from those countries which have rejected them will certainly be in an unenviable position.

Finally, the creation of the International Labour Office, provides a means by which the spirit of Conference survives and may exert its influence on those who have not realised its significance. The establishment of the Office was one of the last, but not the least, of the acts of the Conference, and therefore merits a slight digression.

It will be remembered that the Governing Body of the Office, as provided in the Treaty, consists of twenty-four members, of whom twelve are appointed by the Governments, six by the employers and six by the workers, and that of the twelve Government members, eight are nominated by the eight States "of chief industrial importance." The three groups met separately to make their elections. The Government group agreed, subject to a protest by India, that the eight States should be the United States, Great Britain, France, Italy, Germany, Japan, Belgium and Switzerland. The last seven accordingly appointed representatives, and the delegates of the remaining countries were called upon to select four of them who should nominate four members to fill the places still vacant, and a fifth who should act as a substitute for the United States, until that country joined the Labour Organisation. The nations chosen were Spain, Canada, Argentina, Poland, and Denmark. The employers and the workers then held their group meetings, to which they elected their six representatives. This procedure was strictly in accordance with the terms of the Treaty, but in practice it revealed a difficulty which had not been foreseen. As will be observed from the full list of the members of the Governing Body printed in the footnote,[1] no less

[1] The full list of the members is as follows: *Government Representatives*: Mr. Arthur Fontaine (France), Councillor of State, Director of the Labour Department, Ministry of Labour (Chairman); Sir Malcolm Delevingne, K.C.B. (Great Britain), Assistant Under Secretary of State, Home Office; Baron Mayor des Planches (Italy), Ex-Ambassador at Washington, Commissioner for Emigration; Dr. Hermann Rüfenacht (Switzerland), Director of the Federal Office of Social Insurance; Mr. Francsizek Sokal (Poland), Director of the Labour

than 20 out of the 24 come from European countries, though two of these will give way to representatives of the United States when that country enters the Labour Organisation. The non-European countries felt strongly that they were under-represented, and their dissatisfaction gave rise to a motion moved by Mr. Gemmill, of South Africa, expressing disapproval of the composition of the Governing Body. This motion was carried by a majority of 44 to 39, but the adoption of the motion could have no immediate practical consequences, inasmuch as the election of the members did not rest with the Conference, but

Department, Ministry of Labour and Social Welfare ;   Senator G. D. Robertson (Canada), Minister of Labour ;   Geheimer Oberregierungsrat Dr. Leymann (Germany) ;   Vicomte de Eza (Spain), Ex-Minister of Public Works ;   Mr. E. Mahaim (Belgium), Professor of International Law, University of Liège ;   Dr. Vedel (Denmark), Director of the Ministry of Interior ;   Mr. de Alvear (Argentina), Argentine Ambassador at Paris ;   Mr. Nagaoka (Japan), Councillor of the Japanese Embassy in Paris ;   *Employers' Representatives* : Mr. Louis Guérin (France), Director of the Linen Industry of France ; Sir Allan Smith, K.B.E., M.P. (Great Britain), President of the National Confederation Employers' Organization ; Mr. F. Hodacz (Czecho-Slovakia), Secretary General of the Federation of Czecho-Slovak Manufacturers ; Mr. Jules Carlier (Belgium), President of the Central Industrial Committee for Belgium ;   Mr. Dietrich Schindler (Switzerland), Director General of the Oerlikon Machine Factory ;   Mr. A. Pirelli (Italy), Director of Pirelli Bros., Milan ;   *Workers' Representatives* :   Mr. Léon Jouhaux (France), Secretary General of the Confédération Générale du Travail ;  Mr. G. H. Stuart-Bunning (Great Britain), Ex-Chairman of the Parliamentary Committee, Trades Union Congress ;  Mr. J. Oudegeest, M.P. (Netherlands), President of the National Association of Labour Unions ;  Mr. A. Herman Lindqvist (Sweden), President of the Second Chamber of the Riksdag, President of the Trade Unions' Associations ;  Mr. P. M. Draper (Canada), Secretary-Treasurer of the Trades and Labour Congress ;  Mr. K. Legien (Germany), Secretary-General of the General Commission of Trade Unions.

with the various groups. It was evident that some remedy must be found for this paradoxical situation, and that a revision of the constitution would probably have to be considered at the next meeting of the Conference with a view to insuring adequate representation to all parts of the world.

The Governing Body met for the first time on Nov. 27th. Its first act was to appoint Mr. Albert Thomas, the famous French Socialist leader and the creator of the French Ministry of Munitions, as the provisional Director of the International Labour Office, an appointment which was subsequently confirmed at a meeting in January, held in Paris. Any one who knows Mr. Albert Thomas's energy, vision and sincerity, will realise that a better choice could hardly have been made. By making his appointment their first business, the Governing Body responded to the strong feeling of the Conference that the immediate creation of the Labour Office was essential, if its own work was to be continued and developed. A Parliament without an administration under its control can be little more than a debating society. Although the International Labour Office will not have direct executive powers, the scope and variety of its functions are clearly indicated by the article of the Peace Treaty providing for its establishment and by the duties already imposed upon it by the Washington Conventions. It will not only act as the clearing house for the collection and distribution of information of every kind on industrial and social questions, but will be able to stimulate and assist the various governments in applying the recommendations of the Conference. Difficulties of application are certain to arise. The Labour Office will often be able to suggest expedients for removing them, drawn from its experience of the practice adopted in other countries. It will also be able to give advice on questions of interpretation, which will tend to promote uniformity, and in cases of extreme difficulty can even suggest reference to the Permanent International Court, when it is established. Moreover, apart from its duties in connection with the ratification and application of Conventions, it will perform an invaluable work in preparing the ground for future Conferences. Experience showed very clearly at Washington that the preliminary work of the Organising Committee, hastily performed by a small, improvised staff, as was inevitable, was nevertheless of the greatest possible value. The Reports which it presented contained the latest information obtained from the various Governments by means of a carefully compiled questionnaire on each of the subjects on the agenda. They gave the delegates the material on which to work, and saved endless discussion by showing clearly from the start the points on which there was already a large measure of agreement, and those which would require considerable discussion and on which attention must therefore be concentrated. What the Organising Committee did for the Washington Conference with very imperfect means, the Inter-

national Labour Office, guided by a strong Governing
Body and far better equipped, will be able to do with
much greater success for future meetings. Being
always in touch with the Governments, the employers
and the trade union movements of the world, it will be
able to gather the most complete information on every
subject within its province ; and it is not too much
to expect that such a collection of material, on
scientific lines and on an international scale, will
throw new light on many industrial problems, which
have hitherto appeared obscure, because sufficient
data were not available to enable them to be viewed
as a whole.

At the beginning of this chapter I disclaimed all
intention of attempting to forecast the future. At
a time when the elements of society are in the crucible,
and many are seeking new formulae for their combination, he would be a rash man who undertook to pass
even a tentative judgment on any of the new forms of
national or international endeavour, which are slowly
beginning to crystallise. The International Labour
Organisation is still in its infancy. It has many
trials before it. Even its membership is incomplete,
since at present it lacks the greatest of all industrial
countries, the United States. But it is impossible
to believe that the American people will refuse to
co-operate with the rest of the world in a movement
for the ordered improvement of the lot of mankind.
The whole idea of international effort is as yet so
novel that it is often regarded with profound sus-

picion.  The consciousness of nationalism, springing from the inborn sense of community of blood, speech, and tradition, which has wrought so much for the progress of the world, is so deep-rooted, that to many any wider view of human relationships still seems inconceivable.  The international idea appears to them either as a dangerous delusion, implying the negation of patriotism and of national individuality, or else at best as what Plato termed " a kind of watery. friendship," lacking any vital and binding principle of cohesion.  It is for the future to find the synthesis which will reconcile these two great forces in human society, and to prove that, just as the family and the tribe have been welded into the nation, not only without merging their identity in it, but rather enriching it by their variety of type and of collective experience, so the nations may be united in the world's commonwealth, without sacrificing anything of their peculiar virtues or of their individual genius, but bringing them as contributions to the common good.  In this direction the Labour Section of the Peace Treaty is a constructive experiment ; and though as yet it is still but an experiment, the Washington Conference may be held at least to have proved that it is well worth the making.

H. B. BUTLER.

# THE TASK OF THE INTERNATIONAL LABOUR OFFICE

BY

## ALBERT THOMAS

Ex-Minister of France

Director of the International Labour Office

I. ORGANISATION OF THE OFFICE

II. THE OFFICE AND THE EVOLUTION OF SOCIAL REFORM

III. THE FUTURE OF THE OFFICE

# CHAPTER IX

## THE TASK OF THE INTERNATIONAL LABOUR OFFICE

THE preceding chapters have dealt with the formation of the International Labour Organisation. They have made clear something of the task that lies before it. What was accomplished at Washington has also been set forth. But it is the establishment of an International Labour Office to give effect to the aims of the Permanent Organisation, which holds the promise of its assured success. Some in fact go so far as to say that while the International Labour Conference constitutes the Parliament of Labour, the International Labour Office represents its Administrative Services. This, however, does not altogether represent the facts correctly. The intention of those who are responsible for the work of the Permanent Organisation is rather to leave the beaten track of what Proudhon called "the political hierarchy," and to strike out on a new and independent path, confident in the solidarity of economic forces of the world.

## I. ORGANISATION OF THE OFFICE

With regard to the relations of the International Labour Office with its Governing Body, a very clear division of duties has been prescribed. The Governing Body lays down the general lines of the work of the office, defines its policy, elects the Director, entrusts him with such special tasks as the needs of the moment require, and generally superintends his operations. The Director, on the other hand, has complete control of the Staff and is wholly responsible for the work of the Office. In all their operations, the Director and the Governing Body work in the closest possible harmony, and every step taken is the result of sympathetic understanding between them. Herein lies a notable difference between the functions of the Secretariat of the League and those of the International Labour Office in relation to their respective Councils. While it is laid down in the Peace Treaty that the Assembly and Council of the League are to be " assisted by a Permanent Secretariat," the relations of the International Labour Office with its Governing Body are of an entirely different nature, since it is definitely allowed to exercise certain executive functions of its own. Another important point is the relative autonomy which is granted to the International Labour Organisation. It is not merely a section of the League of Nations, nor a section of its Permanent Secretariat. On the contrary, it has the power to initiate its own policy and to carry it out as a completely independent body.

Following the Washington Conference, the Governing Body of the International Labour Organisation met in London in March 1920 to complete the organisation of the Labour Office. In the following paragraphs an outline of this organisation is given, showing the different sections of the Office and the special branch of its work with which each section will deal.

*The Diplomatic Section.* As already stated, the object of the International Labour Organisation is—through the conventions and recommendations of International Labour Conference—to facilitate the relatively uniform progress of labour reforms through the legislatures of the member states. Before the varied technical problems which underlie these reforms can be considered by the Conference and expressed in terms of conventions and recommendations, much heavy and intricate work must be done by the International Labour Office. An important share of this work devolves upon the section of the Office which, for want of a better name, has been termed the Diplomatic Section. This section will make all necessary preparations for the annual International Labour Conference. It will submit agenda for these conferences to the Governing Body, and, subject to their approval, will circulate the agenda and questionnaires to the member states. On the basis of the replies received, it will prepare reports and draft

conventions for consideration at the Conferences.
It is interesting to follow the procedure when a convention or recommendation has been adopted by an
International Labour Conference. By virtue of
Article 405 of the Peace Treaty the General Secretary
of the League of Nations transmits the authentic
texts of these conventions or recommendations to
each of the Governments concerned.[1] Within the
period of one year—or 18 months at the most—each
Government is under obligation to submit these
authentic texts for ratification to its competent
legislative or other authority. It is the business of the
International Labour Office through its Diplomatic
Section to see that the member states observe these
obligations promptly and fully. The Office, with
the concurrence of the delegates to the Conference
or of the organisations which appointed them, can
approach any member state to urge that the conventions and recommendations of the Conference be
submitted promptly to its legislature for ratification.
The Office through its Diplomatic Section must also
assist the member states generally in dealing with the
difficulties which must arise in interpreting conventions or recommendations, and in adapting them
so as to harmonise with the customs, traditions and
general conditions in various countries. When the
conventions and recommendations of the Conference
have been finally ratified and adopted as national
laws by the legislatures of the member states, it will

[1] Appendix I. p. 282.

be the business of the Diplomatic Section of the Office to see that these new laws are fully and properly enforced.[1]  It will also be its duty to deal with the complaints of interested parties with regard to their enforcement.[2]  Should a complaint disclose the need for an inquiry [3] to ascertain the facts, the Diplomatic Section may advise that a commission for this purpose be appointed on the spot.  It will further be responsible for seeing that effect is given to the recommendations of any such commission, and if necessary it must submit the questions in dispute to the International Court of Justice set up under the League of Nations.[4]  Although the League will doubtless supervise closely the whole field of its activities through its own organisation, it is only through the action of the International Labour Office that the juridical and executive powers of the League can be exercised with regard to the special questions with which the Labour Office has been constituted to deal.

*Scientific or Intelligence Section.*  An important task of the International Labour Office will consist in collecting and distributing information on all subjects relating to the international adjustment of the conditions of industrial life and labour.  This information will be kept up to date and published periodically in French, English, and such other languages as the Governing Body may recommend, in an official

[1] Appendix I. Article 408, p. 284.
[2] Appendix I. Articles 409 and 411, pp. 284-5.
[3] Appendix I. Articles 411-415, pp. 285-7.
[4] Appendix I. Article 416, p. 287.

organ of the Office, which will deal with problems of industry and employment of international interest.[1] The Scientific Section will thus carry out a great social work of incalcuable general value, upon which the deliberations and decisions of the Conference will be based. This work will involve the rapid and constant collection and classification of accurate information on technical subjects of infinite variety from every quarter of the world, and the perfection of a distributing organisation through which this information will readily be available in any country as and when it is required for the purpose of labour reforms. Among other heads of information, the Scientific Section will have to issue a digest of labour legislation in all member states. In this respect the International Labour Office will continue the work carried on for many years at Basle by the International Association for Labour Legislation. The Scientific Section will also be responsible for perfecting an intelligence service, drawing its information from the Press in all countries, and for supplying the answer to any request for information that may be received on matters pertaining to the work of the Office.

It is clear from the nature of their tasks that both the Diplomatic and Scientific Sections of the Office will need the assistance of specialised staffs to carry out their work. Accordingly the organisation of the Office includes no less than fourteen *Technical Sections* as originally planned, each of which will consist of a

[1] Appendix I. Article 396, p 279

small group of specialists. A short description of each of these Technical Sections will serve to indicate the great scope, complexity and importance of the work of the International Labour Office.

*Maritime Section.* Conditions of labour at sea are very different from those on land. Seamen as a class are keenly alive to this fact. They had accordingly demanded that special international conferences should be summoned to deal with maritime labour problems under the auspices of an International Maritime Labour Office. The whole work of social legislation, however, would have been complicated, and much of the existing organisation for furthering the interests of workers as a whole would have been dislocated, if effect had been given to the principle of creating separate international offices to deal with sectional labour interests. Happily, this difficulty was appreciated by the seamen. They agreed, therefore, that a special commission should be appointed to watch their interests in the International Labour Office as an integral part of that organisation, and thus to obviate the need of creating a separate Maritime Office. A Maritime Section of the International Labour Office has accordingly been formed to prepare the way for this commission, and to organise the first International Seamen's Conference which it has been arranged to hold at Genoa in June 1920.

*Unemployment Section.* The decisions of the Washington Conference on the subject of unemployment,[1]

_____
[1] Appendix III. pp. 305-9.

as well as the vital importance and social menace of this great problem, made the creation of this section an immediate necessity. The Conference fully realised the need of appointing a commission to study the whole question of unemployment from an international point of view. This task involves setting up special machinery to carry out a quarterly survey of the official unemployment returns of the member states, and generally to centralise and co-ordinate an international organisation for dealing with this problem as a whole. Therefore unemployment—together with emigration and immigration, which are closely related to it—are already being considered systematically with a view to finding practical solutions by a special staff of the International Labour Office.

*Agricultural Section.* While the Peace Treaty was under preparation, the Commission on International Labour Legislation made it clear that the activities of the Permanent Labour Organisation were not to be limited to the spheres of industry and commerce alone, but were also to include the domain of agriculture. The Washington Conference confirmed this principle. As in the case of seamen, special circumstances, such as variations of climate and the need of concentrated efforts during seed time and harvest differentiate the conditions of agricultural labour from those which apply generally to other industries. The question of adapting labour reforms to agricultural workers is to be an important item on the agenda of the International Labour Conference of 1921, and an

Agricultural Section of the International Labour Office has been formed to deal with the interests of the countless millions of men engaged in the production of food throughout the world.

*Hours of Work Section.* This section of the office is to be entrusted with a complicated and difficult problem in the practical application of the convention passed at the Washington Conference limiting hours of work in industrial undertakings to eight in the day and forty eight in the week.[1] This principle will require careful adjustment to suit the conditions of labour in tropical countries and countries in which special circumstances have to be taken into account.

*Health Section.* This Section will collect all medical, hygienic and general information necessary to enable the Labour Conference to secure workers against the dangers of occupational accidents and illness through preventive measures, and to ensure for them healthy working conditions.[2]

*Emigration Section.* The work of this section will require very soon to be detached from the general section dealing with unemployment and employment exchanges. A Safety Section will also shortly require to be detached from the Health Section.

*Protection of Women and Maternity Section.* There is no need to emphasise the importance of the work of this section which will be based on the foundations laid at the Washington Conference.[3] With the

---

[1] Appendix III. p. 294.  [2] Appendix III. p. 322.
[3] Appendix III. p. 310.

exception of a few questions such as maternity which necessitate special regulations and benefits for women only, the whole tendency of labour reform is to put the working woman, as regards wages and industrial conditions generally, on the same level as the working man.   The work of the International Labour Office will accordingly be based upon this principle, and for this reason no section will be devoted specially to women's conditions as distinct from men's, except the Section which I have just mentioned.

*Home Work Section.*   Is the industrial worker who carries on his occupation at home to remain outside the scope and benefit of labour legislation ?   Can or should he be brought within the scope and benefits of industrial reforms ?   These are important questions which must be considered by the Labour Office.

*Industrial Technique and Production Section.*   No study of the international limitation of hours of work can be undertaken successfully without keeping the question of production in the very fore-front. Any organisation which has as its aim the initiation and maintenance of better conditions of labour must give this problem its most careful attention.   Even now it is questioned in many countries whether the reduction of hours of work will not prove detrimental to trade and industry.   In our desire to free the world of producers from conditions of poverty and squalor, are we by limiting production plunging them into conditions even worse than before ?   A section of the Office will carefully consider whether production cannot by some means be maintained, or even increased, in spite of a reduction of the hours of work.

*Wages Section.* One great problem to which this section will devote itself is that of minimum wages. It will also consider the whole question of remuneration and aim at finding a fair balance between the cost of living and the reward of labour.

*Social Insurance Section.* Enquiries have already been received from more than one State with regard to the development of social insurance, with which the International Labour Office will deal through a special section.

*Education Section.* The work of this section will not be confined to technical, industrial, or professional subjects. It will embrace the whole field of general education. At the Washington Conference age limits were proposed, below which no child may be employed in industrial work. If these proposals are adopted by the legislatures of member states, a great opportunity for developing the rising generation, at the most plastic age both mentally and physically lies open to the world. The International Labour Office will strive to make the most of this opportunity by considering the best and most practical schemes of general as well as of technical education.

*Co-operative Section.* It was foreseen when the Peace Treaty was under consideration that the Office would not confine its activities as regards the workers to the question of industrial conditions alone, but would also deal with questions concerning their

conditions of life generally. This wider sphere of the
work of the Office may perhaps be carried out most
efficaciously through the co-operative movement
among workers in the great centres of industry. The
Co-operative Section of the Office will not, however,
limit its activities to the Co-operative movement
so far as it deals only with the supply of food, but will
foster the extension of this system to problems such
as housing and transport facilities which vitally concern the welfare of workers. The co-operative movement to-day is a strong international movement in
which the Labour Office is bound to take an active
interest. It must be remembered that every worker
is a consumer as well as a producer. A Co-operative
Society is therefore the true complement of a Trade
Union. The former safeguards the interests of the
worker as a consumer, just as the latter safeguards
his interests as a producer.

The above paragraphs shortly describe the organisation with which the International Labour Office
commences its tremendous task. It cannot expect to
enrol in its service all the highest international
authorities upon the infinite variety of questions with
which it will have to deal, and to bring them together
in one centre. But each particular section of the
Office must become a centre of information under
different heads, collected from the various authorities
in all parts of the world. Each section must strive
to stimulate both ideas and research with regard to
its own problems and become a true clearing-house

for inter-communication between the authorities of every country.

As the work of the Office develops, its original organisation may be modified. Some sections may be amalgamated and others split up. It may be that the full scope of the work of the Office has not yet been fully envisaged. The Peace Treaty in Article 396 [1] gives the International Labour Conference powers to carry out any special investigation through the Labour Office, and states that the functions and powers of the Office may be amplified by the Conference. Already some members of the Governing Body are looking forward to the time when the authority of the Office will have attained a moral force which will enable it, in times of industrial unrest, to exercise the functions of adjudication and conciliation between employer and employed. The Office has already been approached for help in the solution of international disputes connected with emigration and unemployment, and it has also organised an enquiry into labour legislation and industrial conditions in Soviet Russia.[2] In neither of these matters has the Office exceeded its true functions and powers, because international labour legislation is essentially a subject which is universal in scope. If any nation inists on remaining outside the permanent labour organisation or will not adopt its conventions, then the whole task of the protection of workers on an international basis

[1] Appendix I. p. 279.
[2] *Labour Conditions in Soviet Russia.* Harrisons & Sons, London.

will become partial and uncertain. It is well therefore that Germany and Austria, although not yet
members of the League of Nations, have been admitted to the International Labour Organisation.
It may even be possible at a later stage to make
some special arrangement with America which will
enable her to take her place in the organisation, and
thus complete the already vast field in which the
International Labour Office will exercise its activities.

## II. THE OFFICE AND THE EVOLUTION OF SOCIAL REFORM

In what spirit will the International Labour Office
discharge its functions ? Will those who control
it rest satisfied with the observance of administrative
routine, the issue of periodical reports and the avoidance of the burdens and responsibilities attaching to
initiative so typical of bureaucratic institutions ?
Such a conception of the functions of the Office
would be an injustice to those responsible for organising it and for directing its activities. It is certain,
moreover, that the workers regard the Office as an
instrument for action which can make its influence
felt in their interests in the highest quarters. The
employers also regard the Office as a creative organisation adaptable to the exigencies of industrial and
commercial developments. The personnel of the
Office, from the Governing Body downwards, is
animated with the desire to make it an institution of
an entirely new type which will concentrate its inde-

pendent powers upon a policy of action. Moreover, it is only by the adoption of such a policy that the Office can hope to survive. Should it fail to utilise the moral and material elements available in each country and combine them for progress, the Office will fail to justify its existence and will die.

In this conception of its functions, what will be the exact position of the Office in the comity of nations and in relation to the widespread impulse towards social reform which characterises the present day ? Some have gone so far as to say that the Office is destined ultimately to become a super-Parliament of Labour to which the national legislatures of all countries will delegate their prerogative of social legislation, and that then the Office will actually promulgate international laws binding upon all peoples. If these speculations ever become realities it will not be in the near future. At present the Conference gives definite shape to social reforms of international scope to which national legislatures may give the force of law. The real compelling force behind the conventions and recommendations of the Conference—as Mr. Barnes points out—is that of public opinion in every country. Some twenty years before the war the education of public opinion on the need of labour legislation for the benefit of workers had commenced in various countries, and national associations had been formed to advocate an uniform system of laws to protect the workers. These associations mainly consisted of economists, jurists and

politicians interested in labour problems. The bulk
of the Trade Unions, if not definitely hostile, at any
rate held aloof from their activities. During the
war the outlook of organised labour underwent a
profound change upon many questions. The great
Trade Unions, in spite of their preoccupation with
class interests, co-operated loyally with every other
section of society in defence of the common interests
of the whole people. With its outlook enlarged,
Labour realised that the interests of the mass of
workers throughout the world were inseparably
bound up with the problems of restoring peace to the
nations and of reconstructing society from the
wreckage of war.

Labour, therefore, took an active part in the making
of peace. To Labour we owe the fact that the
Treaty of Peace laid the foundation of an international
labour charter through the nucleus of an organisation
—namely the existing International Labour Organisation—the function of which is to secure for workers
in every country better conditions of life and labour.
By this act Organised Labour throughout the world
is now identified directly with this great international
movement to legislate for the benefit of workers, and
its co-operation has given the movement a force and
scope which has advanced it at a bound far beyond
the pioneer efforts commenced a quarter of a century
ago. Moreover the Washington Conference by its
first conventions and recommendations has laid
the basis of a vast and comprehensive scheme of

social reconstruction. It is a happy augury for the future that employers, as a whole, have willingly helped in laying this foundation of a new order in a spirit of sympathy and understanding with the workers and with a clear recognition of the fact that they and their workers share what are common interests. Such are the social impulses which give its democratic constitution to the International Labour Organisation with its representative employers and workers sitting in consultation with the delegates of governments, and working with them to solve international social and industrial problems on truly progressive lines.

Thus one of the main functions of the International Labour Office will be to keep in close touch with the great Trade Unions and Associations of Employers in every country. It is to be hoped that these bodies will actively assist the Office in its work, for their friendly co-operation will immensely facilitate the realisation of its aims. The fact of keeping in constant touch with the aspirations of the workers and the difficulties of employers will in itself militate against any danger of the International Labour Office becoming a lifeless institution operating in bureaucratic grooves—even if its duties were not by their nature calculated to combat lethargic tendencies and to demand alert, resourceful handling. These duties may at any time become delicate as well as difficult. For instance, they may involve the settlement of questions on which employers and workers are in acute conflict. They may again—unless negotiated with the utmost skill and care—give rise to an impression that the Office is attempting to interfere in the domestic affairs of some nation so as to constitute an infringement of its sovereign rights. It must be remembered that the point at which purely social and economic problems become definitely political is not always easy to define. In cases where such elements of difficulty are present, any action taken by the Office will necessitate anxious consideration and the exercise of infinite tact. But however difficult its task may be, the Office cannot flinch from taking action when it is necessary. To do so would be to declare its impotence and to sound its death-knell.

It is possible that the discharge of its more delicate functions may, at a later stage, necessitate an expansion of the Office by adding to it something in the nature of a political section to keep it closely in touch with the employers' and workers' organisations. At present, however, it seemed better that such functions should be performed personally by the Director with the assistance of specially chosen colleagues. Further, the task of maintaining contact simultaneously and effectively with the movements for social reform in every country, and with the various organisations of workers and employers in each of them in the present era of almost universal social and industrial unrest, will, as the work of the Office develops, involve enlarging its organisation by establishing special correspondents or offices in different centres. These correspondents will have to be capable of following intelligently the social movements in each country and must keep in close touch with both the employers and workers' organisations. This supplementary organisation might with advantage be extended to include arrangements for systematic publicity, so as to make known through its local agents throughout the world the constitutions and functions of the International Labour Office. At the same time—if necessary by a separate branch of this organisation —public opinion in different countries might be educated regarding the various vital questions with which the Office will deal from time to time, together with the nature of its work as a whole and the principles upon which it is carried on. The nature of the machinery through which the Office will attain these objects may differ in various countries. The Italian Government, for instance, has founded a Secretariat for International Labour Legislation supported by both employers and organised labour, which may prove the most effective way of attaining them in Italy. Whatever methods are adopted however, the object will be the same in every country, namely, to keep the International Labour Office in close touch with associations of workers and employers and to secure the support of public opinion for its great aim of attaining through peaceful and constructive methods those great social reforms which the mass of humanity awaits to-day with eager impatience.

### III. THE FUTURE OF THE OFFICE

Since its creation, the Office has been in a truly paradoxical situation. Despite the criticism of some extremists, it has had from the first the support of organised labour in the great Trade Unions of various countries. Powerful representative bodies of organised labour, such as the Congress of the Confédération Général du Travail of France, the British Trades Union Congress, and the Belgian Trade Union Committee have formally voted resolutions supporting the Office. The first beginnings of its work at the Washington Conference are now before the world. It must be remembered, however, that twelve months at least from the date of its assembling may elapse before the Office can point to the first practical results of its labours—in laws passed by the legislatures of the member states on the conventions and recommendations of the Washington Conference. It is right, therefore, that judgment on the utility of the Office and prophecies as to its future should alike be postponed for a while. In the Revolution of 1848 the workers declared that they gave " three months of suffering " to the service of the Republic. Will the workers of the twentieth century give twelve months' patience to the service of the International Labour Office before they expect to enjoy the true benefits of its work ? Is this too much to ask in the present condition of the world ? Is it too much to ask for a task which may take years of patient work to accomplish ? Is it too much to ask for efforts which certainly give the world at least a temporary stability and a starting-point for future reconstruction. Is it too much to ask for efforts which will give mankind constant opportunities in the future for schemes of progress to benefit the toiling millions of workers ?

Some may hesitate to answer these questions because they fear that the influence of the Office with its elements representing governments and employers may militate against the rapid and complete realisation of social reforms, and that its policy may be deflected from bold progressive principles to conservative and dilatory measures which the workers regard as inimical to their true interests. Above all, the more extreme workers' groups may fear that their advanced theories of social progress, through communism or even bolshevism, may suffer by the efforts of the Office to bring about social reforms through the constitutional channels of national legislatures instead of by revolutionary methods, coupled with its policy of basing these efforts upon the conception of good relations and of common interests between employers and workers, so as to enable social reforms to be carried out under conditions of industrial peace and prosperity.

Needless to say, the International Labour Office will not exceed the functions laid down for it with the help and approval of organised labour by championing any one of the multiplicity of conflicting interests which it will be its work to harmonise into constructive schemes for ordered progress in social reform.  One important consideration, however, must always be borne in mind.  It is the conviction expressed so strongly by labour leaders as well as employers at the conclusion of the war, that if the great work of social reconstruction and industrial recovery which now occupies the world is to be carried out successfully, by constitutional methods, during this troubled period—when the minds of men are still confused by the fearful upheaval which for so long threatened civilisation itself with destruction—it must be based upon new and generous conceptions of social justice for the worker, and carried out with the aid of the great Trade Unions.

The future of the International Labour Office is dedicated to the accomplishment of this immense task.  Those whose duty it will be to complete it, stage by stage, from materials consisting of a mass of intricate and exact detail collected from over forty different countries, will feel glad that they are privileged to spend their energies in building one of the main foundations of a new world in which truer conceptions of justice and universal brotherhood will prevail among mankind.

ALBERT THOMAS.

# APPENDIX I

# THE LABOUR SECTIONS OF THE PEACE TREATY

## GENERAL PRINCIPLES

## PERMANENT ORGANISATION

### CHAP. I. ORGANISATION
### CHAP. II. PROCEDURE
### CHAP. III. GENERAL

## RESOLUTIONS

# THE LABOUR SECTIONS OF THE PEACE TREATY

## GENERAL PRINCIPLES

### ARTICLE 427.

THE High Contracting Parties, recognising that the well-being, physical, moral, and intellectual, of industrial wage-earners is of supreme international importance, have framed, in order to further this great end, the permanent machinery provided for in Section I., and associated with that of the League of Nations.

They recognise that differences of climate, habits and customs, of economic opportunity and industrial tradition, make strict uniformity in the conditions of labour difficult of immediate attainment. But holding, as they do, that labour should not be regarded merely as an article of commerce, they think that there are methods and principles for regulating labour conditions which all industrial communities should endeavour to apply so far as their special circumstances will permit.

Among these methods and principles, the following seem to the High Contracting Parties to be of special and urgent importance :—

*First.*—The guiding principle above enunciated that labour should not be regarded merely as a commodity or article of commerce.

S 273

*Second.*—The right of association for all lawful purposes by the employed as well as by the employers.

*Third.*—The payment to the employed of a wage adequate to maintain a reasonable standard of life as this is understood in their time and country.

*Fourth.*—The adoption of an eight hours' day or a forty-eight hours' week as the standard to be aimed at where it has not already been attained.

*Fifth.*—The adoption of a weekly rest of at least twenty-four hours, which should include Sunday wherever practicable.

*Sixth.*—The abolition of child labour and the imposition of such limitations on the labour of young persons as shall permit the continuation of their education and assure their proper physical development.

*Seventh.*—The principle that men and women should receive equal remuneration for work of equal value.

*Eighth.*—The standard set by law in each country with respect to the conditions of labour should have due regard to the equitable economic treatment of all workers lawfully resident therein.

*Ninth.*—Each State should make provision for a system of inspection in which women should take part, in order to ensure the enforcement of the laws and regulations for the protection of the employed.

Without claiming that these methods and principles are either complete or final, the High Contracting Parties are of opinion that they are well fitted to guide the policy of the League of Nations ; and that, if adopted by the industrial communities who are members of the League, and safeguarded in practice by an adequate system of inspection, they will confer lasting benefits upon the wage earners of the world.

## PERMANENT ORGANISATION

### PREAMBLE

Whereas the League of Nations has for its object the establishment of universal peace, and such a peace can be established only if it is based upon social justice ;

And whereas conditions of labour exist involving such injustice, hardship and privation to large numbers of people as to produce unrest so great that the peace and harmony of the world are imperilled ; and an improvement of those conditions is urgently required : as, for example, by the regulation of the hours of work, including the establishment of a maximum working day and week, the regulation of the labour supply, the prevention of unemployment, the provision of an adequate living wage, the protection of the worker against sickness, disease and injury arising out of his employment, the protection of children, young persons and women, provisions for old age and injury, protection of the interests of workers when employed in countries other than their own, recognition of the principle of freedom of association, the organisation of vocational and technical education and other measures ;

Whereas also the failure of any nation to adopt humane conditions of labour is an obstacle in the way of other nations which desire to improve the conditions in their own countries ;

The High Contracting Parties, moved by sentiments of justice and humanity, as well as by the desire to secure the permanent peace of the world, agree to the following :—

## CHAPTER I

### ORGANISATION

### ARTICLE 387.

A permanent organisation is hereby established for the promotion of the objects set forth in the Preamble.

The original Members of the League of Nations shall be the original Members of this organisation, and hereafter membership of the League of Nations shall carry with it membership of the said organisation.

### ARTICLE 388.

The permanent organisation shall consist of (i) a General Conference of Representatives of the Members and (ii) an International Labour Office controlled by the Governing Body described in Article 7.

### ARTICLE 389.

The meetings of the General Conference of Representatives of the Members shall be held from time to time as occasion may require, and at least once in every year. It shall be composed of four Representatives of each of the Members, of whom two shall be Government Delegates and the two others shall be Delegates representing respectively the employers and the workpeople of each of the Members.

Each Delegate may be accompanied by advisers, who shall not exceed two in number for each item on the agenda of the meeting. When questions specially affecting women are to be considered by the Conference, one at least of the advisers should be a woman.

The Members undertake to nominate non-Government Delegates and advisers chosen in agreement with the industrial organisations, if such organisations exist, which are most

representative of employers or workpeople, as the case may
be, in their respective countries.

Advisers shall not speak except on a request made by the
Delegate whom they accompany and by the special authorisa-
tion of the President of the Conference, and may not vote.

A Delegate may by notice in writing addressed to the
President appoint one of his advisers to act as his deputy,
and the adviser, while so acting, shall be allowed to speak
and vote.

The names of the Delegates and their advisers will be
communicated to the International Labour Office by the
Government of each of the Members.

The credentials of Delegates and their advisers shall be
subject to scrutiny by the Conference, which may, by two-
thirds of the votes cast by the Delegates present, refuse to
admit any Delegate or adviser whom it deems not to have
been nominated in accordance with this Article.

## ARTICLE 390.

Every Delegate shall be entitled to vote individually on
all matters which are taken into consideration by the Conference.

If one of the Members fails to nominate one of the non-
Government Delegates whom it is entitled to nominate, the
other non-Government Delegate shall be allowed to sit and
speak at the Conference, but not to vote.

If in accordance with Article 3 the Conference refuses
admission to a Delegate of one of the Members, the provisions
of the present Article shall apply as if that Delegate had not
been nominated.

## ARTICLE 391.

The meetings of the Conference shall be held at the seat
of the League of Nations, or at such other place as may be
decided by the Conference at a previous meeting by two-
thirds of the votes cast by the Delegates present.

## ARTICLE 392.

The International Labour Office shall be established at the seat of the League of Nations as part of the organisation of the League.

## ARTICLE 393.

The International Labour Office shall be under the control of a Governing Body consisting of 24 persons, appointed in accordance with the following provisions :—

The Governing Body of the International Labour Office shall be constituted as follows :—

Twelve persons representing the Governments,
Six persons elected by the Delegates to the Conference representing the employers,
Six persons elected by the Delegates to the Conference representing the workers.

Of the 12 persons representing the Governments eight shall be nominated by the Members which are of the chief industrial importance, and four shall be nominated by the Members selected for the purpose by the Government Delegates to the Conference, excluding the Delegates of the eight Members mentioned above.

Any question as to which are the Members of the chief industrial importance shall be decided by the Council of the League of Nations.

The period of office of the members of the Governing Body will be three years. The method of filling vacancies and other similar questions may be determined by the Governing Body subject to the approval of the Conference.

The Governing Body shall, from time to time, elect one of its members to act as its Chairman, shall regulate its own procedure and shall fix its own times of meeting. A special meeting shall be held if a written request to that effect is made by at least 10 members of the Governing Body.

## ARTICLE 394.

There shall be a Director of the International Labour Office, who shall be appointed by the Governing Body, and, subject to the instructions of the Governing Body, shall be responsible for the efficient conduct of the International Labour Office and for such other duties as may be assigned to him.

The Director or his deputy shall attend all meetings of the Governing Body.

## ARTICLE 395.

The staff of the International Labour Office shall be appointed by the Director, who shall, so far as is possible with due regard to the efficiency of the work of the Office, select persons of different nationalities. A certain number of these persons shall be women.

## ARTICLE 396.

The functions of the International Labour Office shall include the collection and distribution of information on all subjects relating to the international adjustment of conditions of industrial life and labour, and particularly the examination of subjects which it is proposed to bring before the Conference with a view to the conclusion of international conventions, and the conduct of such special investigations as may be ordered by the Conference.

It will prepare the agenda for the meetings of the Conference.

It will carry out the duties required of it by the provisions of this part of the present Treaty in connection with international disputes.

It will edit and publish in French and English, and in such other languages as the Governing Body may think desirable, a periodical paper dealing with problems of industry and employment of international interest.

Generally, in addition to the functions set out in this article, it shall have such other power and duties as may be assigned to it by the Conference.

## ARTICLE 397.

The Government Departments of any of the Members which deal with questions of industry and employment may communicate directly with the Director through the Representative of their Government on the Governing Body of the International Labour Office, or failing any such Representative, through such other qualified official as the Government may nominate for the purpose.

## ARTICLE 398.

The International Labour Office shall be entitled to the assistance of the Secretary-General of the League of Nations in any matter in which it can be given.

## ARTICLE 399.

Each of the Members will pay the travelling and subsistence expenses of its Delegates and their advisers and of its Representatives attending the meetings of the Conference or Governing Body, as the case may be.

All the other expenses of the International Labour Office and of the meetings of the Conference or Governing Body shall be paid to the Director by the Secretary-General of the League of Nations out of the general funds of the League.

The Director shall be responsible to the Secretary-General of the League for the proper expenditure of all moneys paid to him in pursuance of this Article.

## CHAPTER II

### PROCEDURE

### ARTICLE 400.

The agenda for all meetings of the Conference will be settled by the Governing Body who shall consider any suggestion as to the agenda that may be made by the Government of any of the Members or by any representative organisation recognised for the purpose of Article 3.

### ARTICLE 401.

The Director shall act as the Secretary of the Conference, and shall transmit the agenda so as to reach the Members four months before the meeting of the Conference, and, through them, the non-Government Delegates when appointed.

### ARTICLE 402.

Any of the Governments of the Members may formally object to the inclusion of any item or items in the agenda. The grounds for such objection shall be set forth in a reasoned statement addressed to the Director, who shall circulate it to all the Members of the Permanent Organisation.

Items to which such objection has been made shall not, however, be excluded from the agenda, if at the Conference a majority of two-thirds of the votes cast by the Delegates present is in favour of considering them.

If the Conference decides (otherwise than under the preceding paragraph) by two-thirds of the votes cast by the Delegates present that any subject shall be considered by the Conference, that subject shall be included in the agenda for the following meeting.

## ARTICLE 403.

The Conference shall regulate its own procedure, shall elect its own President, and may appoint committees to consider and report on any matter.

Except as otherwise expressly provided in this part of the present Treaty, all matters shall be decided by a simple majority of the votes cast by the Delegates present.

The voting is void unless the total number of votes cast is equal to half the number of the Delegates attending the Conference.

## ARTICLE 404.

The Conference may add to any committees which it appoints technical experts, who shall be assessors without power to vote.

## ARTICLE 405.

When the Conference has decided on the adoption of proposals with regard to an item in the agenda, it will rest with the Conference to determine whether these proposals should take the form : (a) of a recommendation to be submitted to the Members for consideration with a view to effect being given to it by national legislation or otherwise, or (b) of a draft international convention for ratification by the Members.

In either case a majority of two-thirds of the votes cast by the Delegates present shall be necessary on the final vote for the adoption of the recommendation or draft convention, as the case may be, by the Conference.

In framing any recommendation or draft convention of general application, the Conference shall have due regard to those countries in which climatic conditions, the imperfect development of industrial organisation, or other special circumstances make the industrial conditions substantially different, and shall suggest the modifications, if any, which it considers may be required to meet the case of such countries.

A copy of the recommendation or draft convention shall be authenticated by the signature of the President of the Conference and of the Director, and shall be deposited with the Secretary-General of the League of Nations. The Secretary-General will communicate a certified copy of the recommendation or draft convention to each of the Members.

Each of the Members undertakes that it will, within the period of one year at most from the closing of the session of the Conference, or if it is impossible owing to exceptional circumstances to do so within the period of one year, then at the earliest practicable moment and in no case later than 18 months from the closing of the session of the Conference, bring the recommendation or draft convention before the authority or authorities within whose competence the matter lies for the enactment of legislation or other action.

In the case of a recommendation, the Members will inform the Secretary-General of the action taken.

In the case of a draft convention, the Member will, if it obtains the consent of the authority or authorities within whose competence the matter lies, communicate the formal ratification of the convention to the Secretary-General and will take such action as may be necessary to make effective the provisions of such convention.

If on a recommendation no legislative or other action is taken to make a recommendation effective, or if the draft convention fails to obtain the consent of the authority or authorities within whose competence the matter lies, no further obligation shall rest upon the Member.

In the case of a federal State, the power of which to enter into conventions on labour matters is subject to limitations, it shall be in the discretion of that Government to treat a draft convention to which such limitations apply as a recommendation only, and the provisions of this article with respect to recommendations shall apply in such case.

The following article shall be interpreted in accordance with the following principle :—

In no case shall any Member be asked or required, as a result of the adoption of any recommendation or draft convention by the Conference, to lessen the protection afforded by its existing legislation to the workers concerned.

## ARTICLE 406.

Any convention so ratified shall be registered by the Secretary-General of the League of Nations, but shall only be binding upon the Members which ratify it.

## ARTICLE 407.

If any convention coming before the Conference for final consideration fails to secure the support of two-thirds of the votes cast by the Delegates present, it shall nevertheless be within the right of any of the Members of the Permanent Organisation to agree to such convention among themselves.

Any convention so agreed to shall be communicated by the Governments concerned to the Secretary-General of the League of Nations, who shall register it.

## ARTICLE 408.

Each of the Members agrees to make an annual report to the International Labour Office on the measures which it has taken to give effect to the provisions of conventions to which it is a party. These reports shall be made in such form and shall contain such particulars as the Governing Body may request. The Director shall lay a summary of these reports before the next meeting of the Conference.

## ARTICLE 409.

In the event of any representation being made to the International Labour Office by an industrial association of employers or of workers that any of the Members has failed to secure in any respect the effective observance within its jurisdiction of any convention to which it is a party, the Governing Body may communicate this representation to the Government against which it is made and may invite that Government to make such statement on the subject as it may think fit.

## ARTICLE 410.

If no statement is received within a reasonable time from the Government in question, or if the statement when received is not deemed to be satisfactory by the Governing Body, the latter shall have the right to publish the representation and the statement, if any, made in reply to it.

## ARTICLE 411.

Any of the Members shall have the right to file a complaint with the International Labour Office if it is not satisfied that any other Member is securing the effective observance of any convention which both have ratified in accordance with the foregoing articles.

The Governing Body may, if it thinks fit, before referring such a complaint to a Commission of Enquiry, as hereinafter provided for, communicate with the Government in question in the manner described in Article 23.

If the Governing Body does not think it necessary to communicate the complaint to the Government in question, or if, when they have made such communication, no statement in reply has been received within a reasonable time which the Governing Body considers to be satisfactory, the Governing Body may apply for the appointment of a Commission of Enquiry to consider the complaint and to report thereon.

The Governing Body may adopt the same procedure either of its own motion or on receipt of a complaint from a Delegate to the Conference.

When any matter arising out of Article 24 or 25 is being

considered by the Governing Body, the Government in question shall, if not already represented thereon, be entitled to send a representative to take part in the proceedings of the Governing Body while the matter is under consideration. Adequate notice of the date on which the matter will be considered shall be given to the Government in question.

## ARTICLE 412.

The Commission of Enquiry shall be constituted in accordance with the following provisions :—

Each of the Members agrees to nominate within six months of the date on which the present Treaty comes into force three persons of industrial experience, of whom one shall be a representative of employers, one a representative of workers, and one a person of independent standing, who shall together form a panel from which the members of the Commission of Enquiry shall be drawn.

The qualifications of the persons so nominated shall be subject to scrutiny by the Governing Body, which may by two-thirds of the votes cast by the representatives present refuse to accept the nomination of any person whose qualifications do not in its opinion comply with the requirements of the present article.

Upon the application of the Governing Body, the Secretary-General of the League of Nations shall nominate three persons, one from each section of this panel, to constitute the Commission of Enquiry, and shall designate one of them as the President of the Commission. None of these three persons shall be a person nominated to the panel by any Member directly concerned in the complaint.

## ARTICLE 413.

The Members agree that, in the event of the reference of a complaint to a Commission of Enquiry under Article 25, they will each, whether directly concerned in the complaint or not, place at the disposal of the Commission all the information in their possession which bears upon the subject-matter of the complaint.

## ARTICLE 414.

When the Commission of Enquiry has fully considered the complaint, it shall prepare a report embodying its findings on all questions relevant to determining the issue between the parties and containing such recommendations as it may think proper as to the steps which should be taken to meet the complaint and the time within which they should be taken.

It shall also indicate in this report the measures, if any, of an economic character against a defaulting Government which it considers to be appropriate, and which it considers other Governments would be justified in adopting.

## ARTICLE 415.

The Secretary-General of the League of Nations shall communicate the report of the Commission of Enquiry to each of the Governments concerned in the complaint, and shall cause it to be published.

Each of these Governments shall within one month inform the Secretary-General of the League of Nations whether or not it accepts the recommendations contained in the report of the Commission ; and if not, whether it proposes to refer the complaint to the Permanent Court of International Justice of the League of Nations.

## ARTICLE 416.

In the event of any Member failing to take the action required by Article 19, with regard to a recommendation or draft Convention, any other Member shall be entitled to refer the matter to the Permanent Court of International Justice.

## ARTICLE 417.

The decision of the Permanent Court of International Justice in regard to a complaint or matter which has been referred to it in pursuance of Article 29 or Article 30 shall be final.

## ARTICLE 418.

The Permanent Court of International Justice may affirm, vary or reserve any of the findings or recommendations of the Commission of Enquiry, if any, and shall in its decision indicate the measures, if any, of an economic character which it considers to be appropriate, and which other Governments would be justified in adopting against a defaulting Government.

## ARTICLE 419.

In the event of any Member failing to carry out within the time specified the recommendations, if any, contained in the report of the Commissions of Enquiry, or in the decision of the Permanent Court of International Justice, as the case may be, any other Member may take against that Member the measures of an economic character indicated in the report of the Commission or in the decision of the Court as appropriate to the case.

## ARTICLE 420.

The defaulting Government may at any time inform the Governing Body that it has taken the steps necessary to comply with the recommendations of the Commission of Enquiry or with those in the decision of the Permanent Court of International Justice, as the case may be, and may request it to apply to the Secretary-General of the League to constitute a Commission of Enquiry to verify its contention. In this case the provisions of Articles 26, 27, 28, 29,

31 and 32 shall apply, and if the report of the Commission of Enquiry or the decision of the Permanent Court of International Justice is in favour of the defaulting Government, the other Governments shall forthwith discontinue the measures of an economic character that they have taken against the defaulting Government.

## CHAPTER III

### GENERAL

### ARTICLE 421.

The Members engage to apply conventions which they have ratified in accordance with the provisions of this part of the present Treaty to their colonies, protectorates and possessions, which are not fully self-governing :—

1. Except where owing to the local conditions the convention is inapplicable, or
2. Subject to such modifications as may be necessary to adapt the convention to local conditions.

And each of the Members shall notify to the International Labour Office the action taken in respect of each of its colonies, protectorates and possessions which are not fully self-governing.

### ARTICLE 422.

Amendments to this part of the present Treaty which are adopted by the Conference by a majority of two-thirds of the votes cast by the Delegates present shall take effect when ratified by the States whose representatives compose the Council of the League of Nations and by three-fourths of the Members.

T

## ARTICLE 423.

Any question or dispute relating to the interpretation of this part of the present Treaty or of any subsequent Convention concluded by the Members in pursuance of the provisions of this part of the present Treaty shall be referred for decision to the Permanent Court of International Justice.

## RESOLUTIONS ADOPTED BY THE COMMISSION

### I.—*Resolution proposed by the Belgian, French and Italian Delegations.*

The Commission expresses the hope that as soon as it may be possible an agreement will be arrived at between the High Contracting Parties with a view to endowing the International Labour Conference under the auspices of the League of Nations with power to take, under conditions to be determined, resolutions possessing the force of international law.

### II.—*Resolution proposed by the Belgian, French and Italian Delegations.*

The Commission, being of opinion that an international code of Labour legislation which will be really effective cannot be secured without the co-operation of all industrial countries, expresses the wish that pending the signature of the Treaty of Peace, which will permit all such countries to be approached, the Peace Conference will communicate the present draft Convention to the neutral powers for their information before finally adopting it.

### III.—*Resolution proposed by the French Delegation.*

The Commission considers that the very special questions concerning the minimum conditions to be accorded to seamen might be dealt with at a special meeting of the International Labour Conference devoted exclusively to the affairs of seamen.

# APPENDIX II [1]

RESOLUTION PASSED AT THE BERNE CONFERENCE 1906

WHEN about to sign the convention concerning nightwork for women, the delegates of Denmark, Spain, France, Great Britain, Italy, Luxemburg, Holland, Portugal, Sweden and Switzerland, being convinced of the value of securing the greatest degree of unity possible concerning the regulations to be promulgated in conformity with the present Convention, resolve that the various points dealt with in the said Convention about which any doubt may arise, be submitted by one or several of the Contracting Parties to the judgment of a Commission upon which each contracting State shall be represented by one delegate and deputy-delegates. Such a Commission would be purely consultative in character. It would in no case be able to carry out investigations nor become involved in any matter which pertains to the administrative or other proceedings of the State concerned. It would submit a report upon any questions referred to it which would be communicated to the contracting States.

This Commission could be called upon among other duties :—(1) To advise as to the relatively uniform conditions upon which States outside Europe could join the Convention together with colonies and protectorates, where climatic conditions and native populations necessitate modifications in details of the Convention ; (2) To act as an intermediary body for the exchange of preliminary views, without prejudice to the initiative of each contracting State, when the

[1] See Ch. vii., p. 183.

High Contracting Parties agree as to the utility of arranging new conferences on the subject of labour.

The Commission would meet at the request of a contracting State not more than once a year, except when the contracting States shall agree to hold supplementary meetings in exceptional circumstances. The Commission would assemble in the capital of each of the contracting European States successively in alphabetical order. It is understood that the contracting States reserve the right to submit to arbitration in uniformity with Article 16 of the Hague Convention, questions of immediate importance, even if the opinion of the Commission has been given on such questions. The delegates referred to, request the Swiss Government, which is good enough to agree formally, to continue *pour parlers* for obtaining the consent to this resolution of those States whose delegates have not yet signed it, up to the close of the proceedings for ratifying the Conventions.

This resolution shall be accepted as an integral part of the Convention by the contracting States, at the convenience of the Swiss Government, when it shall have received the consent of all the States signatory to the Convention.

BERNE, 26 *September*, 1906.

# APPENDIX III

Sunderland House,
Curzon Street,
London, 15 *January*, 1920.

The Draft Conventions and Recommendations here reprinted were adopted by the International Labour Conference at its meeting held in Washington on 28 November, 1919, with the exception of the Draft Convention concerning the employment of women before and after childbirth, which was adopted at the meeting held in Washington on 29 November, 1919.

The texts of the Draft Conventions and Recommendations as here presented are true copies of the texts authenticated by the signatures of the President and the Secretary General of the International Labour Conference and deposited with the Secretary General of the League of Nations.

## DRAFT CONVENTIONS AND RECOMMENDATIONS ADOPTED BY THE INTERNATIONAL LABOUR CONFERENCE AT WASHINGTON.

PAGE

Draft Convention limiting the hours of work in industrial undertakings to eight in the day and forty-eight in the week - - - - - - - 294

Draft Convention concerning unemployment - - 305

Recommendation concerning unemployment - - 308

293

PAGE

Recommendation concerning reciprocity of treatment
of foreign workers - - - - - - 310

Draft Convention concerning the employment of
women before and after childbirth - - - 310

Draft Convention concerning employment of women
during the night - - - - - - 315

Recommendation concerning the prevention of anthrax 319

Recommendation concerning the protection of women
and children against lead poisoning - - - 320

Recommendation concerning the establishment of
Government Health Services - - - - 322

Draft Convention fixing the minimum age for admission of children to industrial employment - - 323

Draft Convention concerning the night work of young
persons employed in industry - - - - 327

Recommendation concerning the application of the
Berne Convention of 1906, on the prohibition
of the use of white phosphorus in the manufacture
of matches - - - - - - - - 332

## DRAFT CONVENTION LIMITING THE HOURS OF WORK IN INDUSTRIAL UNDERTAKINGS TO EIGHT IN THE DAY AND FORTY-EIGHT IN THE WEEK.

The General Conference of the International Labour Organisation of the League of Nations,

Having been convened at Washington by the Government of the United States of America, on the 29th day of October, 1919, and

Having decided upon the adoption of certain proposals with regard to the " application of the principle of the 8-hours day or of the 48-hours week," which is the first item in the agenda for the Washington meeting of the Conference, and

Having determined that these proposals shall take the form of a draft international convention,

adopts the following Draft Convention for ratification by the Members of the International Labour Organisation, in accordance with the Labour Part of the Treaty of Versailles of 28 June, 1919, and of the Treaty of St. Germain of 10 September, 1919 :

## ARTICLE 1.

For the purpose of this Convention, the term " industrial undertaking " includes particularly :

(a) Mines, quarries, and other works for the extraction of minerals from the earth.

(b) Industries in which articles are manufactured, altered, cleaned, repaired, ornamented, finished, adapted for sale, broken up or demolished, or in which materials are transformed ; including shipbuilding and the generation, transformation, and transmission of electricity or motive power of any kind.

(c) Construction, reconstruction, maintenance, repair, alteration, or demolition of any building, railway, tramway, harbour, dock, pier, canal, inland waterway, road, tunnel, bridge, viaduct, sewer, drain, well, telegraphic or telephonic installation, electrical undertaking, gas work, water work, or other work of construction, as well as the preparation for or laying the foundations of any such work or structure.

(d) Transport of passengers or goods by road, rail, sea or inland waterway, including the handling of goods at docks, quays, wharves or warehouses, but excluding transport by hand.

The provisions relative to transport by sea and on inland waterways shall be determined by a special conference dealing with employment at sea and on inland waterways.

The competent authority in each country shall define the line of division which separates industry from commerce and agriculture.

ARTICLE 2.

The working hours of persons employed in any public or private industrial undertaking or in any branch thereof, other than an undertaking in which only members of the same family are employed, shall not exceed eight in the day and forty-eight in the week, with the exceptions hereinafter provided for.

(a) The provisions of this Convention shall not apply to persons holding positions of supervision or management, nor to persons employed in a confidential capacity.

(b) Where by law, custom, or agreement between employers' and workers' organisations, or, where no such organisations exist, between employers' and workers' representatives, the hours of work on one or more days of the week are less than eight, the limit of eight hours may be exceeded on the remaining days of the week by the sanction of the competent public authority, or by agreement between such organisations or representatives; provided, however, that in no case under the provisions of this paragraph shall the daily limit of eight hours be exceeded by more than one hour.

(c) Where persons are employed in shifts it shall be permissible to employ persons in excess of eight hours in any one day and forty-eight hours in any one week, if the average number of hours over a period of three weeks or less does not exceed eight per day and forty-eight per week.

ARTICLE 3.

The limit of hours of work prescribed in Article 2 may be exceeded in case of accident, actual or threatened, or in case of urgent work to be done to machinery or plant, or in case of

" force majeure," but only so far as may be necessary to avoid serious interference with the ordinary working of the undertaking.

## ARTICLE 4.

The limit of hours of work prescribed in Article 2 may also be exceeded in those processes which are required by reason of the nature of the process to be carried on continuously by a succession of shifts, subject to the condition that the working hours shall not exceed fifty-six in the week on the average. Such regulation of the hours of work shall in no case affect any rest days which may be secured by the national law to the workers in such processes in compensation for the weekly rest day.

## ARTICLE 5.

In exceptional cases where it is recognised that the provisions of Article 2 cannot be applied, but only in such cases, agreements between workers' and employers' organisations concerning the daily limit of work over a longer period of time may be given the force of regulations, if the Government, to which these agreements shall be submitted, so decides.

The average number of hours worked per week, over the number of weeks covered by any such agreement, shall not exceed forty-eight.

## ARTICLE 6.

Regulations made by the public authority shall determine for industrial undertakings :

(a) The permanent exceptions that may be allowed in preparatory or complementary work which must necessarily be carried on outside the limits laid down for the general working of an establishment, or for certain classes of workers whose work is essentially intermittent.

(*b*) The temporary exceptions that may be allowed, so that establishments may deal with exceptional cases of pressure of work.

These regulations shall be made only after consultation with the organisations of employers and workers concerned, if any such organisations exist. These regulations shall fix the maximum of additional hours in each instance, and the rate of pay for overtime shall not be less than one and one-quarter times the regular rate.

## ARTICLE 7.

Each Government shall communicate to the International Labour Office :

(*a*) A list of the processes which are classed as being necessarily continuous in character under Article 4 ;

(*b*) Full information as to working of the agreements mentioned in Article 5 ; and

(*c*) Full information concerning the regulations made under Article 6 and their application.

The International Labour Office shall make an annual report thereon to the General Conference of the International Labour Organisation.

## ARTICLE 8.

In order to facilitate the enforcement of the provisions of this Convention, every employer shall be required :

(*a*) To notify by means of the posting of notices in conspicuous places in the works or other suitable place, or by such other method as may be approved by the Government, the hours at which work begins and ends, and where work is carried on by shifts, the hours at which each shift begins and ends. These hours shall be so fixed that the duration of the work shall not exceed the limits prescribed by this Convention, and when so notified they shall not be changed except with such notice and in such manner as may be approved by the Government.

(*b*) To notify in the same way such rest intervals accorded during the period of work as are not reckoned as part of the working hours.

(*c*) To keep a record in the form prescribed by law or regulation in each country of all additional hours worked in pursuance of Articles 3 and 6 of this Convention.

It shall be made an offence against the law to employ any person outside the hours fixed in accordance with paragraph (*a*), or during the intervals fixed in accordance with paragraph (*b*).

## ARTICLE 9.

In the application of this Convention to Japan the following modifications and conditions shall obtain :

(*a*) The term "industrial undertaking" includes particularly—

The undertakings enumerated in paragraph (*a*) of Article 1 ;

The undertakings enumerated in paragraph (*b*) of Article 1, provided there are at least ten workers employed ;

The undertakings enumerated in paragraph (*c*) of Article 1, in so far as these undertakings shall be defined as "factories" by the competent authority ;

The undertakings enumerated in paragraph (*d*) of Article 1, except transport of passengers or goods by road, handling of goods at docks, quays, wharves, and warehouses, and transport by hand ; and,

Regardless of the number of persons employed, such of the undertakings enumerated in paragraphs (*b*) and (*c*) of Article 1 as may be declared by the competent authority either to be highly dangerous or to involve unhealthy processes.

(*b*) The actual working hours of persons of fifteen years of age or over in any public or private industrial undertaking, or in any branch thereof, shall not exceed fifty-seven in the week, except that in the raw-silk industry the limit may be sixty hours in the week.

(c) The actual working hours of persons under fifteen years of age in any public or private industrial undertaking, or in any branch thereof, and of all miners of whatever age engaged in underground work in the mines, shall in no case exceed forty-eight in the week.

(d) The limit of hours of work may be modified under the conditions provided for in Articles 2, 3, 4, and 5 of this Convention, but in no case shall the length of such modification bear to the length of the basic week a proportion greater than that which obtains in those Articles.

(e) A weekly rest period of twenty-four consecutive hours shall be allowed to all classes of workers.

(f) The provision in Japanese factory legislation limiting its application to places employing fifteen or more persons shall be amended so that such legislation shall apply to places employing ten or more persons.

(g) The provisions of the above paragraphs of this Article shall be brought into operation not later than 1 July, 1922, except that the provisions of Article 4 as modified by paragraph (d) of this Article shall be brought into operation not later than 1 July, 1923.

(h) The age of fifteen prescribed in paragraph (c) of this Article shall be raised, not later than 1 July, 1925, to sixteen.

ARTICLE 10.

In British India the principle of a sixty-hour week shall be adopted for all workers in the industries at present covered by the factory acts administered by the Government of India, in mines, and in such branches of railway work as shall be specified for this purpose by the competent authority. Any modification of this limitation made by the competent authority shall be subject to the provisions of Articles 6 and 7 of this Convention. In other respects the provisions of this

Convention shall not apply to India, but further provisions limiting the hours of work in India shall be considered at a future meeting of the General Conference.

### ARTICLE 11.

The provisions of this Convention shall not apply to China, Persia, and Siam, but provisions limiting the hours of work in these countries shall be considered at a future meeting of the General Conference.

### ARTICLE 12.

In the application of this Convention to Greece, the date at which its provisions shall be brought into operation in accordance with Article 19 may be extended to not later than 1 July, 1923, in the case of the following industrial undertakings :

    (1) Carbon-bisulphide works,
    (2) Acids works,
    (3) Tanneries,
    (4) Paper mills,
    (5) Printing works,
    (6) Sawmills,
    (7) Warehouses for the handling and preparation of tobacco,
    (8) Surface mining,
    (9) Foundries,
    (10) Lime works,
    (11) Dye works,
    (12) Glassworks (blowers),
    (13) Gas works (firemen),
    (14) Loading and unloading merchandise ;

and to not later than 1 July, 1924, in the case of the following industrial undertakings :

    (1) Mechanical industries : Machine shops for engines, safes, scales, beds, tacks, shells (sporting), iron foundries,

bronze foundries, tin shops, plating shops, manufactories of hydraulic apparatus ;

(2) Constructional industries : Lime-kilns, cement works, plasterers' shops, tile yards, manufactories of bricks and pavements, potteries, marble yards, excavating and building work ;

(3) Textile industries : Spinning and weaving mills of all kinds, except dye works ;

(4) Food industries : Flour and grist-mills, bakeries, macaroni factories, manufactories of wines, alcohol, and drinks, oil works, breweries, manufactories of ice and carbonated drinks, manufactories of confectioners' products and chocolate, manufactories of sausages and preserves, slaughterhouses, and butcher shops ;

(5) Chemical industries : Manufactories of synthetic colours, glassworks (except the blowers), manufactories of essence of turpentine and tartar, manufactories of oxygen and pharmaceutical products, manufactories of flaxseed oil, manufactories of glycerine, manufactories of calcium carbide, gas works (except the firemen) ;

(6) Leather industries : Shoe factories, manufactories of leather goods ;

(7) Paper and printing industries : Manufactories of envelopes, record books, boxes, bags, bookbinding, lithographing, and zinc-engraving shops ;

(8) Clothing industries : Clothing shops, underwear and trimmings, workshops for pressing, workshops for bed coverings, artificial flowers, feathers, and trimmings, hat and umbrella factories ;

(9) Woodworking industries : Joiners' shops, coopers' sheds, wagon factories, manufactories of furniture and chairs, picture-framing establishments, brush and broom factories ;

(10) Electrical industries : Power houses, shops for electrical installations ;

(11) Transportation by land : Employees on railroads and street cars, firemen, drivers, and carters.

# APPENDIX III 303

### ARTICLE 13.

In the application of this convention to Roumania the date at which its provisions shall be brought into operation in accordance with Article 19 may be extended to not later than 1 July, 1924.

### ARTICLE 14.

The operation of the provisions of this Convention may be suspended in any country by the Government in the event of war or other emergency endangering the national safety.

### ARTICLE 15.

The formal ratifications of this Convention, under the conditions set forth in Part XIII of the Treaty of Versailles of 28 June, 1919, and of the Treaty of St. Germain of 10 September, 1919, shall be communicated to the Secretary General of the League of Nations for registration.

### ARTICLE 16.

Each Member of the International Labour Organisation which ratifies this Convention engages to apply it to its colonies, protectorates and possessions which are not fully self-governing :

(a) Except where owing to the local conditions its provisions are inapplicable ; or

(b) Subject to such modifications as may be necessary to adapt its provisions to local conditions.

Each Member shall notify to the International Labour Office the action taken in respect of each of its colonies, protectorates and possessions which are not fully self-governing.

### ARTICLE 17.

As soon as the ratifications of two Members of the International Labour Organisation have been registered with the

Secretariat, the Secretary General of the League of Nations shall so notify all the Members of the International Labour Organisation.

## ARTICLE 18.

This Convention shall come into force at the date on which such notification is issued by the Secretary General of the League of Nations, and it shall then be binding only upon those Members which have registered their ratifications with the Secretariat. Thereafter this Convention will come into force for any other Member at the date on which its ratification is registered with the Secretariat.

## ARTICLE 19.

Each Member which ratifies this Convention agrees to bring its provisions into operation not later than 1 July, 1921, and to take such action as may be necessary to make these provisions effective.

## ARTICLE 20.

A Member which has ratified this Convention may denounce it after the expiration of ten years from the date on which the Convention first comes into force, by an act communicated to the Secretary General of the League of Nations for registration. Such denunciation shall not take effect until one year after the date on which it is registered with the Secretariat.

## ARTICLE 21.

At least once in ten years the Governing Body of the International Labour Office shall present to the General Conference a report on the working of this convention, and shall consider the desirability of placing on the agenda of the Conference the question of its revision or modification.

## DRAFT CONVENTION CONCERNING
## UNEMPLOYMENT.

The General Conference of the International Labour Organisation of the League of Nations,

Having been convened at Washington by the Government of the United States of America, on the 29th day of October, 1919, and

Having decided upon the adoption of certain proposals with regard to the " question of preventing or providing against unemployment," which is the second item in the agenda for the Washington meeting of the Conference, and

Having determined that these proposals shall take the form of a draft international convention,

adopts the following Draft Convention for ratification by the Members of the International Labour Organisation, in accordance with the Labour Part of the Treaty of Versailles of 28 June, 1919, and of the Treaty of St. Germain of 10 September, 1919 :

### Article 1.

Each Member which ratifies this Convention shall communicate to the International Labour Office, at intervals as short as possible and not exceeding three months, all available information, statistical or otherwise, concerning unemployment, including reports on measures taken or contemplated to combat unemployment. Whenever practicable, the information shall be made available for such communication not later than three months after the end of the period to which it relates.

### Article 2.

Each Member which ratifies this Convention shall establish a system of free public employment agencies under the control of a central authority. Committees, which shall include representatives of employers and of workers, shall be appointed to advise on matters concerning the carrying on of these agencies.

Where both public and private free employment agencies exist, steps shall be taken to coordinate the operations of such agencies on a national scale.

The operations of the various national systems shall be coordinated by the International Labour Office in agreement with the countries concerned.

### ARTICLE 3.

The Members of the International Labour Organisation which ratify this Convention and which have established systems of insurance against unemployment shall, upon terms being agreed between the members concerned, make arrangements whereby workers belonging to one Member and working in the territory of another shall be admitted to the same rates of benefit of such insurance as those which obtain for the workers belonging to the latter.

### ARTICLE 4.

The formal ratifications of this Convention under the conditions set forth in Part XIII of the Treaty of Versailles of 28 June, 1919, and the Treaty of St. Germain of 10 September, 1919, shall be communicated to the Secretary General of the League of Nations for registration.

### ARTICLE 5.

Each Member of the International Labour Organisation which ratifies this Convention engages to apply it to its colonies, protectorates and possessions which are not fully self-governing :

(*a*) Except where owing to the local conditions its provisions are inapplicable ; or

(*b*) Subject to such modifications as may be necessary to adapt its provisions to local conditions.

Each Member shall notify to the International Labour Office the action taken in respect of each of its colonies, protectorates and possessions which are not fully self-governing.

## ARTICLE 6.

As soon as the ratifications of three Members of the International Labour Organisation have been registered with the Secretariat, the Secretary General of the League of Nations shall so notify all the Members of the International Labour Organisation.

## ARTICLE 7.

This Convention shall come into force at the date on which such notification is issued by the Secretary General of the League of Nations, but it shall then be binding only upon those Members which have registered their ratifications with the Secretariat. Thereafter this Convention will come into force for any other Member at the date on which its ratification is registered with the Secretariat.

## ARTICLE 8.

Each Member which ratifies this Convention agrees to bring its provisions into operation not later than 1 July, 1921, and to take such action as may be necessary to make these provisions effective.

## ARTICLE 9.

A Member which has ratified this Convention may denounce it after the expiration of ten years from the date on which the Convention first comes into force, by an act communicated to the Secretary General of the League of Nations for registration. Such denunciation shall not take effect until one year after the date on which it is registered with the Secretariat.

ARTICLE 10.

At least once in ten years the Governing Body of the International Labour Office shall present to the General Conference a report on the working of this convention, and shall consider the desirability of placing on the agenda of the Conference the question of its revision or modification.

## RECOMMENDATIONS CONCERNING UNEMPLOYMENT.

The General Conference of the International Labour Organisation of the League of Nations,

Having been convened at Washington by the Government of the United States of America on the 29th day of October, 1919, and

Having decided upon the adoption of certain proposals with regard to the " question of preventing or providing against unemployment," which is the second item in the agenda for the Washington meeting of the Conference, and

Having determined that these proposals shall take the form of a recommendation,

adopts the following Recommendation, to be submitted to the Members of the International Labour Organisation for consideration with a view to effect being given to it by national legislation or otherwise, in accordance with the Labour Part of the Treaty of Versailles of 28 June, 1919, and of the Treaty of St. Germain of 10 September, 1919 :

## I.

The General Conference recommends that each Member of the International Labour Organisation take measures to prohibit the establishment of employment agencies which charge fees or which carry on their business for profit. Where such agencies already exist, it is further recommended that they be permitted to operate only under Government licenses, and that all practical measures be taken to abolish such agencies as soon as possible.

## II.

The General Conference recommends to the Members of the International Labour Organisation that the recruiting of bodies of workers in one country with a view to their employment in another country should be permitted only by mutual agreement between the countries concerned and after consultation with employers and workers in each country in the industries concerned.

## III.

The General Conference recommends that each Member of the International Labour Organisation establish an effective system of unemployment insurance, either through a Government system or through a system of Government subventions to associations whose rules provide for the payment of benefits to their unemployed members.

## IV.

The General Conference recommends that each Member of the International Labour Organisation coordinate the execution of all work undertaken under public authority, with a view to reserving such work as far as practicable for periods of unemployment and for districts most affected by it.

## RECOMMENDATION CONCERNING RECIPROCITY OF TREATMENT OF FOREIGN WORKERS.

The General Conference of the International Labour Organisation of the League of Nations,

> Having been convened at Washington by the Government of the United States of America on the 29th day of October, 1919, and
>
> Having decided upon the adoption of certain proposals with regard to the " question of preventing or providing against unemployment," which is the second item in the agenda for the Washington meeting of the Conference, and
>
> Having determined that these proposals shall take the form of a recommendation,

adopts the following recommendation to be submitted to the Members of the International Labour Organisation for consideration with a view to effect being given to it by national legislation or otherwise, in accordance with the Labour Part of the Treaty of Versailles of 28 June, 1919, and of the Treaty of St Germain of 10 September, 1919 :

The General Conference recommends that each Member of the International Labour Organisation shall, on condition of reciprocity and upon terms to be agreed between the countries concerned, admit the foreign workers (together with their families) employed within its territory, to the benefit of its laws and regulations for the protection of its own workers, as well as to the right of lawful organisation as enjoyed by its own workers.


## DRAFT CONVENTION CONCERNING THE EMPLOYMENT OF WOMEN BEFORE AND AFTER CHILDBIRTH.

The General Conference of the International Labour Organisation of the League of Nations,

Having been convened at Washington by the Government of the United States of America on the 29th day of October 1919, and

Having decided upon the adoption of certain proposals with regard to " women's employment, before and after childbirth, including the question of maternity benefit," which is part of the third item in the agenda for the Washington meeting of the Conference, and

Having determined that these proposals shall take the form of a draft international convention,

adopts the following draft Convention for ratification by the Members of the International Labour Organisation, in accordance with the Labour Part of the Treaty of Versailles of 28 June, 1919, and of the Treaty of St. Germain of 10 September, 1919 :

## ARTICLE 1.

For the purpose of this Convention, the term " industrial undertaking " includes particularly :

(a) Mines, quarries, and other works for the extraction of minerals from the earth.

(b) Industries in which articles are manufactured, altered, cleaned, repaired, ornamented, finished, adapted for sale, broken up or demolished, or in which materials are transformed ; including shipbuilding and the generation, transformation, and transmission of electricity or motive power of any kind.

(c) Construction, reconstruction, maintenance, repair, alteration, or demolition of any building, railway, tramway, harbour, dock, pier, canal, inland waterway, road, tunnel, bridge, viaduct, sewer, drain, well, telegraphic or telephonic installation, electrical undertaking, gas work, water work, or other work of construction, as well as the preparation for or laying the foundation of any such work or structure.

(*d*) Transport of passengers or goods by road, rail, sea, or inland waterway, including the handling of goods at docks, quays, wharves, and warehouses, but excluding transport by hand.

For the purpose of this Convention, the term " commercial undertaking " includes any place where articles are sold or where commerce is carried on.

The competent authority in each country shall define the line of division which separates industry and commerce from agriculture.

## ARTICLE 2.

For the purpose of this Convention, the term " woman " signifies any female person, irrespective of age or nationality, whether married or unmarried, and the term " child " signifies any child whether legitimate or illegitimate.

## ARTICLE 3.

In any public or private industrial or commercial undertaking, or in any branch thereof, other than an undertaking in which only members of the same family are employed, a woman—

(*a*) Shall not be permitted to work during the six weeks following her confinement.

(*b*) Shall have the right to leave her work if she produces a medical certificate stating that her confinement will probably take place within six weeks.

(*c*) Shall, while she is absent from her work in pursuance of paragraphs (*a*) and (*b*), be paid benefits sufficient for the full and healthy maintenance of herself and her child, provided either out of public funds or by means of a system of insurance, the exact amount of which shall be determined by the competent authority in each country, and as an additional benefit shall be entitled to free attendance by a doctor or certified midwife. No mistake of the medical adviser in estimating the date of confinement shall preclude a woman from receiving these benefits from the date of the medical certificate up to the date on which the confinement actually takes place.

(*d*) Shall in any case, if she is nursing her child, be allowed half an hour twice a day during her working hours for this purpose.

## ARTICLE 4.

Where a woman is absent from her work in accordance with paragraphs (*a*) or (*b*) of Article 3 of this Convention, or remains absent from her work for a longer period as a result of illness medically certified to arise out of pregnancy or confinement and rendering her unfit for work, it shall not be lawful, until her absence shall have exceeded a maximum period to be fixed by the competent authority in each country, for her employer to give her notice of dismissal during such absence nor to give her notice of dismissal at such a time that the notice would expire during such absence.

## ARTICLE 5.

The formal ratifications of this Convention, under the conditions set forth in Part XIII of the Treaty of Versailles of 28 June, 1919, and of the Treaty of St. Germain of 10 September, 1919, shall be communicated to the Secretary General of the League of Nations for registration.

## ARTICLE 6.

Each Member of the International Labour Organisation which ratifies this Convention engages to apply it to its colonies, protectorates and possessions which are not fully self-governing :

(*a*) Except where, owing to the local conditions, its provisions are inapplicable ; or

(b) Subject to such modifications as may be necessary to adapt its provisions to local conditions.

Each Member shall notify to the International Labour Office the action taken in respect of each of its colonies, protectorates and possessions which are not fully self-governing.

## ARTICLE 7.

As soon as the ratifications of Two members of the International Labour Organisation have been registered with the Secretariat, the Secretary General of the League of Nations shall so notify all the Members of the International Labour Organisation.

## ARTICLE 8.

This Convention shall come into force at the date on which such notification is issued by the Secretary General of the League of Nations, but it shall then be binding only upon those Members which have registered their ratifications with the Secretariat. Thereafter this Convention will come into force for any other Member at the date on which its ratification is registered with the Secretariat.

## ARTICLE 9.

Each Member which ratifies this Convention agrees to bring its provisions into operation not later than 1 July, 1922, and to take such action as may be necessary to make these provisions effective.

## ARTICLE 10.

A Member which has ratified this Convention may denounce it after the expiration of ten years from the date on which the Convention first comes into force, by an act communicated to the Secretary General of the League of Nations for registration. Such denunciation shall not take effect until one year after the date on which it is registered with the Secretariat.

## ARTICLE 11.

At least once in ten years the Governing Body of the International Labour Office shall present to the General Conference a report on the working of this Convention, and shall consider the desirability of placing on the agenda of the Conference the question of its revision or modification.

## DRAFT CONVENTION CONCERNING EMPLOYMENT OF WOMEN DURING THE NIGHT.

The General Conference of the International Labour Organisation of the League of Nations,

Having been convened at Washington by the Government of the United States of America, on the 29th day of October, 1919, and

Having decided upon the adoption of certain proposals with regard to " women's employment : during the night," which is part of the third item in the agenda for the Washington meeting of the Conference, and

Having determined that these proposals shall take the form of a draft international convention,

adopts the following Draft Convention for ratification by the Members of the International Labour Organisation, in accordance with the Labour Part of the Treaty of Versailles of 28 June, 1919, and of the Treaty of St Germain of 10 September, 1919 :

## ARTICLE 1.

For the purpose of this Convention, the term " industrial undertaking " includes particularly :

(a) Mines, quarries, and other works for the extraction of minerals from the earth ;

(b) Industries in which articles are manufactured, altered, cleaned, repaired, ornamented, finished, adapted for sale, broken up or demolished, or in which materials are transformed ; including shipbuilding, and the generation, transformation, and transmission of electricity or motive power of any kind ;

(c) Construction, reconstruction, maintenance, repair, alteration, or demolition of any building, railway, tramway, harbour, dock, pier, canal, inland waterway, road, tunnel, bridge, viaduct, sewer, drain, well, telegraphic or telephonic installation, electrical undertaking, gas work, water work or other work of construction, as well as the preparation for or laying the foundations of any such work or structure.

The competent authority in each country shall define the line of division which separates industry from commerce and agriculture.

### ARTICLE 2.

For the purpose of this Convention, the term "night" signifies a period of at least eleven consecutive hours, including the interval between ten o'clock in the evening and five o'clock in the morning.

In those countries where no Government regulation as yet applies to the employment of women in industrial undertakings during the night, the term " night " may provisionally, and for a maximum period of three years, be declared by the Government to signify a period of only ten hours, including the interval between ten o'clock in the evening and five o'clock in the morning.

### ARTICLE 3.

Women without distinction of age shall not be employed during the night in any public or private industrial undertaking, or in any branch thereof, other than an undertaking in which only members of the same family are employed.

## Article 4.

Article 3 shall not apply :

(a) In cases of *force majeure*, when in any undertaking there occurs an interruption of work which it was impossible to foresee, and which is not of a recurring character.

(b) In cases where the work has to do with raw materials or materials in course of treatment which are subject to rapid deterioration, when such night work is necessary to preserve the said materials from certain loss.

## Article 5.

In India and Siam, the application of Article 3 of this Convention may be suspended by the Government in respect to any industrial undertaking, except factories as defined by the national law. Notice of every such suspension shall be filed with the International Labour Office.

## Article 6.

In industrial undertakings which are influenced by the seasons and in all cases where exceptional circumstances demand it, the night period may be reduced to ten hours on sixty days of the year.

## Article 7.

In countries where the climate renders work by day particularly trying to the health, the night period may be shorter than prescribed in the above articles, provided that compensatory rest is accorded during the day.

### ARTICLE 8.

The formal ratifications of this Convention, under the conditions set forth in Part XIII of the Treaty of Versailles of 28 June, 1919, and of the Treaty of St. Germain of 10 September, 1919, shall be communicated to the Secretary General of the League of Nations for registration.

### ARTICLE 9.

Each Member of the International Labour Organisation which ratifies this Convention engages to apply it to its colonies, protectorates and possessions which are not fully self-governing :

(a) Except where owing to the local conditions its provisions are inapplicable ; or

(b) Subject to such modifications as may be necessary to adapt its provisions to local conditions.

Each Member shall notify to the International Labour Office the action taken in respect of each of its colonies, protectorates and possessions which are not fully self-governing.

### ARTICLE 10.

As soon as the ratifications of two Members of the International Labour Organisation have been registered with the Secretariat, the Secretary General of the League of Nations shall so notify all the Members of the International Labour Organisation.

### ARTICLE 11.

This Convention shall come into force at the date on which such notification is issued by the Secretary General of the League of Nations, but it shall then be binding only upon those Members which have registered their ratifications with the Secretariat. Thereafter this Convention will come into force for any other Member at the date on which its ratification is registered with the Secretariat.

## ARTICLE 12.

Each Member which ratifies this Convention agrees to bring its provisions into operation not later than 1 July, 1922, and to take such action as may be necessary to make these provisions effective.

## ARTICLE 13.

A Member which has ratified this Convention may denounce it after the expiration of ten years from the date on which the Convention first comes into force, by an act communicated to the Secretary General of the League of Nations for registration. Such denunciation shall not take effect until one year after the date on which it is registered with the Secretariat.

## ARTICLE 14.

At least once in ten years, the Governing Body of the International Labour Office shall present to the General Conference a report on the working of this Convention, and shall consider the desirability of placing on the agenda of the Conference the question of its revision or modification.

## RECOMMENDATION CONCERNING THE PREVENTION OF ANTHRAX.

The General Conference of the International Labour Organisation of the League of Nations,

Having been convened at Washington by the Government of the United States of America on the 29th day of October, 1919, and

Having decided upon the adoption of certain proposals with regard to " women's employment : unhealthy processes," which is part of the third item in the agenda for the Washington meeting of the Conference ; and

Having determined that these proposals shall take the form of a recommendation,

adopts the following recommendation, to be submitted to the Members of the International Labour Organisation for consideration with a view to effect being given to it by national legislation or otherwise, in accordance with the Labour Part of the Treaty of Versailles of 28 June, 1919, and the Treaty of St. Germain of 10 September, 1919 :

The General Conference recommends to the Members of the International Labour Organisation that arrangements should be made for the disinfection of wool infected with anthrax spores, either in the country exporting such wool or, if that is not practicable, at the port of entry in the country importing such wool.

## RECOMMENDATION CONCERNING THE PROTECTION OF WOMEN AND CHILDREN AGAINST LEAD POISONING.

The General Conference of the International Labour Organisation of the League of Nations,

Having been convened at Washington by the Government of the United States of America on the 29th day of October, 1919, and

Having decided upon the adoption of certain proposals with regard to " women's and children's employment : unhealthy processes," which is part of the third and fourth items in the agenda for the Washington meeting of the Conference, and

Having determined that these proposals shall take the form of a recommendation, adopts the following Recommendation, to be submitted to the Members of the International Labour Organisation for consideration with a view to effect being given to it by national legislation or otherwise, in accordance with the Labour Part of the Treaty of Versailles of 28 June, 1919, and of the Treaty of St. Germain of 10 September, 1919 :

The General Conference recommends to the Members of the International Labour Organisation that in view of the danger involved to the function of maternity and to the physical development of children, women and young persons under the age of eighteen years be excluded from employment in the following processes :

(*a*) In furnace work in the reduction of zinc or lead ores.

(*b*) In the manipulation, treatment, or reduction of ashes containing lead, and in the desilverizing of lead.

(*c*) In melting lead or old zinc on a large scale.

(*d*) In the manufacture of solder or alloys containing more than ten per cent. of lead.

(*e*) In the manufacture of litharge, massicot, red lead, white lead, orange lead, or sulphate, chromate or silicate (frit) of lead.

(*f*) In mixing and pasting in the manufacture or repair of electric accumulators.

(*g*) In the cleaning of workrooms where the above processes are carried on.

It is further recommended that the employment of women and young persons under the age of eighteen years in processes involving the use of lead compounds be permitted only subject to the following conditions :

(*a*) Locally applied exhaust ventilation, so as to remove dust and fumes at the point of origin.

(*b*) Cleanliness of tools and workrooms.

(*c*) Notification to Government authorities of all cases of lead poisoning, and compensation therefor.

(*d*) Periodic medical examination of the persons employed in such processes.

(e) Provision of sufficient and suitable cloakroom, washing, and mess-room accommodation, and of special protective clothing.

(f) Prohibition of bringing food or drink into work rooms.

It is further recommended that in industries where soluble lead compounds can be replaced by non-toxic substances, the use of soluble lead compounds should be strictly regulated.

For the purpose of this Recommendation, a lead compound should be considered as soluble if it contains more than five per cent. of its weight (estimated as metallic lead) soluble in a quarter of one per cent. solution of hydrochloric acid.

## RECOMMENDATION CONCERNING THE ESTABLISHMENT OF GOVERNMENT HEALTH SERVICES.

The General Conference of the International Labour Organisation of the League of Nations,

Having been convened at Washington by the Government of the United States of America on the 29th day of October, 1919, and

Having decided upon the adoption of certain proposals with regard to " women's employment : unhealthy processes," which is part of the third item in the agenda for the Washington meeting of the Conference, and

Having determined that these proposals shall take the form of a recommendation,

adopts the following Recommendation, to be submitted to the Members of the International Labour Organisation for consideration with a view to effect being given to it by national legislation or otherwise, in accordance with the Labour Part of the Treaty of Versailles of 28 June, 1919, and the Treaty of St. Germain of 10 September, 1919 :

The General Conference recommends that each Member of the International Labour Organisation which has not already done so should establish as soon as possible, not only a system of efficient factory inspection, but also in addition thereto a Government service especially charged with the duty of safeguarding the health of the workers, which will keep in touch with the International Labour Office.

## DRAFT CONVENTION FIXING THE MINIMUM AGE FOR ADMISSION OF CHILDREN TO INDUSTRIAL EMPLOYMENT.

The General Conference of the International Labour Organisation of the League of Nations,

Having been convened by the Government of the United States of America at Washington, on the 29th day of October, 1919, and

Having decided upon the adoption of certain proposals with regard to the " employment of children : minimum age of employment," which is part of the fourth item in the agenda for the Washington meeting of the Conference, and

Having determined that these proposals shall take the form of a draft international convention,

adopts the following Draft Convention for ratification by the Members of the International Labour Organisation, in accordance with the Labour Part of the Treaty of Versailles of 28 June, 1919, and of the Treaty of St. Germain of 10 September, 1919 :

### ARTICLE 1.

For the purpose of this convention, the term " industrial undertaking " includes particularly :

(a) Mines, quarries and other works for the extraction of minerals from the earth.

(b) Industries in which articles are manufactured, altered, cleaned, repaired, ornamented, finished, adapted for sale, broken up or demolished, or in which minerals are transformed ; including shipbuilding, and the generation, transformation, and transmission of electricity and motive power of any kind.

(c) Construction, reconstruction, maintenance, repair, alteration, or demolition of any building, railway, tramway, harbour, dock, pier, canal, inland waterway, road, tunnel, bridge, viaduct, sewer, drain, well, telegraphic or telephonic installation, electrical undertaking, gas work, water work, or other work of construction, as well as the preparation for or laying the foundations of any such work or structure.

(d) Transport of passengers or goods by road or rail or inland waterway, including the handling of goods at docks, quays, wharves, and warehouses, but excluding transport by hand.

The competent authority in each country shall define the line of division which separates industry from commerce and agriculture.

## ARTICLE 2.

Children under the age of fourteen years shall not be employed or work in any public or private industrial undertaking, or in any branch thereof, other than an undertaking in which only members of the same family are employed.

## ARTICLE 3.

The provisions of Article 2 shall not apply to work done by children in technical schools, provided that such work is approved and supervised by public authority.

## ARTICLE 4.

In order to facilitate the enforcement of the provisions of this Convention, every employer in an industrial undertaking shall be required to keep a register of all persons under the age of sixteen years employed by him, and of the dates of their births.

### ARTICLE 5.

In connection with the application of this Convention to Japan, the following modifications of Article 2 may be made :

(a) Children over twelve years of age may be admitted into employment if they have finished the course in the elementary school ;

(b) As regards children between the ages of twelve and fourteen already employed, transitional regulations may be made.

The provision in the present Japanese law admitting children under the age of twelve years to certain light and easy employments shall be repealed.

### ARTICLE 6.

The provisions of Article 2 shall not apply to India, but in India children under twelve years of age shall not be employed,

(a) In manufactories working with power and employing more than ten persons ;

(b) In mines, quarries, and other works for the extraction of minerals from the earth ;

(c) In the transport of passengers or goods, or mails, by rail, or in handling of goods at docks, quays, and wharves, but excluding transport by hand.

### ARTICLE 7.

The formal ratifications of this Convention, under the conditions set forth in Part XIII of the Treaty of Versailles of 28 June, 1919, and of the Treaty of St. Germain of 10 September, 1919, shall be communicated to the Secretary General of the League of Nations for registration.

## ARTICLE 8.

Each member of the International Labour Organisation which ratifies this Convention engages to apply it to its colonies, protectorates and possessions which are not fully self-governing :

    (*a*) Except where owing to the local conditions its provisions are inapplicable ; or

    (*b*) Subject to such modifications as may be necessary to adapt its provisions to local conditions.

Each Member shall notify to the International Labour Office the action taken in respect to each of its colonies, protectorates and possessions which are not fully self-governing.

## ARTICLE 9.

As soon as the ratifications of two Members of the International Labour Organisation have been registered with the Secretariat, the Secretary General of the League of Nations shall so notify all the members of the International Labour Organisation.

## ARTICLE 10.

This Convention shall come into force at the date on which such notification is issued by the Secretary General of the League of Nations, but it shall then be binding only upon those Members which have registered their ratifications with the Secretariat. Thereafter this Convention will come into force for any other Member at the date on which its ratification is registered with the Secretariat.

## ARTICLE 11.

Each Member which ratifies this Convention agrees to bring its provisions into operation not later than 1 July, 1922, and to take such action as may be necessary to make these provisions effective.

### ARTICLE 12.

A Member which has ratified this Convention may denounce it after the expiration of ten years from the date on which the Convention first comes into force, by an act communicated to the Secretary General of the League of Nations for registration. Such denunciation shall not take effect until one year after the date on which it is registered with the Secretariat.

### ARTICLE 13.

At least once in ten years, the Governing Body of the International Labour Office shall present to the General Conference a report on the working of this Convention, and shall consider the desirability of placing on the agenda of the Conference the question of its revision or modification.

## DRAFT CONVENTION CONCERNING THE NIGHT WORK OF YOUNG PERSONS EMPLOYED IN INDUSTRY.

The General Conference of the International Labour Organisation of the League of Nations,

Having been convened by the Government of the United States of America at Washington, on the 29th day of October, 1919, and

Having decided upon the adoption of certain proposals with regard to the " employment of children : during the night," which is part of the fourth item in the agenda for the Washington meeting of the Conference, and

Having determined that these proposals shall take the form of a draft international convention,

adopts the following Draft Convention for ratification by the Members of the International Labour Organisation, in accordance with the Labour Part of the Treaty of Versailles of

28 June, 1919, and of the Treaty of St. Germain of 10 September, 1919 ;

### ARTICLE 1.

For the purpose of this Convention, the term " industrial undertaking " includes particularly :

(a) Mines, quarries, and other works for the extraction of minerals from the earth.

(b) Industries in which articles are manufactured, altered, cleaned, repaired, ornamented, finished, adapted for sale, broken up, or demolished, or in which materials are transformed ; including shipbuilding, and the generation, transformation, and transmission of electricity or motive power of any kind.

(c) Construction, reconstruction, maintenance, repair, alteration, or demolition of any building, railway, tramway, harbour, dock, pier, canal, inland waterway, road, tunnel, bridge, viaduct, sewer, drain, well, telegraphic or telephonic installation, electrical undertaking, gas work, water work, or other work of construction as well as the preparation for or laying the foundations of any such work or structure.

(d) Transport of passengers or goods by road or rail, including the handling of goods at docks, quays, wharves, and warehouses, but excluding transport by hand.

The competent authority in each country shall define the line of division which separates industry from commerce and agriculture.

### ARTICLE 2.

Young persons under eighteen years of age shall not be employed during the night in any public or private industrial undertaking, or in any branch thereof, other than an undertaking in which only members of the same family are employed. except as hereinafter provided for.

Young persons over the age of sixteen may be employed during the night in the following industrial undertakings on work which, by reason of the nature of the process, is required to be carried on continuously day and night :

(a) Manufacture of iron and steel ; processes in which reverberatory or regenerative furnaces are used, and galvanizing of sheet metal or wire (except the pickling process).

(b) Glass works.

(c) Manufacture of paper.

(d) Manufacture of raw sugar.

(e) Gold mining reduction work.

## ARTICLE 3.

For the purpose of this Convention, the term "night" signifies a period of at least eleven consecutive hours, including the interval between ten o'clock in the evening and five o'clock in the morning.

In coal and lignite mines work may be carried on in the interval between ten o'clock in the evening and five o'clock in the morning, if an interval of ordinarily fifteen hours, and in no case of less than thirteen hours, separates two periods of work.

Where night work in the baking industry is prohibited for all workers, the interval between nine o'clock in the evening and four o'clock in the morning may be substituted in the baking industry for the interval between ten o'clock in the evening and five o'clock in the morning.

In those tropical countries in which work is suspended during the middle of the day, the night period may be shorter than eleven hours if compensatory rest is accorded during the day.

## ARTICLE 4.

The provisions of Article 2 and 3 shall not apply to the night work of young persons between the ages of sixteen and eighteen years in cases of emergencies which could not have been controlled or foreseen, which are not of a periodical character, and which interfere with the normal working of the industrial undertaking.

## ARTICLE 5.

In the application of this Convention to Japan, until 1 July, 1925, Article 2 shall apply only to young persons under fifteen years of age and thereafter it shall apply only to young persons under sixteen years of age.

## ARTICLE 6.

In the application of this Convention to India, the term " industrial undertaking " shall include only " factories " as defined in the Indian Factory Act, and Article 2 shall not apply to male young persons over fourteen years of age.

## ARTICLE 7.

The prohibition of night work may be suspended by the Government, for young persons between the ages of sixteen and eighteen years, when in case of serious emergency the public interest demands it.

## ARTICLE 8.

The formal ratifications of this Convention, under the conditions set forth in Part XIII of the Treaty of Versailles of 28 June, 1919, and of the Treaty of St Germain of 10 September, 1919, shall be communicated to the Secretary General of the League of Nations for registration.

## ARTICLE 9.

Each Member of the International Labour Organisation which ratifies this Convention engages to apply it to its colonies, protectorates and possessions which are not fully self-governing :

(a) Except where owing to the local conditions its provisions are inapplicable ; or

(b) Subject to such modifications as may be necessary to adapt its provisions to local conditions.

Each Member shall notify to the International Labour Office the action taken in respect of each of its colonies, protectorates and possessions which are not fully self-governing.

## ARTICLE 10.

As soon as the ratifications of two Members of the International Labour Organisation have been registered with the Secretariat the Secretary General of the League of Nations shall so notify all the Members of the International Labour Organisation.

## ARTICLE 11.

This Convention shall come into force at the date on which such notification is issued by the Secretary General of the League of Nations, and it shall then be binding only upon those Members which have registered their ratifications with the Secretariat. Thereafter this Convention will come into force for any other Member at the date on which its ratification is registered with the Secretariat.

## ARTICLE 12.

Each Member which ratifies this Convention agrees to bring its provisions into operation not later than 1 July, 1922, and to take such action as may be necessary to make these provisions effective.

## ARTICLE 13.

A Member which has ratified this Convention may denounce it after the expiration of ten years from the date on which the

Convention first comes into force, by an act communicated to the Secretary General of the League of Nations for registration. Such denunciation shall not take effect until one year after the date on which it is registered with the Secretariat.

ARTICLE 14.

At least once in ten years the Governing Body of the International Labour Office shall present to the General Conference a report on the working of this Convention, and shall consider the desirability of placing on the agenda of the Conference the question of its revision or modification.

ARTICLE 15.

The French and English texts of this Convention shall both be authentic.

## RECOMMENDATION CONCERNING THE APPLICATION OF THE BERNE CONVENTION OF 1906, ON THE PROHIBITION OF THE USE OF WHITE PHOSPHORUS IN THE MANUFACTURE OF MATCHES.

The General Conference of the International Labour Organisation of the League of Nations,

Having been convened at Washington by the Government of the United States of America on the 29th day of October, 1919, and

Having decided upon the adoption of a proposal with regard to the " extension and application of the International Convention adopted at Berne in 1906 on the prohibition of the use of white phosphorus in the manufacture of matches," which is part of the fifth item in the agenda for the Washington meeting of the Conference, and

Having determined that this proposal shall take the form of a recommendation,

adopts the following Recommendation, to be submitted to the Members of the International Labour Organisation for consideration with a view to effect being given to it by national legislation or otherwise, in accordance with the Labour Part of the Treaty of Versailles of 28 June, 1919, and the Treaty of St. Germain of 10 September, 1919 :

The General Conference recommends that each Member of the International Labour Organisation, which has not already done so, should adhere to the International Convention adopted at Berne in 1906 on the prohibition of the use of white phosphorus in the manufacture of matches.

# APPENDIX IV

## DRAFT CONVENTIONS AND RECOMMENDATIONS[1] ADOPTED BY THE INTERNATIONAL LABOUR CONFERENCE—GENOA, 1920.

### RECOMMENDATION CONCERNING THE LIMITATION OF HOURS OF WORK IN THE FISHING INDUSTRY.

IN view of the declaration in the Treaties of Peace that all industrial communities should endeavour to adopt, so far as their special circumstances will permit, "an eight-hours' day or a forty-eight hours' week as the standard to be aimed at where it has not already been attained," the International Labour Conference recommends that each Member of the International Labour Organisation enact legislation limiting in this direction the hours of work of all workers employed in the fishing industry, with such special provisions as may be necessary to meet the conditions peculiar to the fishing industry in each country ; and that in framing such legislation each Government consult with the organisations of employers and the organisations of workers concerned.

### RECOMMENDATION CONCERNING THE LIMITATION OF HOURS OF WORK IN INLAND NAVIGATION.

### I.

That each Member of the International Labour Organisation should, if it has not already done so, enact legislation

---

[1] The formal preamble to each Convention and Recommendation is omitted, the material portions only being reprinted in this Appendix.

limiting in the direction of the above declaration in the Treaties of Peace the hours of work of workers employed in inland navigation, with such special provisions as may be necessary to meet the climatic and industrial conditions peculiar to inland navigation in each country, and after consultation with the organisations of employers and the organisations of workers concerned.

## II.

That those Members of the International Labour Organisation whose territories are riparian to waterways which are used in common by their boats should enter into agreements for limiting in the direction of the aforesaid declaration, the hours of work of persons employed in inland navigation on such waterways, after consultation with the organisations of employers and the organisations of workers concerned.

## III.

That such national legislation and such agreements between riparian countries should follow as far as possible the general lines of the Draft Convention concerning hours of work adopted by the International Labour Conference at Washington, with such exceptions as may be necessary for meeting the climatic or other special conditions of the countries concerned.

## IV.

That, in the application of this Recommendation, each Member of the International Labour Organisation should determine for itself, after consultation with the organisations of employers and the organisations of workers concerned, what is inland navigation as distinguished from maritime navigation, and should communicate its determination to the International Labour Office.

## V.

That each Member of the International Labour Organisation should report to the International Labour Office, within two years after the adjournment of the Genoa Conference, the progress which it has made in the direction of this Recommendation.

### Recommendation concerning the Establishment of National Seamen's Codes.

In order that, as a result of the clear and systematic codification of the national law in each country, the seamen of the world, whether engaged on ships of their own or foreign countries, may have a better comprehension of their rights and obligations, and in order that the task of establishing an International Seamen's Code may be advanced and facilitated, the International Labour Conference recommends that each Member of the International Labour Organisation undertake the embodiment in a seamen's code of all its laws and regulations relating to seamen in their activities as such.

### Draft Convention Fixing the Minimum Age for Admission of Children to Employment at Sea.

#### Article 1.

For the purpose of this Convention, the term " vessel " includes all ships and boats, of any nature whatsoever, engaged in maritime navigation, whether publicly or privately owned ; it excludes ships of war.

#### Article 2.

Children under the age of fourteen years shall not be employed or work on vessels, other than vessels upon which only members of the same family are employed.

#### Article 3.

The provisions of Article 2 shall not apply to work done by children on school-ships or training-ships, provided that such work is approved and supervised by public authority.

# APPENDIX IV 337

## ARTICLE 4.

In order to facilitate the enforcement of the provisions of this Convention, every shipmaster shall be required to keep a register of all persons under the age of sixteen years employed on board his vessel, or a list of them in the articles of agreement, and of the dates of their births.

## ARTICLE 5.

Each Member of the International Labour Organisation which ratifies this Convention engages to apply it to its colonies, protectorates, and possessions which are not fully self-governing :

(a) Except where owing to the local conditions its provisions are inapplicable ; or

(b) Subject to such modifications as may be necessary to adapt its provisions to local conditions.

Each Member shall notify to the International Labour Office the action taken in respect to each of its colonies, protectorates, and possessions which are not fully self-governing.

## ARTICLE 6.

The formal ratifications of this Convention under the conditions set forth in Part XIII of the Treaty of Versailles of 28 June, 1919, of the Treaty of St. Germain of 10 September, 1919, of the Treaty of Neuilly of 27 November, 1919, and of the Treaty of the Grand Trianon of 4 June, 1920, shall be communicated to the Secretary-General of the League of Nations for registration.

## ARTICLE 7.

As soon as the ratifications of two Members of the International Labour Organisation have been registered with the Secretariat, the Secretary General of the League of Nations

Y

shall so notify all the Members of the International Labour Organisation.

## ARTICLE 8.

This convention shall come into force at the date on which such notification is issued by the Secretary General of the League of Nations, but it shall then be binding only upon those Members which have registered their ratifications with the Secretariat. Thereafter this Convention will come into force for any other Member at the date on which its ratification is registered with the Secretariat.

## ARTICLE 9.

Subject to the provisions of Article 8, each Member which ratifies this Convention agrees to bring its provisions into operation not later than 1 July, 1922, and to take such action as may be necessary to make these provisions effective.

## ARTICLE 10.

A Member which has ratified this Convention may denounce it after the expiration of ten years from the date on which the Convention first comes into force, by an act communicated to the Secretary General of the League of Nations for registration. Such denunciation shall not take effect until one year after the date on which it is registered with the Secretariat.

## ARTICLE 11.

At least once in ten years, the Governing Body of the International Labour Office shall present to the General Conference a report on the working of this Convention, and shall consider the desirability of placing on the agenda of the Conference the question of its revision or modification.

### RECOMMENDATION CONCERNING UNEMPLOYMENT INSURANCE FOR SEAMEN.

The General Conference, with a view to securing the application to seamen of Part III of the Recommendation concerning Unemployment adopted at Washington on 28 November, 1919, recommends that each Member of the International Labour Organisation should establish for seamen an effective system of insurance against unemployment arising out of ship-wreck or any other cause, either by means of Government insurance or by means of Government subventions to industrial organisations whose rules provide for the payment of benefits to their unemployed members.

### DRAFT CONVENTION CONCERNING UNEMPLOYMENT INDEMNITY IN CASE OF LOSS OR FOUNDERING OF THE SHIP.

#### ARTICLE 1.

For the purpose of this Convention, the term " seamen " includes all persons employed on any vessel engaged in maritime navigation.

For the purpose of this Convention, the term " vessel " includes all ships and boats, of any nature whatsoever, engaged in maritime navigation, whether publicly or privately owned ; it excludes ships of war.

#### ARTICLE 2.

In every case of loss or foundering of any vessel, the owner or person with whom the seaman has contracted for service on board the vessel shall pay to each seaman employed thereon an indemnity against unemployment resulting from such loss or foundering.

This indemnity shall be paid for the days during which the seaman remains in fact unemployed at the same rate as the wages payable under the contract, but the total indemnity

Y 2

payable under this Convention to any one seaman may be limited to two months' wages.

## ARTICLE 3.

Seamen shall have the same remedies for recovering such indemnities as they have for recovering arrears of wages earned during the service.

## ARTICLE 4.

Each Member of the International Labour Organisation which ratifies this Convention engages to apply it to its colonies, protectorates and possessions which are not fully self-governing :

(a) Except where owing to the local conditions its provisions are inapplicable ; or

(b) Subject to such modifications as may be necessary to adapt its provisions to local conditions.

Each Member shall notify to the International Labour Office the action taken in respect of each of its colonies, protectorates and possessions which are not fully self-governing.

(*The six concluding Articles of this Draft Convention are identical with the six concluding Articles of the Draft Convention relating to the Employment of Children at Sea.*)

## DRAFT CONVENTION FOR ESTABLISHING FACILITIES FOR FINDING EMPLOYMENT FOR SEAMEN.

### ARTICLE 1.

For the purpose of this Convention, the term " seamen " includes all persons, except officers, employed as members of the crew on vessels engaged in maritime navigation.

### ARTICLE 2.

The business of finding employment for seamen shall not be carried on by any person, company, or other agency, as a commercial enterprise for pecuniary gain ; nor shall any fees be charged directly or indirectly by any person, company or other agency, for finding employment for seamen on any ship.

The law of each country shall provide punishment for any violation of the provision of this Article.

## ARTICLE 3.

Notwithstanding the provisions of Article 2, any person, company or agency, which has been carrying on the work of finding employment for seamen as a commercial enterprise for pecuniary gain, may be permitted to continue temporarily under Government licence, provided that such work is carried on under Government inspection and supervision, so as to safeguard the rights of all concerned.

Each Member which ratifies this Convention agrees to take all practicable measures to abolish the practice of finding employment for seamen as a commercial enterprise for pecuniary gain as soon as possible.

## ARTICLE 4.

Each Member which ratifies this Convention agrees that there shall be organised and maintained an efficient and adequate system of public employment offices for finding employment for seamen without charge. Such system may be organised and maintained, either :

(1) by representative associations of shipowners and seamen jointly under the control of a central authority, or,

(2) in the absence of such joint action, by the State itself.

The work of all such employment offices shall be administered by persons having practical maritime experience.

Where such employment offices of different types exist, steps shall be taken to co-ordinate them on a national basis.

## ARTICLE 5.

Committees consisting of an equal number of representatives of shipowners and seamen shall be constituted to advise on matters concerning the carrying on of these offices; the Government in each country may make provision for further defining the powers of these committees, particularly with reference to the committees' selection of their chairmen from outside their own membership, to the degree of state supervision, and to the assistance which such committees shall have from persons interested in the welfare of seamen.

## ARTICLE 6.

In connection with the employment of seamen, freedom of choice of ship shall be assured to seamen and freedom of choice of crew shall be assured to shipowners.

## ARTICLE 7.

The necessary guarantees for protecting all parties concerned shall be included in the contract of engagement or articles of agreement, and proper facilities shall be assured to seamen for examining such contract or articles before and after signing.

## ARTICLE 8.

Each Member which ratifies this Convention will take steps to see that the facilities for employment of seamen provided for in this Convention shall, if necessary by means of public offices, be available for the seamen of all countries which ratify this Convention, and where the industrial conditions are generally the same.

## ARTICLE 9.

Each country shall decide for itself whether provisions similar to those in this Convention shall be put in force for deck-officers and engineer-officers.

### ARTICLE 10.

Each Member which ratifies this Convention shall communicate to the International Labour Office all available information, statistical or otherwise, concerning unemployment among seamen and concerning the work of its seamen's employment agencies.

The International Labour Office shall take steps to secure the co-ordination of the various national agencies for finding employment for seamen, in agreement with the Governments or organisations concerned in each country.

### ARTICLE 11.

Each Member of the International Labour Organisation which ratifies this Convention engages to apply it to its colonies, protectorates and possessions which are not fully self-governing :

(a) Except where owing to the local conditions its provisions are inapplicable ; or

(b) Subject to such modifications as may be necessary to adapt its provisions to local conditions.

Each Member shall notify to the International Labour Office the action taken in respect of each of its colonies, protectorates and possessions which are not fully self-governing.

(*The six concluding Articles of this Draft Convention are identical with the six concluding Articles of the Draft Convention relating to the Employment of Children at Sea.*)

# APPENDIX V

## MEMBER STATES AND GOVERNING BODY OF THE INTERNATIONAL LABOUR ORGANISATION

### MEMBER STATES.

Argentine Republic.
Austria.
Belgium.
Bolivia.
Brazil.
British Empire.
    Australia.
    Canada.
    India.
    New Zealand.
    South Africa.
Chili.
China.
Colombia.
Cuba.
Czecho-Slovakia.
Denmark.
Ecuador.
France.
Germany.
Greece.
Guatemala.
Haiti.

Hedjaz.
Honduras.
Italy.
Japan.
Liberia.
Netherlands.
Nicaragua.
Norway.
Panama.
Paraguay.
Persia.
Peru.
Poland.
Portugal.
Roumania.
Salvador.
Serb-Croat-Slovene State.
Siam.
Spain.
Sweden.
Switzerland.
Uruguay.
Venezuela.

# APPENDIX V 345

## Governing Body.

I. One representative of the Government of each of the following Twelve Member States of the Permanent Labour Organisation :

| | |
|---|---|
| Argentine. | Great Britain. |
| Belgium. | Italy. |
| Canada. | Japan. |
| Denmark. | Poland. |
| France. | Spain. |
| Germany. | Switzerland. |

II. Six representatives of the Employers :

Mr. Carlier (Belgium).
Mr. Guerin (France).
Mr. Hodacz (Czecho-Slovakia).
Mr. Pirelli (Italy).
Mr. Schindler (Switzerland).
Sir Allan Smith (Great Britain).

III. Six representatives of the Workers :

Mr. Stuart Bunning (Great Britain).
Mr. Draper (Canada).
Mr. Jouhaux (France).
Mr. Legien (Germany).
Mr. Lindquist (Sweden).
Mr. Oudegeest (Netherlands).

Chairman of the Governing Body—Mr. Arthur Fontaine (France).

Directors of the International Labour Office—Director, Mr. Albert Thomas (France) ; Deputy Director, Mr. H. B. Butler, C.B. (Great Britain).

GLASGOW : PRINTED AT THE UNIVERSITY PRESS BY ROBERT MACLEHOSE AND CO. LTD.